# CareerJournal.com

# RESUME

## GUIDE FOR

# $100,000+
# EXECUTIVE
# JOBS

## WILLIAM E. MONTAG

JOHN WILEY & SONS, INC.

ISBN 0-471-23287-4

For Debbie,

Michael Hamilton, Senior Editor, John Wiley & Sons, Inc.,

Tony Lee, Editor in Chief, CareerJournal.com,

And all my past clients . . .

# Contents

# Introduction

**REALITY CHECK**

To capitalize on luck and timing, your marketing package must be in the hands of the decision maker at exactly the right moment. A job search is, and will always be, a numbers game. Widespread failure to play the game has benefited those who do, including clients of Montag Associates who have employed our patented Expansionist Theory and the World Wide Web to outmarket, outmaneuver, and outdistance the competition.

Describing your career and job search Web site as "The Premier Career Site for Executives, Managers, and Professionals" might well sound like Madison Avenue hype—unless that Web site is owned and operated by *CareerJournal* from *The Wall Street Journal*. It is with great pleasure that I join forces with *CareerJournal* for this sequel to earlier bestsellers. This expanded entry will help you launch your search with the same competitive edge held by clients of Montag Associates: They have enjoyed a placement success rate that far surpasses even the best performance of the outplacement industry. As demonstrated through real-life case histories featured throughout the text, clients who combined our power packaging in Part I with our Expansionist Theory and 24/7 online job search strategies in Part II have repeatedly outmarketed, outsmarted, and outclassed the competition. This new entry is intended to help you achieve the same results.

The *24/7 Online Job Search Directory* (Chapter 11), featuring market-tested career and job search Web sites, was researched—via quality online research sources—and developed from the bottom up. Each Web site was visited, revisited, researched, and probed. As of this writing, all of the Web sites in the directory are active. Of course, this does not guarantee that ongoing consolidations within the dot-com business sector won't claim some of the listed Web sites. However, many of these Web sites are owned and operated by the most dynamic and durable names in the job search industry— Korn/Ferry International, Heidrick & Struggles, Spencer Stuart, A.T Kearney, Whitehead Mann Group, The Whitney Group, DHR International, CareerJournal, ExecuNet, Futurestep, CareerBuilder, and TMP Worldwide Executive Search's Monster Division. Other enduring names in the 24/7 *Directory* include the Riley Guide, Quintessential Careers, Kennedy Information, Peter Weddle, and Pam Dixon's Online Job Search Companion. As for consolidations taking place in the industry (for example, CareerBuilder acquired the Headhunter Web site), you will be able to keep up with such changes through the real-time career centers (e.g., www.rileyguide.com and www .quintcareers.com) included in the 24/7 directory.

## ABOUT PART I: MARKET-TESTED POWER PACKAGING

As you, the intelligent manager, pick up and browse through yet another resume book, just as I have done for the past two decades, your doubts and skepticism are understandable. The universe of resume books on the market is hardly populated with Pulitzer Prize candidates.

As a Fortune 100 manager, veteran writer, and executive career consultant, I've been an outspoken critic of the past and current crop of generally weak and outdated resume books. The acute shortage of quality, marketing-oriented resume books in the increasingly hostile circa 2002 job market creates a serious void at a time when effective self-marketing is critical. I wrote this book to demonstrate how resumes can be written better, based on an intense decade of successfully packaging and marketing discriminating management-level clients into a wide spectrum of companies ranging from international growth companies (e.g., General Electric, Daimler-Benz, IBM, 3M Corporation, and Westdeutsche Landesbank) to mid-size and emerging start-up companies.

Since virtually every resume book on the market says that it is either good, better, or best, how can you objectively differentiate and identify those books that can really help you with the critical job search self-marketing process as we enter the twenty-first century?

Let's demonstrate how and why this book *is* superior.

To assist you within an economic environment characterized by corporate downsizing, rapid turnover, zero job security, and perpetual job searches, this workbook offers the following critically important *features and advantages* that clearly separate and distinguish it:

▶ *Superior Quality Sample Resumes and Cover Letters.* Based directly on more than 60 real-life client case histories, the market-tested and proven samples in this book successfully generated quality interviews and six-figure career moves. These are samples of unmatched quality from which to extract, borrow, and adapt key words, phrases, sentences, and paragraphs as you develop your own power package.

▶ *A Uniquely Strong Focus on Defining and Packaging Marketable Skills and Achievements.* Unlike almost all other resume books on the market, this workbook deemphasizes and subordinates the narrative job descriptions (*often misrepresented as achievements* by many books) that clutter most resumes; it also totally eliminates other nonselling information.

The twenty-first century job market continues to respond favorably to the skills and achievement-oriented resumes featured in this workbook—and because major online job search Web sites such as www.CareerJournal.com focus on defining your major accomplishments and skills/key words, the resumes developed herein will facilitate and expedite your twenty-first century online job search. In fact, the skills and accomplishment sections of CareerJournal .com's ResumeBuilder feature correspond exactly to the skills and accomplishment sections of the power packages that you will develop in Part I.

*Note: An Important Word about Resume Format:* As detailed on pages 12 and 29, this book demonstrates and recommends the combination functional and chronological format in developing your resume marketing package. This market-tested format positions your Career Skills/Knowledge and Career Achievements on page one (functional format) and your chronological employment history on page two (chronological format). Based on more than a decade of measuring market response through clients who made successful career moves, I strongly recommend this marketing-driven format. If for reasons of convention (remember that conventional methods have helped produce a 99 percent rejection rate), you choose to use the chronological format, refer to Appendix I for an example of how to convert from the combination format to the chronological format.

▶ *An Unparalleled Emphasis on the Marketing Cover Letter.* Unlike the majority of resume books on the market, this workbook treats the cover letter and resume as *coequal* and *totally inseparable* components of the total marketing package. While other books frequently highlight the importance of the letter, they often undermine this importance by merely tacking on a chapter near the end of the book that contains a *few* mediocre to poor sample letters, *none* of which are related to the sample resumes.

Every sample resume in this book has a corresponding cover letter—*no* other books on the market can make this claim. Based on a frequently heard comment from my management clients, "The cover letter got me the interview," I have no doubts about the importance of the letter.

▶ *A More Representative Cross Section of Sample Resumes and Cover Letters.* By deliberately excluding many highly specialized, often irrelevant job positions that provide filler for countless resume books, this workbook concentrates on presenting the several mainstream categories and subcategories of management-level positions into which most managers fall.

▶ *An Intense Focus on Real-Life Success Stories.* The narrative and samples in this book reflect the market-tested and proven methods and techniques that resulted in successful career moves for satisfied clients.

▶ *A Respect for the Intelligence and Experience of the Reader/ Manager.* This workbook steadfastly avoids the insultingly simplistic advice that permeates the universe of resume books: There are no references to paper size, paper color, typos, spelling, or photocopying.

▶ *A Respect for and Focus on Market Response.* Simply stated, the power-packaging techniques and real-life samples in this book achieved the desired results for managers just like you—they produced positive interviews and job offers in an increasingly tough and selective marketplace which is, of course, the *ultimate* and only relevant judge of quality.

If you have not been in the job market for some time and/or have not prepared or updated your resume in recent years, I have included, for your convenience, two data-gathering chapters. They help you recall, organize, and document the necessary information to complete your marketing resume and cover letter. Chapters 2 and 3 help you focus on and define your marketable skills and achievements, which are the major components of your resume and cover letter package.

## ABOUT PART II: LAUNCHING A JOB SEARCH CAMPAIGN IN THE TWENTY-FIRST CENTURY

### REALITY CHECK

In comparing restrictive search theories to our patented Expansionist Theory, remember this simple truth: You can never be guilty of making too many contacts, but you can certainly be guilty of making too few. Widespread failure to heed this fact has ceded a big competitive edge to our clients who beat the competition with high-volume marketing that wins job offers.

The resume and cover letter package drafted through the market-tested process in Part I gives you a competitive that will facilitate and expedite your search. This power packaging, combined with aggressive use of our multistep, high-volume Expansionist Theory and 24/7 Online Job Search Directory in Part II, continues to be a winning formula for clients who repeatedly outmarket their peers by at least 1,000 percent—achieving a placement success rate that buries the competition. Our clients and readers get results, and so will you.

### A Word about Some Icons of the World Wide Web

My online research not only revealed the quality Web sites contained in the 24/7 Directory; it also revealed the names of those trailblazers who have made the Web an essential job search tool. In alphabetical order, they are: Margaret F. Dikel (www.rileyguide.com), Pam Dixon (www.pamdixon.com), Dr. Randall S. Hansen (www.quintcareers .com), Dave Opton (www.execunet.com), and Peter Weddle (www .weddles.com). As detailed in Chapter 11, their early vision brought critically needed organization, creativity, and discipline to the untamed Internet. These five Web explorers have secured a place in Internet history.

# Part I

# Market-Tested Power Packaging

──────── **REALITY CHECK** ────────

In the career and job search game, the only thing that really matters is results. As demonstrated through real-life case histories, clients who combined our market-tested resume and cover letter packages with our Expansionist Theory have enjoyed a placement success rate that far surpassed the outplacement industry norm.

# 1

# Frequently Asked Questions with Market-Tested Answers

Your most important job search/marketing tools are your resume and cover letter. As you think through the following questions and answers, please remember three market-tested philosophies that guided the development of this workbook:

*Philosophy 1.* Conventional, simplistic, and dogmatic how-to advice published in the past has helped to produce a 99% nationwide rejection rate for resumes—hardly a ringing endorsement for perpetuating past practices and advice.

*Philosophy 2.* The only opinion that really matters in judging the quality and effectiveness of your marketing resume and cover letter package is the opinion and response of the marketplace. The real-life sample resume and cover letter packages in this workbook were well-received by the marketplace, resulting in successful career moves up to six-figure salaries at the senior vice-president level.

*Philosophy 3.* Individuals need to be professional marketeers in planning their job search campaigns and developing their marketing presentation packages. The increasingly volatile, hostile, and challenging white-collar job market of the twenty-first century will require and demand nothing less.

Q: Why doesn't my old resume generate more *quality* interviews and multiple quality offers?

A: The marketing resume and cover letter package should, but rarely does, present your strongest possible case so as to increase your chances of landing on the potential candidate pile rather than on the no pile allotted to 99% of all resumes. Most resumes reach the no pile for a sadly legitimate reason—they fail to market and sell the individual.

Resumes are rejected for other reasons (e.g., a true nonmatch or lack of needed technical skills or credentials). However, based on two decades of experience, I have concluded that the overriding reason for the nationwide rejection rate of 99% is that most resumes simply do not achieve their intended goal of marketing and selling the candidate.

Q: How then do I present my strongest possible case?

A: You achieve this by focusing on and presenting, in your resume and cover letter, a well thought out, well-crafted, and hard-hitting presentation of your marketable skills and achievements. When you cut through all the superficial theories postulated about resume content, the undeniable fact is that you will (and should) ultimately be judged by the reader/decision maker based on your applicable skills and past accomplishments.

Few decision makers care much about the extended and detailed job descriptions that fill most resumes. While the resume and cover letter packages that you develop here will include brief job descriptions as secondary data, the primary emphasis will be on developing the strongest possible achievement statements (i.e., success stories) and skills definition sections of the resume and cover letter.

Strong, hard-hitting achievement statements convey this message: "Since I directed these successful efforts, accomplished these management goals, resolved these major problems, and achieved these targeted results for past employers, I can do the same for you."

Q: Should my resume be no longer than one page? How critical is the cover letter?

A: Epitaph for the One-Page Resume Theory: Once and for all, let's put this overaged turkey of a theory to rest.

A key principle behind the oft-quoted one-page resume theory is indeed a sound one, stating that your presentation must be succinct and to the point because you only have 15 seconds of the reader's review time to make your best case. So far, so good.

It is the interpretation and application of this principle, namely, that the resume must therefore be one page, that is all wet. In fact, the principle that you must present your best case as succinctly as possible for a 15-second review process leads instead to the following conclusion: If you don't first sell the reader with your marketing cover letter, you are not likely to sell the reader at all!

As detailed in Chapter 5, the marketing cover letter is the single most critical document that you will produce. While the resume must be as strong as the letter, the cover letter must do 98% of the initial marketing. I can state this un-equivocally, based on my experience in the marketplace and on feedback from clients.

The cover letter is a chance to speak to the reader/inter-viewer. By developing the type of skills and achievement-oriented letters outlined in Chapter 5, you give yourself the same competitive edge that led to my clients' successful career moves into international growth companies as well as emerging mid-size and start-up companies. Failure to de-velop a hard-hitting, creative, achievement and skills-oriented cover letter results in a missed opportunity.

As for the resume, by using the recommended combina-tion format (see next question), which positions your skills and achievements on page one (functional format) and all employer names, dates, and job descriptions on page two (chronological format), you accomplish the following: All the marketing (i.e., communication of your skills and achievements) is indeed contained on the first page of the resume so that if the reader only reviews page one, that is okay.

The cover letter and first page of your two-page resume should and (by applying this book's techniques) will con-tain 99% of your marketable selling points. This is a sound application of the principle behind the outmoded one-page resume theory. Decades of firsthand experience and the success of my white-collar clients, 98% of whom had two-page resumes, indicate that the rule that the resume must absolutely not exceed one page is simplistic tripe.

Q: What resume format should I use?

A: The typical analysis of the chronological versus functional versus combination formats is frequently characterized by lengthy lists of simplistic pros and cons that complicate the decision-making process and divert attention from the most critical factors to consider in determining the optimum format, namely, the impact of and market response to the various format styles.

Based on a busy decade of measuring market response through clients who made successful career moves, my experience has been that the format producing the greatest market impact is the one that best highlights and sells your most marketable assets—your accomplishments and skills. I, therefore, recommend (and demonstrate throughout this book) the combination functional (page one) and chronological (page two) format, which is, in most instances, the most marketing-driven format for presenting your skills and achievements.

Grouping and presenting your skills and achievements on page one of the resume while presenting your reverse chronological listing of employers (with dates, job titles, and job descriptions) on page two has several marketing advantages:

▶ First of all, and most importantly, by grouping your skills and achievements together on page one of the resume, you are presenting your most marketable and highest impact information first—a sound application of fundamental marketing principles. Remember you are the product, and the resume and cover letter package is your chief preinterview sales tool. You should, therefore, develop your chief sales tool using the same proven marketing principles and techniques that apply to any product.

▶ Second, by using this recommended combination format, you are demonstrating your respect for the employer's valuable and limited time by not forcing the reviewer to read and sort through a bunch of job descriptions, dates, and other low-impact, nonselling data better presented in the chronological section (page two).

If for reasons of convention (remember that conventional methods have helped produce a 99% rejection rate), you choose to use the chronological format, refer to Appendix I for an example of how to convert from the combination format to chronological format.

Q: Should my resume always include an objective statement?

A: An objective statement should always be included somewhere in your resume and cover letter marketing package but not necessarily in the resume itself. In fact, safe rules of thumb are that:

1. An objective statement will *always* be included in the marketing cover letter.

2. An objective statement will be included *less frequently* or *not at all* in the resume.

Q: Why is this so?

A: Including an objective statement in *both* the resume and cover letter is unnecessarily redundant.

Since the recipient of the marketing package will, in most instances, read the cover letter first, the objective statement must always appear in the letter, which is developed as a high-powered marketing tool in Chapter 5. It is, therefore, not necessary also to include an objective statement in the resume. Moreover, by not including the objective statement on the resume, you make the resume less restrictive, thereby leaving the door open to targeting multiple objectives each of which can be readily expressed by simply modifying the objective statements in the cover letter.

It is obviously not forbidden also to include the objective statement on the resume. However, if you decide to include it, have a better reason than "the Sunday newspaper supplement says the objective should always be on the resume." Such Sunday-supplement advice has been a major contributor to the extremely high rejection rate for resumes.

# 2

# Defining Your
# Success Stories
# and Skills

Chapters 2 and 3 are designed for those of you who have not been on the job market for some time and/or who have not prepared or updated your resume in recent years. These chapters will help you recall, organize, and document the important information needed to complete your marketing resume and cover letter package in Chapters 4 and 5.

In particular, these chapters will help you to focus on and define your marketable credentials, skills, and achievements, which are, of course, the major components of your resume and letter packages. When you have completed these sections, you will have a database of information from which to effectively communicate your credentials, skills, and achievements both in the marketing resume and during interviews when you verbally tell your story of accomplishment.

## WRITING YOUR SUCCESS STORIES/
## ACCOMPLISHMENT STATEMENTS

Success stories emphasizing and communicating results achieved are the most effective way to demonstrate that you are a leader and an achiever who can assume a leadership role in the new company's organization. They convey the message: "Since I directed these successful efforts, accomplished these management goals, resolved these major problems, and achieved these targeted results for my past companies, I can do the same for you."

Describe, and whenever possible quantify, your success stories focusing on the bottom-line impact of your accomplishments. Describe what you personally accomplished either individually or as a member of the management team, in areas such as these: measurable contributions to survival and profits during recessionary times; improvements to ROI (return on investment) and ROA (return on assets); specific management goals achieved; major roadblocks overcome; serious problems turned around; major projects completed; tough challenges met; contributions to revenue and/or profit growth; productivity improvements instituted; efficiencies implemented; cost reductions achieved; staffs upgraded or turned around.

Think through the specific goals or objectives you were to achieve and/or the problems you were to overcome and describe the steps you specifically executed to help achieve the goals or overcome the problems. Write out the specific accomplishments and the bottom-line impact of these accomplishments on the operating performance of your company, division, or department.

Remember to let your ego flow. Also remember that understatement of facts and achievements is just as bad as overstatement. If you don't fully communicate your achievements to prospective companies, another management candidate who did will very likely get the interview and offer. Do not worry at this point about writing quality or style—simply describe your achievements/success stories (i.e., tell your story) using your individual style and phraseology.

Following are real-life examples of success story notes, followed by the strong achievement statements developed from them. These achievement statements, excerpted from resumes that generated six-figure-salary job interviews, are similar to the ones you will develop in Chapter 4.

## EXAMPLE 1

Corporate Director of Admin. & Property Services; consolidated/colocated facilities: Examples: 29 warehouses consolidated into 4—annual savings $5.8 million; reduced HQ space by lease buyout—reduced from 90,000 square feet to 62,000 square feet = 30% reduction—saved $4.6 million over term of lease; negotiated buyout of redundant space—cost avoidance of $48,000 × 6 years—yield $250K cash in hand; developed facilities standards program for corporation that aids in identifying requirements, budget levels, and establishing space standards—yielded a 20% reduction in space requirements over previous planning methods—yielded annual savings of $3,400,000.

*Written Achievement Statement*

- Consolidated 29 Acme warehouses down to 4, generating annual savings of $5.8 million; saved $4.6 million by reducing headquarters space 30%; introduced uniform facility standards that reduced total space requirements 20% saving another $3.4 million annually.

## EXAMPLE 2

Vice President International Banking Group; comprised of California and Europe; responsibilities: consolidate; asset sales; capital markets; project financing; thrust of group—toward investment banking; emphasis—lucrative fees and deal-making; generated $6.5 million revenue; 270 banking relationships; 1/3 or 90 at-risk; only lost 8; saved over 90% of the business that could have been lost; new transaction business; new corporate clients generated—international clients—Fortune 500 Domestic Deals.

*Written Achievement Statement*

- As Vice President of the International Banking Group, produced revenue of $6.5 million through aggressive client development and by saving 90% of the seriously at-risk accounts: accelerated the ROA by focusing on corporate finance, investment banking, and asset sales.

Note the emphasis on using strong, descriptive, hard-hitting, and market-tested words and phrases to describe the accomplishments extracted from the success story notes. High-impact words and phrases, such as *turned around, accelerated, executed, generated, initiated, created, instituted, restructured, upgraded, negotiated, expanded, resolved,* are critical components in expressing the importance and impact of your accomplishments.

Use the following list of high-impact words and phrases—extracted from real-life resumes and letters—as a guide in selecting the strongest and most accurate terms to describe, define, and convey the impact of your accomplishments.

As you write your own success story achievement statements both here and in Chapter 4, be sure to refer to Chapters 6 and 7 for a cross section of sample resumes and cover letters. Feel free to borrow and extract from these well-written, well-received success stories and achievement statements.

# HIGH-IMPACT WORDS AND PHRASES FROM REAL-LIFE RESUMES AND LETTERS

abated
abolished
accelerated
achieved
actively participated
aggressively
applied
assumed a key role
authored
built
chaired
closed
codeveloped
codirected
cofounded
cold-called
collected
comanaged
communicated
completed
computerized
conducted
consolidated
contributed
controlled
convinced
coordinated
corrected
cost-effectively
created
critiqued
dealt effectively
defined
delivered
designed
developed and applied
directed
doubled
earned
eliminated
emphasized

enforced
established
exceeded
executed
exercised
expanded
expedited
facilitated
filled
focused
formulated
fostered
founded
gained
generated
ground-breaking
helped
implemented
improved
increased
initiated
instituted
instructed
integrated
interviewed
introduced
investigated
lectured
led
leveraged
maintained
managed
marketed
motivated
negotiated
orchestrated
organized
outmaneuvered
overcame
oversaw
penetrated

performed
permitted
persuaded
planned
played a key role
played an early and
   central role
played a pivotal role
positioned
prepared
presented
prevented
produced
profitably
project managed
promoted
proposed
prospected
protected
provided
published
quadrupled
ranked
received
recommended
recruited
reduced
removed
renegotiated
replaced
researched
resolved
restored
restructured
satisfied
saved
saving
scoped out
selected
selected by
self-financed

| | | |
|---|---|---|
| set up | taught | was able to |
| signed | tightened | was awarded |
| significantly | took the lead in | was chosen |
| sold | trained | was requested |
| staffed | tripled | was selected |
| started | troubleshooted | was singled out |
| stopped | turned around | well-received |
| substituted | uncovered | withstood |
| supervised | upgraded | yielded |

## DEFINING YOUR SKILLS, KNOWLEDGE, AND FUNCTIONAL EXPERTISE

Thinking through your management responsibilities in light of the preceding success stories (and referring to the following list of possible skills, knowledge, and functional expertise), list your skills and areas of knowledge applied in your highest impact positions. Think of your marketable skills and knowledge as the tools used to achieve your success stories. Be exhaustive in listing your skills, knowledge, and functional expertise; do not be concerned about prioritizing and editing them until later.

Refer to Chapters 6 and 7 for a cross section of sample cover letters and resumes that include well-worded, well-organized, and well-received skills definition sections. Feel free to borrow and extract directly from these samples.

## SKILLS, KNOWLEDGE, AND FUNCTIONAL EXPERTISE

*General management*

*Sales/marketing executive*

Sales/marketing management
Client development
Major account development
Quota achievement strategies
Proposals/presentations
Marketing materials/brochure development
Group marketing/seminars/speeches
Trade show participation
Closing skills
Customer service
Marketing
Strategic planning
Market research skills
Advertising/media

*Operations executive*

Research and development
Product research
Product development
Engineering
Manufacturing
Materials management
Production and inventory control
Procurement operations
Distribution operations
Receiving operations
Warehousing operations
Facilities operations

*Finance/administration*

Administrative services
Mergers and acquisitions
Finance/accounting
Controller operations
Accounting operations
Budgeting
Capital appropriations
Auditing operations

Cost reduction strategies
Credit operations

*Treasury operations*

Cash management
Investment/borrowing strategies
Basis point reductions
Foreign exchange strategies
Securities industry
Banking relations

*Human resources management*

Recruiting strategies
Training and development
Organizational development
Benefits administration
Labor relations
Outplacement
Public relations

*Information technology (IT)*

IT executive
Computer operations
Software applications/development
Spreadsheets/MS Excel
Graphics/MS PowerPoint

*Brokerage executive*

Investment banking
Asset management
Real estate/property management
Leasing executive

*Entrepreneurial*

Start-up operations
Financing/capitalization

*Turnaround strategies*

Project management
Planning skills

Problem-solving
Staff supervision/development
Coordination skills

*Communications*

Chief Information Officer (CIO)
Negotiating skills
Verbal communication
Written communication
Multilingual (specify)

# 3

## Defining Other Vital Information

As previously discussed, this chapter and Chapter 2 have been included for those of you who have not been on the job market for some time and/or who have not prepared or updated your resume in recent years. These chapters will help you recall, organize, and document the important information needed to complete your marketing resume and cover letter package in Chapters 4 and 5.

While the success stories and marketable skills defined in Chapter 2 are the most important components of your resume and cover letter package, the information gathered here may well further strengthen your marketing package and overall marketability.

### DATA COLLECTION: INTERNATIONAL CREDENTIALS, LICENSES, ACTIVITIES, AND OTHER ACHIEVEMENTS

What foreign languages do you speak?

_____ Fluent _____ Knowledgeable _____ Weak _____

_____ Fluent _____ Knowledgeable _____ Weak _____

_____ Fluent _____ Knowledgeable _____ Weak _____

What foreign languages do you read and/or write?

_____ Fluent _____ Knowledgeable _____ Weak _____

_____ Fluent _____ Knowledgeable _____ Weak _____

_____ Fluent _____ Knowledgeable _____ Weak _____

Where have you traveled and/or worked internationally? List all countries visited, with approximate dates and reason for the visit:

Since we operate in an increasingly global economy, citing international work assignments, languages, and other global activities may well have substantial market value.

Marketable licenses and/or other certifications (e.g., real estate, brokerage, private pilot):

Marketable business-related group memberships, chairmanships, and other elected or appointed positions (including relevant skills acquired and accomplishments):

Marketable volunteer activities that might be applicable (i.e., have some market impact) to your career move:

Documents authored and/or published; government-issued patents or copyrights:

Potentially marketable avocations including sports-related activities, licensed activities, serious hobbies, and other nonwork-related pastimes:

CAUTIONARY NOTE: Whether or not you will actually include any of the preceding licenses, volunteer activities, or avocations in your final marketing package depends on the answer to the following question: Does this information really contribute to marketing myself? Do not include obviously superfluous or filler information in your resume marketing package. Almost everybody does it, but the

99% nationwide rejection rate for resumes is hardly an endorsement for perpetuating past practices in developing marketing resumes and cover letters.

## DATA COLLECTION: EDUCATION AND MARKETABLE TRAINING

Undergraduate and graduate level education

Undergraduate College _____ From _____ To _____

City, State _____

Degree _____ Year _____

Major/Minor Course Study _____

Still-marketable academic honors/achievements (cumulative GPA, GPA in major, ranking, special honors, scholarships, etc.)

_____

_____

Still-marketable leadership activities/sports achievements

_____

Other marketable accomplishments (e.g., well-received studies/projects, international studies)

_____

_____

Graduate School _____ From _____ To _____

City, State _____

Degree _____ Year _____

Major/Minor Course Study _____

Still-marketable academic honors/achievements (cumulative GPA, GPA in major, ranking, special honors, scholarships, etc.)

_____

Other marketable accomplishments (e.g., well-received papers, international studies)

_____

Other institution (e.g., additional undergraduate or graduate school attended)

Name _____ From _____ To _____

City, State _____

Degree _____ Year _____

Major Course Study _____

Still-marketable academic honors/achievements (cumulative GPA, GPA in major, ranking, special honors, scholarships, etc.)

_____

_____

Still-marketable leadership activities/sports achievements

_____

Other marketable accomplishments (well-received papers/studies/projects, international studies, etc.)

_____

_____

List other marketable training courses and/or seminars completed:

1. _____

2. _____

3. _____

4. _____

5. _____

6. _____

7. _____

8. _____

# DATA COLLECTION: MILITARY EXPERIENCE
(IF APPLICABLE AND STILL MARKETABLE)

Branch _____

Dates: From _____ To _____

Final Rank _____

Number of Promotions _____

Formal Honors (including reasons)

_____

_____

_____

Describe three to five significant achievements during your military service:

1.

2.

3.

4.

5.

## DATA COLLECTION: CHRONOLOGICAL
## EMPLOYMENT HISTORY

Provide the following information for *each* company by which you were employed starting with your current or most recent employer. This chronological information will assist you in completing page two of your combination functional and chronological formatted resume, which contains skills and accomplishments on page one (extracted from Chapter 2) and chronological work history, including job descriptions, on page two (extracted from this chapter).

Company Name _____ City _____ State _____

Dates of Employment: From _____ To _____

Company's Products or Services _____

Most Recent Job Title _____ Dates in position: From _____ To _____

Describe the scope and responsibilities of this position. Include major projects and/or functional work responsibilities for which you are accountable; number of employees under your direct supervision; amount of your revenue, expense, and capital budgets; other relevant data.

Your *Previous* Job Title _____ Dates in position: From _____ To _____

Describe the scope and responsibilities of this position:

Your *Previous* Job Title _____ Dates in position: From _____ To _____

Describe the scope and responsibilities of this position:

# 4

## Developing and Writing Your Marketing Resume

As you, the sophisticated manager, start the process of developing your updated resume, please keep in mind that my approach to developing the marketing resume is based on an intense period of successfully packaging and marketing discriminating management-level clients into a wide spectrum of companies ranging from international growth companies to mid-size and emerging start-up companies.

To facilitate and accelerate the process of developing the strongest possible resume package, this book includes (what the marketplace has characterized as) superior quality sample resumes from which to develop your own high-impact resume. Based directly on more than 50 real-life client case histories, the market-tested and proven samples featured in this chapter and in Chapters 6 and 7 provide unmatched quality resumes from which to extract, borrow, and adapt key words, phrases, sentences, and paragraphs as you develop your own power package.

As you generate your marketing package following the techniques outlined in this chapter, you will also note a uniquely strong focus on defining your marketable skills and achievements. Unlike almost all other resume texts, this workbook plays down and subordinates the narrative job descriptions (often misrepresented as achievements by many books) that clutter most resumes; it also totally eliminates other nonselling information.

Remember that the marketplace has responded favorably to the skills and achievement-oriented resumes featured here. The power-packaging techniques in this book achieved the desired results for managers just like you—they produced positive interviews and job offers in an increasingly tough and selective marketplace, which is, of course, the ultimate and only relevant judge of quality.

## HOW TO DEVELOP YOUR MARKETING RESUME

Those of you who have not been on the job market for some time and/or who have not updated your resume in recent years have probably, as suggested earlier, completed Chapters 2 and 3. You have written out and documented your marketable skills, success stories/accomplishments, experiences, honors, and education. Armed with this database, you have at your fingertips all the information that you will need to complete your resume marketing package and marketing cover letter.

The challenge now is to sort through this material to select the most marketable facts. You can select and group together your most marketable skills delineated in Chapter 2. You can likewise review, select, and rewrite for presentation your most marketable achievements based on your success stories, formulated in Chapter 2.

Before you start putting together the marketing resume, let me reiterate a point about format. In developing the resume package, this chapter will be demonstrating and recommending the previously discussed combination format, which positions Career Skills/Knowledge and Career Achievements on page one (functional format) and the chronological employment data on page two (chronological format).

As discussed earlier, I strongly recommend the combination format. The marketplace has responded very favorably to this marketing-driven format. However, should you choose to develop a purely chronological resume, refer to Appendix I, which demonstrates how to convert to the chronological format.

As you develop the resume, feel free to refer to the more than 50 real-life, market-tested, and proven sample resumes in Chapters 6 and 7:

> ▶ Directly borrow and adapt for your own use key words, phrases, and/or sentences from the real-life samples most closely resembling your field, background, and objectives.

▶ Modify the borrowed phrases and sentences to fit your own experiences and background.

## PAGE ONE

### Education/Credentials

First, let's briefly address the issue of where to position your education and related credentials. Many how-to books advise you to place education at the end of the resume, particularly if you have several years of experience beyond graduation. Well, whether education is positioned first or last is hardly the biggest issue in the world—it certainly will not make or break your resume marketing package.

Having said that, it is my marketing-driven opinion that the education information should, in most cases, be positioned up front on page one unless there are concrete reasons, such as the lack of a degree, to position education information at the end. My recommendation is based on the premise that education and related credentials are *always* a key component of your overall profile even if you are a veteran manager with 30 years experience. While your accumulated job skills and achievements should and do become the most important factors in marketing yourself, your education credentials will follow you and be a part of your total profile for your whole life.

Devoting a few lines to your education at the beginning of the resume doesn't take up much space and instantly informs the reader that you have the baseline academic credentials. Remember that even in classified ads for executive level positions, companies almost always include academic requirements along with the other qualifications to fill the job.

If you ultimately choose to position your education and related credentials toward the end, do it for a logical reason and not because conventional how-to books and other simplistic advice say you should. Remember that conventional methods and simplistic and dogmatic how-to advice from the past have helped produce a 99% nationwide rejection rate for resumes.

The following examples and the resumes in Chapters 6 and 7 include other types of credentials including (relevant and marketable) languages, international travel, licenses, publications, and business memberships. When going through your notes from Chapters 2 and 3, if you feel that certain credentials have some market value (the key criteria) include them in the resume at this point. You can always edit them out later after you see the complete resume package come together.

The following real-life examples of Education/Credentials sections are taken from resumes that generated quality interviews and successful career moves up to the six-figure-salary, senior vice-president level.

## EXAMPLE 1

## EDUCATION

B.S.   Honors   Finance      Georgetown University      1980

## EXAMPLE 2

## EDUCATION/CREDENTIALS

M.B.A.   Honors   University of Paris Graduate School of Business      1985

International: Bilingual French and English; solid knowledge of Mideastern languages; traveled to over 60 nations

Certifications: Commercial Pilot's License; Black Belt Karate; Championship Skier

## EXAMPLE 3

## EDUCATION

M.B.A.   Finance/Marketing   University of Virginia   1976
B.S.       Statistics              UCLA                        1974

## EXAMPLE 4

## EDUCATION/CREDENTIALS

B.S.   Electrical Engineering    International University   Comprehensive Six-Year Program
B.A.   Business Administration   Lehman College             Managerial Studies

International:   Traveled throughout Europe, Asia, South America, and North America
Languages:       Fluent French and Spanish

## EXAMPLE 5

## EDUCATION

B.A.   Kent State University      1962

(In this last example, the Education section was positioned at the end of the resume to subordinate the graduation date.)

**Career Skills/Knowledge**

This section focuses on presenting the relevant, transferable, and marketable skills and knowledge that you documented in Chapter 2. These are the tools that you have accumulated and applied to achieve the bottom-line results and accomplishments that we will address after we have completed the Skills section. By presenting multiple primary and secondary skills, you provide the future employer with a succinct listing of valuable (and therefore marketable) skills and talents that you will apply to achieve bottom-line results for your future company.

Presenting your primary and secondary skills and knowledge also allows you to demonstrate the diversity and multiplicity of talents and abilities in your arsenal of experience. This critical advantage helps avoid the simplistic and narrow-minded stereotyping that frequently accompanies the resume review process (e.g., he/she is a manufacturing type or he/she is a technical type). Such premature and superficial stereotyping during the critical 15- to 30-second resume review cycle frequently results in a quick trip to the terminal no pile. This simplistic stereotyping is particularly costly and frustrating since most veteran managers possess multiple, diverse, and transferable talents and experiences that permit them to market themselves toward as many as three to five different (albeit sometimes related) objectives.

Like the successfully placed clients whose Skills/Knowledge sections are shown here, use this section to show your diversity of talents. As demonstrated, you will extract and develop a two-column list of skills: the left column should reflect your primary skills (aimed at your primary objective); the right column should reflect your secondary skills, which may be just as strong as your primary skills but are designated as secondary because they are not quite as relevant to your primary objective.

As also shown in the following examples, you may well develop a second (and possibly third, fourth, etc.) version of your resume (and Skills section) to market yourself to different objectives. For example, the primary skills in Version 1 may become the secondary skills in Version 2, whereas the secondary skills in Version 1 may become the primary skills in Version 2.

As you develop your Skills section, refer to your Chapter 2 notes and feel free to borrow directly from the examples provided here. Also refer to and borrow from the sample resumes in Chapters 6 and 7, which contain a cross section of well-worded, well-organized, and well-received Skills sections. Remember that you do not have to get it perfect the first time; through several drafts, you can and will perform the editing changes necessary to present your skills in the most marketable way.

Following are examples of the Skills/Knowledge sections of resumes that generated quality interviews and successful career moves up to the six-figure-salary, senior vice-president level.

## EXAMPLE 1: JOHN Q. SAMPLE

| | |
|---|---|
| Career Move Achieved | Vice President of a major Fortune 500 high-tech company/industry leader |
| Background | Six-figure-salary executive with multiple objectives: Version 1 below reflects the first objective aimed at securing a finance/administration executive position. Version 2 reflects a second objective aimed at securing a corporate property management executive position. |

### Version 1

### CAREER SKILLS/KNOWLEDGE

- Finance/administration management
- General management
- Strategic/operational planning
- General/administrative services
- Financial planning & analysis
- Procurement operations
- Facilities/telecommunications
- Training operations
- Logistics services
- Global transportation

- Property management
- Development/construction
- Occupancy growth strategies
- Premium rate strategies
- Consolidation strategies
- Lease management/negotiations
- Site selection/space planning
- Budgeting/accountability
- Government regulations
- Environmental guidelines

### Version 2

### CAREER SKILLS/KNOWLEDGE

- Property management
- Development/construction
- Occupancy growth strategies
- Premium rate strategies
- Consolidation strategies
- Lease management/negotiations
- Site selection/space planning
- Budgeting/accountability
- Government regulations
- Environmental guidelines

- Finance/administration management
- General management
- Strategic/operational planning
- General/administrative services
- Financial planning & analysis
- Procurement operations
- Facilities/telecommunications
- Training operations
- Logistics services
- Global transportation

## EXAMPLE 2: DAVID Q. SAMPLE

Career Move Achieved     Senior Vice President of major European-based financial institution

Background     Six-figure-salary executive with multiple fast-track objectives: Version 1 below reflects goal of securing a senior investment banking position; Version 2 reflects second goal of securing a corporate marketing/sales executive position.

*Version 1*

### CAREER SKILLS/KNOWLEDGE

| | |
|---|---|
| o Banking executive | o Marketing/sales executive |
| o International banking | o General management |
| o Investment banking | o Start-up operations |
| o Corporate/capital markets | o Major client development |
| o Acquisitions/joint ventures | o Competitive maneuvering |
| o Subsidiary recapitalization | o Expansion/turnaround strategies |
| o Project financing/syndicates | o Revenue/profit growth |
| o Trade financing/foreign exchange | o Organizational development |

*Version 2*

### CAREER SKILLS/KNOWLEDGE

| | |
|---|---|
| o Marketing/sales executive | o Financial executive |
| o General management | o International banking |
| o Start-up operations | o Investment banking |
| o Major client development | o Corporate/capital markets |
| o Competitive maneuvering | o Acquisitions/joint ventures |
| o Expansion/turnaround strategies | o Subsidiary recapitalization |
| o Revenue/profit growth | o Project financing/syndicates |
| o Organizational development | o Trade financing/foreign exchange |

## EXAMPLE 3: MATTHEW Q. SAMPLE

Career Move Achieved    Executive position within the transportation industry

Background    Over-50 executive under intense pressure to find a position: Version 1 reflects product management/sales objective; Version 2 reflects strategic planning objective.

*Version 1*

### CAREER SKILLS/KNOWLEDGE

o Marketing/sales management
o Revenue/profit turnaround
o Product management/market development
o National accounts programs
o Sales productivity growth
o Competitor intelligence systems
o Business ownership/leveraged buyouts
o Advertising/promotions
o Operations turnaround

o Strategic planning
o Business plans/market research
o Market growth/segmentation
o ROI growth strategies
o Profit/investment optimization
o Economic modeling/pricing
o Supply/demand analysis
o Finance/controller operations
o Cash-flow/financing/bank relations

*Version 2*

### CAREER SKILLS/KNOWLEDGE

o Strategic planning
o Business plans/market research
o Market growth/segmentation
o ROI growth strategies
o Profit/investment optimization
o Economic modeling/pricing
o Supply/demand analysis
o Finance/controller operations
o Cash-flow/financing/bank relations

o Marketing/sales management
o Revenue profit turnaround
o Product management
o National accounts programs
o Sales productivity growth
o Competitor intelligence systems
o Business ownership/leveraged buyouts
o Advertising/promotions
o Operations turnaround

## EXAMPLE 4: WILLIAM Q. SAMPLE

Career Move Achieved    General management position with a European-based company

Background    Over-50 executive with broad-based international experience: Version 1 reflects international sales/marketing objective; Version 2 reflects international operations objective.

*Version 1*

### CAREER SKILLS/KNOWLEDGE

o Sales/marketing executive
o International sales/markets
o European relations
o Strategic/marketing plans
o Market share strategies
o Major client development
o Competitive maneuvering
o Exchange rate strategies
o Organizational development
o Staff supervision/development

o Operations/materials/engineering
o Purchasing operations
o Cost controls/reductions
o Global distribution/logistics
o Heavy industry clients
o Aircraft engine market
o Engineering operations
o Electrical/systems engineering
o New product design
o Plant operating systems design

*Version 2*

### CAREER SKILLS/KNOWLEDGE

o Operations/materials/engineering
o Purchasing operations
o Cost controls/reductions
o Global distribution/logistics
o Heavy industry clients
o Aircraft engine market
o Engineering operations
o Electrical/systems engineering
o New product design
o Plant operating systems design

o Sales/marketing executive
o International sales/markets
o European relations
o Strategic/marketing plans
o Market share strategies
o Major client development
o Competitive maneuvering
o Exchange rate strategies
o Organizational development
o Staff supervision/development

## Career Achievements

More than any other single factor, your achievements (see Chapter 2) help sell you to prospective employers. Here you want to convey the message, "Since I directed these successful efforts, accomplished these management goals, resolved these major problems, and achieved these targeted results for my past companies, I can do the same for you."

Armed with the information assembled in Chapter 2 and the real-life samples from Chapters 6 and 7 (for reference throughout the writing process), you can proceed with confidence to write up the strongest possible list of major achievements. At this stage, you should not yet be concerned with prioritizing or judging whether ultimately to include or exclude any particular achievement. As you systematically go through your Chapter 2 notes and borrow from the samples in Chapters 6 and 7, you should write achievement statements for *all* your success stories. You can and will play editor later.

Consider the following examples of effective, interview-generating achievement statements developed from the type of raw success story notes formulated in Chapter 2.

## EXAMPLE 1: SUCCESS STORY NOTES

Executive Vice President Administration—Prototype Corporation: Direct annual budget—expense—of $65 million plus control additional $15 million in expenses allocated to other cost centers—equals total operating budget of $80 million; $80 million organization; direct 12 major functions including property management; profitably oversee 56 global locations—2 million sq. ft.—office, manufacturing, distribution, field offices. Annual lease expense/facility contracts—$50,000,000; most leased except some mfg. and R&D—contract negotiations critical. Manage assets—company owned—with asset value of approximately $100 million—located worldwide.

*Written Achievement Statement Based on Notes*

- As Executive Vice President of Administration at Prototype Corporation, profitably directed an $80 million operation spanning 56 international locations representing over two million square feet: responsibilities executed in directing 12 major departments include the management of $100 million in company assets and the negotiation of $50 million in facility contracts related to properties located worldwide.

## EXAMPLE 2: SUCCESS STORY NOTES

Milestones as Exec. V.P. of Administration: (1) Completed 300K sq. ft. research facility—months ahead of schedule—several million $ under budget of 52 million—8.4% under. (2) Also took lead in consolidating 15 locations/sites down to 4—primarily included research and administrative types of facilities; estimated annual savings of at least 5 million $—savings based on reducing sq. ft., rental $, and some infrastructure cost reductions. (3) Also consolidated & relocated—mfg. and branch offices; forcefully renegotiated leasehold agreements; eliminated duplication, improved communication, productivity, and efficiencies. Integrated and consolidated operations to gain efficiencies and productivity worldwide—total savings of $50 million over several years and significant increase in productivity.

*Written Achievement Statements Based on Notes*

- Generated multiyear savings of $50 million and accelerated productivity growth through a major consolidation of Prototype's manufacturing and branch office network: aggressively renegotiated expensive leasehold agreements, eliminated redundant operations, and instituted global efficiencies.
- Consolidated 15 research and administrative sites into 4, generating an annual savings of $5 million for Prototype through reductions in square footage and rental expense; also directed the successful completion of an important 300,000 square foot research facility which was finished well ahead of schedule and several million dollars under budget.

## EXAMPLE 3: SUCCESS STORY NOTES

Corporate Director of Admin. & Property Services; consolidated/co-located facilities: Examples: 29 warehouses consolidated into 4—annual savings $5.8 million; reduced HQ space by lease buyout—reduced from 90,000 square feet to 62,000 square feet = 30% reduction—saved $4.6 million over term of lease; negotiated buyout of redundant space—cost avoidance of $48,000 × 6 years—yield $250K cash in hand; developed facilities standards program for corporation that aids in identifying requirements, budget levels, and establishing space standards—yielded a 20% reduction in space requirements over previous planning methods—yielded annual savings of $3,400,000.

*Written Achievement Statement Based on Notes*

- Consolidated 29 Acme warehouses down to 4, generating annual savings of $5.8 million; saved $4.6 million by reducing headquarters

space 30%; introduced uniform facility standards that reduced total space requirements 20%, saving another $3.4 million annually.

## EXAMPLE 4: SUCCESS STORY NOTES

Vice President International Banking Group; comprises California
and Europe; responsibilities: consolidate; asset sales; capital markets; project financing. Thrust of group—toward investment banking;
emphasis—lucrative fees and deal-making; generated $6.5 million
revenue; 270 banking relationships; 1/3 or 90 at-risk; only lost 8;
saved over 90% of the business that could have been lost; new transaction business; new corporate clients generated—international
clients—Fortune 500 Domestic Deals.

*Written Achievement Statement Based on Notes*

• As Vice President of the International Banking Group, produced
  revenue of $6.5 million through aggressive client development
  and by saving 90% of the seriously at-risk accounts: accelerated
  the ROA by focusing on corporate finance, investment banking,
  and asset sales.

Note again the emphasis on using strong market-tested words
and phrases to describe the accomplishments extracted from the
success story notes. High-impact terms such as *turned around, accelerated, executed, generated, initiated, created, instituted, restructured, upgraded, negotiated, expanded, resolved* are critical components in
expressing the importance and dimension of your accomplishments.
Use the word list on pages 17 and 18 as a guide in selecting the
strongest and most accurate terms to describe, define, and convey
the impact of your accomplishments.

Refer to the following examples and the resumes in Chapters 6
and 7:

▶ Directly borrow and adapt for your own use the action words,
  phrases, and/or sentences from the real-life samples most
  closely resembling your field, background, and objectives.

▶ Modify the borrowed phrases and sentences to fit your own
  experience and background.

Following are examples of the Career Achievements sections of
resume packages that generated quality interviews and successful
career moves up to the six-figure-salary, senior vice-president level.

## EXAMPLE 1: JOHN Q. SAMPLE

Career Move Achieved    Vice President of a Fortune 500
high-tech company/industry leader

### CAREER ACHIEVEMENTS

o As Corporate Director of Administration & Property Services, assumed a central role in Acme's turnaround to profitability: generated tens of millions of dollars in cost reductions and cash flow through aggressive property consolidations, upgraded services and procurement, and enforced management accountability.

o Promoted five grade levels during my last four years at ABC Company based on achieving all major P&L goals in directing the $19 million Corporate Administration and Property Management Department.

o Consolidated 29 Acme warehouses down to 4, generating annual savings of $5.8 million; saved $4.6 million by reducing corporate headquarters space 30%; introduced uniform facility standards which reduced total space requirements 20%, generating another $3.4 million in annual cost savings.

o As head of Acme's $230 million purchasing operation, introduced an aggressive multiple-sourcing program which improved the margins of two major product lines by 7% and 9% respectively.

o Overcame powerful organizational resistance to produce over $3 million cash and annual savings of $2.1 million by persuading the chairman to sell off Acme's corporate yacht.

o Generated annual cost savings of over $800,000 by installing a Novell network and upgrading ABC Company's distribution, travel, and other corporate services.

o Productively managed ABC Company's property holdings, achieving 97% occupancy of 800,000 square feet at premium rates; developed a sophisticated model which helped save $7 million on the cost of an out-of-control $40 million building project at ABC.

## EXAMPLE 2: DAVID Q. SAMPLE

Career Move Achieved    Senior Vice President of major
international financial institution

### CAREER ACHIEVEMENTS

o As Vice President of ABC's International Banking Group, produced revenue of $6.5 million through aggressive client development and by saving 90% of the at-risk accounts: accelerated the ROA by focusing on corporate finance, investment banking, and asset sales.

o As Vice President of Corporate Banking at ABC's Southern California headquarters, leveraged my international contacts to market corporate and capital market products generating $5 million in added net income: achieved 250% growth in fees from capital market products.

o Was recruited away and promoted by ABC to start and manage the new International Energy Group: established and directed the lending operation generating over $500 million in new client bookings in only 18 months with an ROA of over 1%.

o As head of Commercial Development in charge of ABC's International Energy Group, initiated and closed several profitable deals including a hard-to-close $600 million project with an international energy company: created and directed a syndicate of major international lenders.

o As Group Officer at Acme International Bank, established and directed operations of a new North American office: achieved and exceeded an aggressive operating plan generating new lending of $300 million and profitability in 5 months instead of the forecasted 10 months.

## EXAMPLE 3: MATTHEW Q. SAMPLE
### (Over-50 Client)

Career Move Achieved    Executive position within the
transportation industry

### CAREER ACHIEVEMENTS

o Upon promotion to Southwestern Sales Director, accelerated sales productivity and major account development achieving a critically needed 35% growth in sales at a pivotal time for the struggling Acme Corporation, which had lost huge market shares due to poor product pricing strategies: achieved highest sales growth and won a major nationwide sales award.

o As Southeastern Sales Director for a troubled division of Acme, turned around profitability becoming the top-ranked Sales Director in the division: instituted aggressive market expansion, national account programs, and strategic planning increasing revenue from $5 million to $23 million in four years; converted a $3 million loss into a $3 million profit.

o Upon being promoted to Product Manager at Acme, created a product management system which accelerated the decision-making process for the pricing, promotion, and distribution of products: increased profits 30% through saturation marketing to growth industries.

o Based on a track record of achievements in sales management and strategic planning, was recruited by corporate headquarters to manage a major group's business evaluation function as part of the restructuring of the strategic planning process: improved declining ROIs by upgrading the pricing structure; saved tens-of-millions of dollars by demonstrating the marginal payback of proposed expenditures.

o Upon promotion to Business Planning Director, orchestrated a multibillion-dollar asset reallocation program which helped triple profits within five years: reallocated over a billion dollars of production assets to growth products; proposed a half-billion-dollar plant conversion which was implemented at half the cost of constructing a new plant.

o Negotiated and closed the leveraged buyout of a $3 million service business formerly owned by the Avery Company: developed a solid business plan which was successfully marketed to major financial institutions with whom I negotiated over a million dollars in financing.

o As owner of a Texas-based venture, turned around sales and operations overcoming most roadblocks except the company's lack of liquidity in a recessionary economy: increased sales 60% in 15 months by upgrading service and promotional programs; restructured cash management; reduced aged receivables 75%; negotiated a 20% reduction in product costs; achieved a 60% increase in productivity.

# EXAMPLE 4: WILLIAM Q. SAMPLE
## (Over-50 Client)

**Career Move Achieved**  General management position with European-based company

## CAREER ACHIEVEMENTS

o Earned multiple promotions up to Executive Vice President of Sales at a U.S. Division of Acme International, one of Europe's largest industrial corporations: created a highly productive sales organization and achieved a fivefold increase in revenue turning the U.S. Division into a $20 million business which now accounts for almost 40% of the subsidiary's global sales.

o In spite of high turnover and chronically unfavorable exchange rates, which adversely impacted the U.S. Division's pricing structure, generated a 500% increase in Acme's customer base through an accelerated client development program which emphasized quality and service to offset the unfavorable pricing.

o In spite of global competition, closed multimillion-dollar clients including Western Electric, AT&T, Boeing, and John Deere: accelerated the AT&T account from zero to $9 million representing half of total sales; generated a ninefold sales increase from the Harvester Division of John Deere; produced an eightfold increase in the Western Electric and Boeing accounts.

o Significantly reduced overhead and logistics expenses and all but eliminated aged receivables and write-offs by creating and enforcing conservative credit policies at Acme; in order to meet scheduled delivery dates through on-time shipments from Europe, also established a first-rate logistics function.

o Earned several promotions up to director within the Engineering Department of a Florida-based division of Essex Corporation: directed high-quality product designs, upgraded operating systems critical to the production process, and effectively troubleshot the complex power supply systems.

Once you have completed the preceding process, you will probably have written out somewhere between 8 and 15 bulleted accomplishment/achievement statements depending on your years and breadth of experience. You can now go through and edit, rework, and reword the bulleted sentences, combine related achievements wherever appropriate and eliminate less important achievements as you prioritize and reorder the achievements based on their relative importance.

In executing the editing process, remember to borrow and adapt key words, phrases, and/or sentences from the proven, marketing-driven samples in Chapters 6 and 7. Develop and pattern your own achievement statements based on these sample resume packages that generated quality interviews and job offers for clients.

## PAGE TWO

### Career Experience

This section is (normally) a reverse chronological listing of the companies/organizations where you have been employed. This information appears on page two of your combination functional (page one: Skills and Achievements sections) and chronological resume.

Use your Chapter 3 notes to record dates of employment, job titles, job descriptions, relevant military experience, and relevant education/training/credentials not included on page one. Be sure to augment your job descriptions with any accomplishments not designated for inclusion in the CAREER ACHIEVEMENTS section.

Following (for your adaptation) are real-life examples of the experience sections of resumes that generated interviews leading to successful career moves. Also refer to Chapters 6 and 7 for a cross section of sample resumes and cover letters representing a full complement of fields, backgrounds, and objectives.

## EXAMPLE 1: JOHN Q. SAMPLE

### CAREER EXPERIENCE

### ACME CORPORATION, Any Town, CA   3/88–Present

Corporate Director of Administration & Property Services
Direct the overall management, planning, site selection, lease negotiations, consolidations, and disposition for property totaling two million square feet. Additionally direct the $230 million purchasing operation and all corporate administrative services.

### ABC COMPANY, Any Town, CA   6/80–3/88

Director of Services & Property   3/85–3/88
Directed services with a staff of 63 and a budget of $19 million: included property management, purchasing, communications, systems, mail, and office equipment placement and maintenance. Reviewed and approved all facilities and construction contracts. Audited almost $100 million in operating expense budgets.

Manager of Administration   2/83–3/85
Developed policies and procedures, negotiated property transactions, and created a model which turned around a $40 million building project.

Senior Facilities Consultant   8/81–2/83
Developed well-received proposals that resulted in the creation of a $12 million Facilities Group.

Senior Consultant   6/80–8/81
Introduced the much needed zero-based budgeting concept to seven major operations.

**REFERENCES PROVIDED UPON REQUEST**

## EXAMPLE 2: DAVID Q. SAMPLE

### CAREER EXPERIENCE

### ABC BANK, Any Town, CA    3/88–Present

INTERNATIONAL BANKING GROUP, Any Town, CA    2/91–Present

Vice President
Responsible for major account development emphasizing high-margin corporate finance and investment banking: acquisitions, recapitalization, and collateralized financing. Upgraded asset quality by addressing and restructuring below-par debt.

CORPORATE BANKING, Any Town, CA    3/88–2/91

Vice President
Created and marketed corporate and capital market products and services to global clients.

### ACME INTERNATIONAL BANK, Any Town, Europe    6/85–3/88

Group Officer (Assistant Vice President), Any Town, British Columbia    4/87–3/88
Managed start-up of a new operation: directed staffing, property selection, facility planning, contract negotiations, and purchasing. Also developed marketing policies and operating procedures.

Officer, Any Town, CA    5/86–4/87
Accelerated global account development quadrupling pre-tax net income to over $4 million.

Officer, Any Town, Europe    6/85–5/86
Established a Credit Group generating over $2 million in fees from new business development.

### REFERENCES PROVIDED UPON REQUEST

## EXAMPLE 3: MATTHEW Q. SAMPLE

### CAREER EXPERIENCE

### ACME CORPORATION, Any City, TX    1976–1992

Business Planning Director—XYZ Division    1989–1992
Designated to orchestrate the development of corporate strategies and upgrade the planning process.

Business Evaluation Director—ABC Division    1986–1989
Designated to reorganize and turn around strategic planning.

Southwestern Sales Director—ABC Division    1982–1986
Developed and directed a high-producing sales team responsible for national account development.

Product Manager—XYZ Division    1978–1982
Created a product management system which accelerated the decision-making process for the pricing, promotion, and distribution of products.

Southeastern Sales Director—XYZ Division    1977–1978
Implemented a Major Account Program; expanded into growth markets; instituted effective competitor data-gathering procedures; created Division's first comprehensive strategic plan.

Senior Marketing Analyst    1976–1977
Executed comprehensive feasibility studies which resulted in the formation of critically needed account development departments. Developed a well-received business plan for a beleaguered venture.

### ESSEX COMPANY, Any City, TX    1992–1994

Senior Consultant
Determined the feasibility of a client's expansion into major European markets: executed comprehensive product demand and competitive studies as a basis for decision making.

### SERVICE VENTURE, Any City, TX    1994–Present

Founder: Directed Marketing, Advertising, Sales, Operations, Finance, and Customer Service.

INTERNATIONAL:    Traveled throughout South America and Europe
LANGUAGES:    Fluent French, Italian, and Spanish

Note: In order to focus on the client's corporate experience, listed the above companies in chronological order instead of reverse chronological order.

## EXAMPLE 4: WILLIAM Q. SAMPLE

### CAREER EXPERIENCE

#### ACME INTERNATIONAL CORPORATION, Any Town, NJ   1984–Present

Executive Vice President of Sales   1987–Present
Direct the Sales Organization with responsibility for direct sales, marketing, strategic planning, client development, import operations, logistics, distribution, and credit.

Vice President of Sales   1984–1987
Directed sales, marketing, strategic planning, and related functions.

#### ESSEX CORPORATION, Any Town, FL   1975–1984

Director of Engineering   1980–1984
Earned several promotions based on engineering achievements in directing low-tolerance design and systems engineering projects. Also successfully planned and executed high-visibility manufacturing projects.

### MILITARY EXPERIENCE

European Military:   Honorably Discharged

**Affiliations:**      Society of U.S. Engineers; Production Engineers of the Northeast
**Citizenship:**       U.S. Citizen

### REFERENCES AVAILABLE UPON REQUEST

Note that the preceding page two Experience Sections are what most people prepare and use as their complete resume. The resultant failure aggressively and succinctly to focus on and highlight your marketable skills and achievements is the single biggest contributor to the nationwide 99% rejection rate. While the chronological Experience section should be included to complete the informational database (and satisfy bureaucratic tendencies to track employment dates), you will not, for the most part, be evaluated and judged based on your ability to write the detailed job descriptions that fill most resumes. You will rather be evaluated and judged on your ability to communicate and highlight your past skills and accomplishments (just as you have done here) as key indicators of your potential to achieve similar bottom-line results for your future employer.

## EDITING THE RESUME

Now that the resume package is complete, you may decide to conduct a final review and editing so that you can make editorial changes, reorganize, and refine your total resume package. During the final editing process, continue to borrow freely and to adapt key words, phrases, and/or sentences from the proven, marketing-driven samples in Chapters 6 and 7. Develop and pattern your own achievement statements based on these resume packages that generated quality interviews and job offers for clients.

Use patience and care because the resume combined with the cover letter (discussed in Chapter 5) is the primary, and often only, means of communicating to potential employers and creating your first impression. Remember the old, but nonetheless true, cliche: "You will NOT get a second chance to create a first impression."

## BRINGING IT ALL TOGETHER

Following are real-life examples of complete resume packages (assembled from the preceding examples) that generated quality interviews and successful career moves up to the senior vice-president level and six-figure salary range.

Note that these examples include, for your optional application, my trademark headers that appear on the same line as your name and provide the reader with a brief two- to five-word description of your background/discipline. These headers have been well-received by the marketplace.

## EXAMPLE 1

**JOHN Q. SAMPLE**          **Administration/Finance Executive**

123 Any Street, Any City, CA XXXXX (619) 555-1234

B.S.     Honors     Finance     Georgetown University     1980

### CAREER SKILLS/KNOWLEDGE

o Finance/administration management
o General management
o Strategic/operational planning
o General/administrative services
o Financial planning & analysis
o Procurement operations
o Facilities/telecommunications
o Training operations
o Logistics services
o Global transportation

o Property management
o Development/construction
o Occupancy growth strategies
o Premium rate strategies
o Consolidation strategies
o Lease management/negotiations
o Site selection/space planning
o Budgeting/accountability
o Government regulations
o Environmental guidelines

### CAREER ACHIEVEMENTS

o As Corporate Director of Administration & Property Services, assumed a central role in Acme's turnaround to profitability: generated tens of millions of dollars in cost reductions and cash flow through aggressive property consolidations, upgraded services and procurement, and enforced management accountability.

o Promoted five grade levels during my last four years at ABC Company based on achieving all major P&L goals in directing the $19 million Corporate Administration and Property Management Department.

o Consolidated 29 Acme warehouses down to 4, generating annual savings of $5.8 million; saved $4.6 million by reducing corporate headquarters space 30%; introduced uniform facility standards which reduced total space requirements 20%, generating another $3.4 million in annual cost savings.

o As head of Acme's $230 million purchasing operation, introduced an aggressive multiple-sourcing program which improved the margins of two major product lines by 7% and 9% respectively.

o Overcame powerful organizational resistance to produce over $3 million cash and annual savings of $2.1 million by persuading the chairman to sell off Acme's corporate yacht.

o Generated annual cost savings of over $800,000 by installing a Novell network and upgrading ABC Company's distribution, travel, and other corporate services.

o Productively managed ABC Company's property holdings, achieving 97% occupancy of 800,000 square feet at premium rates; developed a sophisticated model which helped save $7 million on the cost of an out-of-control $40 million building project at ABC.

## CAREER EXPERIENCE

### ACME CORPORATION, Any Town, CA   3/88–Present

Corporate Director of Administration & Property Services
Direct the overall management, planning, site selection, lease negotiations, consolidations, and disposition for property totaling two million square feet. Additionally direct the $230 million purchasing operation and all corporate administrative services.

### ABC COMPANY, Any Town, CA   6/80–3/88

Director of Services & Property   3/85–3/88
Directed services with a staff of 63 and a budget of $19 million: included property management, purchasing, communications, systems, mail, and office equipment placement and maintenance. Reviewed and approved all facilities and construction contracts. Audited almost $100 million in operating expense budgets.

Manager of Administration   2/83–3/85
Developed policies and procedures, negotiated property transactions, and created a model which turned around a $40 million building project.

Senior Facilities Consultant   8/81–2/83
Developed well-received proposals that resulted in the creation of a $12 million Facilities Group.

Senior Consultant   6/80–8/81
Introduced the much needed zero-based budgeting concept to seven major operations.

## REFERENCES PROVIDED UPON REQUEST

## EXAMPLE 2

| DAVID Q. SAMPLE | International Sales/Finance |
|---|---|

**123 Any Street, Any City, CA XXXXX (619) 555-1234**

| M.B.A. | Honors | University of Paris Graduate School of Business | 1985 |

| International: | Bilingual French and English; solid knowledge of Mideastern languages; traveled to over 60 nations |
|---|---|
| Certifications: | Commercial Pilot's License; Black Belt Karate; Championship Skier |

### CAREER SKILLS/KNOWLEDGE

o Marketing/sales executive
o General management
o Start-up operations
o Major client development
o Competitive maneuvering
o Expansion/turnaround strategies
o Revenue/profit growth
o Organizational development

o Financial executive
o International banking
o Investment banking
o Corporate/capital markets
o Acquisitions/joint ventures
o Subsidiary recapitalization
o Project financing/syndicates
o Trade financing/foreign exchange

### CAREER ACHIEVEMENTS

o As Vice President of ABC's International Banking Group, produced revenue of $6.5 million through aggressive client development and by saving 90% of the at-risk accounts: accelerated the ROA by focusing on corporate finance, investment banking, and asset sales.

o As Vice President of Corporate Banking at ABC's Southern California headquarters, leveraged my international contacts to market corporate and capital market products generating $5 million in added net income: achieved 250% growth in fees from capital market products.

o Was recruited away and promoted by ABC to start and manage the new International Energy Group: established and directed the lending operation generating over $500 million in new client bookings in only 18 months with an ROA of over 1%.

o As head of Commercial Development in charge of ABC's International Energy Group, initiated and closed several profitable deals including a hard-to-close $600 million project with an international energy company: created and directed a syndicate of major international lenders.

o As Group Officer at Acme International Bank, established and directed operations of a new North American office: achieved and exceeded an aggressive operating plan generating new lending of $300 million and profitability in five months instead of the forecasted ten months.

DAVID Q. SAMPLE                                                         Page 2

## CAREER EXPERIENCE

### ABC BANK, Any Town, CA   3/88–Present

INTERNATIONAL BANKING GROUP, Any Town, CA   2/91–Present

Vice President
Responsible for major account development emphasizing high-margin corporate finance and investment banking: acquisitions, recapitalization, and collateralized financing. Upgraded asset quality by addressing and restructuring below-par debt.

CORPORATE BANKING, Any Town, CA   3/88–2/91

Vice President
Created and marketed corporate and capital market products and services to global clients.

### ACME INTERNATIONAL BANK, Any Town, Europe   6/85–3/88

Group Officer (Assistant Vice President), Any Town, British Columbia   4/87–3/88
Managed start-up of a new operation: directed staffing, property selection, facility planning, contract negotiations, and purchasing. Also developed marketing policies and operating procedures.

Officer, Any Town, CA   5/86–4/87
Accelerated global account development quadrupling pre-tax net income to over $4 million.

Officer, Any Town, Europe   6/85–5/86
Established a Credit Group generating over $2 million in fees from new business development.

## REFERENCES PROVIDED UPON REQUEST

# EXAMPLE 3

**MATTHEW Q. SAMPLE**   **Product Management/Strategic Planning/Sales**

**123 Any Street, Any Town, TX  XXXXX  (214) 555-1234**

| | | | |
|---|---|---|---|
| M.B.A. | Finance/Marketing | University of Virginia | 1976 |
| B.S. | Statistics | UCLA | 1974 |

## CAREER SKILLS/KNOWLEDGE

o  Marketing/sales management

o  Revenue/profit turnaround

o  Product management/market development

o  National accounts programs

o  Sales productivity growth

o  Competitor intelligence systems

o  Business ownership/leveraged buyouts

o  Advertising/promotions

o  Operations turnaround

o  Strategic planning

o  Business plans/market research

o  Market growth/segmentation

o  ROI growth strategies

o  Profit/investment optimization

o  Economic modeling/pricing

o  Supply/demand analysis

o  Finance/controller operations

o  Cash-flow/financing/bank relations

## CAREER ACHIEVEMENTS

o  Upon promotion to Southwestern Sales Director, accelerated sales productivity and major account development achieving a critically needed 35% growth in sales at a pivotal time for the struggling Acme Corporation, which had lost huge market shares due to poor product pricing strategies: achieved highest sales growth and won a major nationwide sales award.

o  As Southeastern Sales Director for a troubled division of Acme, turned around profitability becoming the top-ranked Sales Director in the division: instituted aggressive market expansion, national account programs, and strategic planning increasing revenue from $5 million to $23 million in four years; converted a $3 million loss into a $3 million profit.

o  Upon being promoted to Product Manager at Acme, created a product management system which accelerated the decision-making process for the pricing, promotion, and distribution of products: increased profits 30% through saturation marketing to growth industries.

o  Based on a track record of achievements in sales management and strategic planning, was recruited by corporate headquarters to manage a major group's business evaluation function as part of the restructuring of the strategic planning process: improved declining ROIs by upgrading the pricing structure; saved tens-of-millions of dollars by demonstrating the marginal payback of proposed expenditures.

o  Upon promotion to Business Planning Director, orchestrated a multibillion-dollar asset reallocation program which helped triple profits within five years: reallocated over a billion dollars of production assets to growth products; proposed a half-billion-dollar plant conversion which was implemented at half the cost of constructing a new plant.

o  Negotiated and closed the leveraged buyout of a $3 million service business formerly owned by the Avery Company: developed a solid business plan which was successfully marketed to major financial institutions with whom I negotiated over a million dollars in financing.

o  As owner of a Texas-based venture, turned around sales and operations overcoming most roadblocks except the company's lack of liquidity in a recessionary economy: increased sales 60% in 15 months by upgrading service and promotional programs; restructured cash management; reduced aged receivables 75%; negotiated a 20% reduction in product costs; achieved a 60% increase in productivity.

## CAREER EXPERIENCE

### ACME CORPORATION, Any City, TX    1976–1992

Business Planning Director—XYZ Division    1989–1992
Designated to orchestrate the development of corporate strategies and upgrade the planning process.

Business Evaluation Director—ABC Division    1986–1989
Designated to reorganize and turn around strategic planning.

Southwestern Sales Director—ABC Division    1982–1986
Developed and directed a high-producing sales team responsible for national account development.

Product Manager—XYZ Division    1978–1982
Created a product management system which accelerated the decision-making process for the pricing, promotion, and distribution of products.

Southeastern Sales Director—XYZ Division    1977–1978
Implemented a Major Account Program; expanded into growth markets; instituted effective competitor data-gathering procedures; created Division's first comprehensive strategic plan.

Senior Marketing Analyst    1976–1977
Executed comprehensive feasibility studies which resulted in the formation of critically needed account development departments. Developed a well-received business plan for a beleaguered venture.

### ESSEX COMPANY, Any City, TX    1992–1994

Senior Consultant
Determined the feasibility of a client's expansion into major European markets: executed comprehensive product demand and competitive studies as a basis for decision-making.

### SERVICE VENTURE, Any City, TX    1994–Present

Founder:  Directed Marketing, Advertising, Sales, Operations, Finance, and Customer Service.

**INTERNATIONAL:**  Traveled throughout South America and Europe
**LANGUAGES:**        Fluent French, Italian, and Spanish

## EXAMPLE 4

**WILLIAM Q. SAMPLE**                    **International Sales Executive**

**123 Any Street Address, Any Town, NJ XXXXX  (201) 555-1234**

B.S.   Electrical Engineering    International University  Comprehensive Six-Year Program
B.A.  Business Administration  Lehman College            Managerial Studies

International:       Traveled throughout Europe, Asia, South America, and North America
Languages:         Fluent French and Spanish

### CAREER SKILLS/KNOWLEDGE

o Sales/marketing executive
o International sales/markets
o European relations
o Strategic/marketing plans
o Market share strategies
o Major client development
o Competitive maneuvering
o Exchange rate strategies
o Organizational development
o Staff supervision/development

o Operations/materials/engineering
o Purchasing operations
o Cost controls/reductions
o Global distribution/logistics
o Heavy industry clients
o Aircraft engine market
o Engineering operations
o Electrical/systems engineering
o New product design
o Plant operating systems design

### CAREER ACHIEVEMENTS

o Earned multiple promotions up to Executive Vice President of Sales at a U.S. Division of Acme International, one of Europe's largest industrial corporations: created a highly productive sales organization and achieved a fivefold increase in revenue turning the U.S. Division into a $20 million business which now accounts for almost 40% of the subsidiary's global sales.

o In spite of high turnover and chronically unfavorable exchange rates, which adversely impacted the U.S. Division's pricing structure, generated a 500% increase in Acme's customer base through an accelerated client development program which emphasized quality and service to offset the unfavorable pricing.

o In spite of global competition, closed multimillion-dollar clients including Western Electric, AT&T, Boeing, and John Deere: accelerated the AT&T account from zero to $9 million representing half of total sales; generated a ninefold sales increase from the Harvester Division of John Deere; produced an eightfold increase in the Western Electric and Boeing accounts.

o Significantly reduced overhead and logistics expenses and all but eliminated aged receivables and write-offs by creating and enforcing conservative credit policies at Acme; in order to meet scheduled delivery dates through on-time shipments from Europe, also established a first-rate logistics function.

o Earned several promotions up to director within the Engineering Department of a Florida-based division of Essex Corporation: directed high-quality product designs, upgraded operating systems critical to the production process and effectively troubleshooted the complex power supply systems.

## CAREER EXPERIENCE

### ACME INTERNATIONAL CORPORATION, Any Town, NJ   1984–Present

Executive Vice President of Sales   1987–Present
Direct the Sales Organization with responsibility for direct sales, marketing, strategic planning, client development, import operations, logistics, distribution, and credit.

Vice President of Sales   1984–1987
Directed sales, marketing, strategic planning, and related functions.

### ESSEX CORPORATION, Any Town, FL   1975–1984

Director of Engineering   1980–1984
Earned several promotions based on engineering achievements in directing low-tolerance design and systems engineering projects. Also successfully planned and executed high-visibility manufacturing projects.

## MILITARY EXPERIENCE

European Military:   Honorably Discharged

**Affiliations:**     Society of U.S. Engineers; Production Engineers of the Northeast
**Citizenship:**     U.S. Citizen

## REFERENCES AVAILABLE UPON REQUEST

# 5

## Developing and Writing Your Marketing Cover Letter

**THE STRATEGIC MARKETING DOCUMENT**

As discussed and detailed in previous chapters, the marketing cover letter combined with a hard-hitting resume is the most critical document that you will produce. Since you have only 15 to 30 seconds of the reviewer's time to market yourself and make your case, if you don't sell the reader with the cover letter, you will very likely not sell the reader at all.

Based on extensive feedback directly from the marketplace and from executive-level clients who have repeatedly stated, "The cover letter got me the interview," I have firmly concluded that the failure to develop a strong, creative achievement and skills-oriented letter results in a missed opportunity.

Unlike the vast majority of resume books on the market, this workbook treats the cover letter and resume as *co-equal* and *inseparable* components of the total marketing package. While other books frequently highlight the importance of the letter, they often undermine this importance by merely tacking on a chapter near the end of the book with a few mediocre-to-poor sample letters, *none* of which are related to the sample resumes.

By developing the type of market-tested and proven letters outlined in this chapter and demonstrated through the more than 60 case histories contained in this book, you give yourself the same competitive edge that led to my clients' successful career moves into international growth companies as well as emerging mid-size and start-up companies.

## DEVELOPING THE COVER LETTER TEXT

While developing the text of the letter, refer to the sample letters in Chapters 6 and 7, which provide a full complement of fields, backgrounds, and objectives.

- ▸ Directly borrow and adapt for your own use key words, phrases, and/or sentences from the real-life samples most closely resembling your field, background, and objectives.
- ▸ Modify the borrowed phrases and sentences to fit your own experiences and background.

### The Introductory Paragraph: A Modular Approach

The introductory paragraph must "grab" the reader to make him or her want to read further. It should include a fact-oriented, hard-hitting capsule overview of your achievements and skills extracted from your already-developed resume.

By *substituting* words and phrases that apply to *you and your experience* for the words in parentheses, you can modify the following introductory paragraphs to fit your own situation. Once you have initially modified the paragraph, then insert additional changes *to reflect your own personality and style*—make sure your final version fits you.

The following modular paragraphs were excerpted from letters that generated quality interviews and job offers:

As a central figure in (Acme Corporation's massive restructuring), I applied executive skills in (finance), (administration), (property management), and (purchasing) to (facilitate Acme's turnaround to profitability). I likewise produced (multimillion-dollar profits for the ABC Company) through (productive management of its administration and property management services) receiving (accelerated promotions up to Director of a $19 million operation).

I have combined (a top business degree, global experience), and executive skills in (sales), (finance), (banking), and (general management) to (establish and direct new operations which have generated millions in revenue for well-respected international companies). Bottom-line contributions to profit have been rewarded with (accelerated promotions, job security, and a six-figure salary package).

I have combined (a top school M.B.A.) with executive skills in (marketing), (sales management), (product management), (strategic planning), and (general management) to (orchestrate a leveraged buyout), (head up a $3 million business), (strategically reposition troubled operations), and (turn around and accelerate sales for weak divisions of the Acme Corporation).

As (Executive Vice President of Sales for the U.S. Division of a European-based corporation), I have applied proficient skills in (international sales), (marketing), (client development), and (operations) to (outmaneuver the competition), (deal with volatile exchange rates), (accelerate growth of the corporate client base), and (achieve a fivefold increase in sales)—(a revenue level that now accounts for 40% of worldwide sales).

I have developed and applied skills in (sales), (marketing), and (operations) to (successfully sell products), (direct plant operations), (generate cost reductions), (achieve quotas), and (upgrade product quality) for (two Seattle-based companies). Results achieved have been rewarded with (promotions and substantial pay raises).

I have (profitably) applied skills in (sales), (marketing), (client development), (real estate brokerage), and (property management) to (sell $10 million worth of product), (earn Million-Dollar-Club status), (profitably manage several apartment buildings), and (generate $5 million in sales in a two-year period).

I have applied skills in (sales), (marketing), (operations), and (project management) to (start up a multimillion-dollar electronics company), (generate half of its total sales), (expand the client base of another high-tech company), and (coordinate total administration of a $300 million project for a major electronics firm).

I have formulated and executed expert (sales and marketing strategies) to (outmaneuver the competition), (penetrate new markets), and (generate record sales in the Los Angeles marketplace) during (the past 15 years with a subsidiary of Acme Industries). This has been rewarded with (up to a six-figure income) and (number one ranking nationally).

## The Letter's Second Paragraph: A Modular Approach

In the second paragraph, you tell the reader why you are writing to the company/firm. Use the same basic approach that you used to develop the introductory paragraph. By substituting words and phrases that apply to you and your experience for the words in parentheses, you can modify the following paragraphs to fit your own situation. Once you have initially modified the paragraph, insert additional changes *to reflect your own personality and style*—make sure your final version fits you.

Following are modular paragraphs from letters that achieved quality interviews and job offers:

I am presenting for your review my skills, achievements, and (talent for accelerating profit margins and turning around unprofitable organizations) so that we can discuss my joining _____ as a member of your (senior management) team.

I am bringing to your attention my skills, achievements, (strategic brainpower), (global network), and (talent for exceeding profit goals under negative economic conditions) so that we can discuss my joining _____ as a member of your (senior management) team.

I am bringing to your attention my skills, achievements, (talent for stimulating sales productivity), and (ability to achieve bottom-line results under the most intense pressure) so that we can discuss my joining _____ as a member of your (senior sales management) team.

I am presenting for your review my skills, achievements, (technical degree), (global contacts), and (talent for creating productive sales forces and achieving aggressive revenue and profit goals) so that we can discuss my joining _____ as a member of your (senior sales management) team.

I am bringing to your attention my skills, achievements, (high energy), (talent for improving job candidate quality), and (track record of cost reductions) so that we can discuss my joining _____ as a member of your (HR Management) Team.

I am bringing to your attention my skills, achievements, (nationwide network of electronics industry contacts), and (ability to produce results under crisis management conditions) so that we can discuss my joining _____ as a member of your (R&D Management) Team.

I am bringing to your attention my skills, achievements, (leasing industry expertise), and (talent for generating bottom-line results within problem operations) so that we can discuss my joining _____ as a member of your (management) team.

**Writing the Second Paragraph Objective Statements**

Your objective statements should not be so restrictive that you are easily eliminated from contention for alternative job opportunities. For example, you can use generic or organizational objectives as alternatives to job titles:

> . . . so that we can discuss my joining the Acme Corporation as a member of your
>
> Senior Management team.
>
> General Management team.
>
> Sales/Marketing Management team.
>
> Financial or Treasury Management team.
>
> Operations/Manufacturing Management team.
>
> Research & Development Management team.
>
> Human Resources Management team.
>
> Engineering Management team.

It is not unusual for people realistically and legitimately to define as many as three to five different objectives. This is an excellent way to broaden your options and create as many different job opportunities as possible by marketing yourself toward multiple objectives.

Multiple objectives require the creation and use of multiple objective statements (and multiple versions of the cover letter and resume package) for marketing and dissemination to multiple functional contacts within the corporate structure.

**The Letter's Third Paragraph**

To develop the letter's third paragraph, simply select and extract some of the major bulleted achievements directly from the already developed resume to reinforce and support the achievements summarized in the first paragraph. The deliberate and necessary redundancy created by including bulleted achievement statements in both the cover letter and resume has met with unqualified success in the marketplace.

The all-important cover letter must be developed as a stand-alone document based on the assumption that the reader will only review the letter—remember that you only get 15 to 30 seconds to make your case; therefore, the reader may well not get past the letter. To be a stand-alone document, the cover letter must necessarily contain key information extracted from and deliberately redundant with the resume.

The success of my clients in the marketplace has proven that intelligent decision makers are impressed by candidates who create comprehensive stand-alone letters that contain vital information excerpted from the resume. Such letters send a positive message to the reader that the candidate is a good communicator who understands and respects the reader's limited review time.

Following are examples of third paragraphs from letters that generated quality interviews and job offers:

## EXAMPLE 1: JOHN Q. SAMPLE

Results achieved to date include:

o Promoted five grade levels during my last four years at ABC Company based on achieving all major P&L goals in directing the $19 million Corporate Administration and Property Management Department.

o As Acme's Corporate Director of Administration & Property Services, generated tens of millions of dollars in cost reductions and cash flow through aggressive property consolidations, upgraded services and procurement, and enforced management accountability.

o Consolidated 29 Acme warehouses down to 4, generating annual savings of $5.8 million; saved $4.6 million by reducing corporate headquarters space 30%; introduced uniform facility standards which reduced total space requirements 20%, generating another $3.4 million in annual cost savings.

o As head of Acme's $230 million purchasing operation, introduced an aggressive multiple-sourcing program which improved the margins of two major product lines by 7% and 9% respectively.

o Productively managed ABC Company's property holdings, achieving 97% occupancy of 800,000 square feet at premium rates; developed a sophisticated model which helped save $7 million on the cost of an out-of-control $40 million building project at ABC.

## EXAMPLE 2: DAVID Q. SAMPLE

Major accomplishments to date include:

o As Vice President of ABC's International Banking Group, produced revenue of $6.5 million through aggressive client development and by saving 90% of the seriously at-risk accounts: accelerated the ROA by focusing on corporate finance, investment banking, and asset sales.

o As Vice President of Corporate Banking at ABC's Southern California headquarters, leveraged my international contacts to market corporate and capital market products generating $5 million in added net income: achieved 250% growth in fees from capital market products.

o Was recruited away and promoted by ABC to start and manage the new International Energy Group: established and directed the lending operation generating over $500 million in new client bookings in only 18 months with an ROA of over 1%.

o As head of Commercial Development in charge of ABC's International Energy Group, initiated and closed several profitable deals including a hard-to-close $600 million project with an international energy company: created and directed a syndicate of major international lenders.

## EXAMPLE 3: MATTHEW Q. SAMPLE

Results achieved to date include:

o Upon promotion to Southwestern Sales Director, accelerated sales productivity and major account development achieving a critically needed 35% growth in sales at a pivotal time for the struggling Acme Corporation, which had lost huge market shares due to poor product pricing strategies: achieved highest sales growth and won a major nationwide sales award.

o As Southeastern Sales Director for a troubled division of Acme, turned around profitability becoming the top-ranked Sales Director in the division: instituted aggressive market expansion, national account programs, and strategic planning increasing revenue from $5 million to $23 million in four years; converted a $3 million loss into a $3 million profit.

o Based on a track record of achievements in sales management and strategic planning, was recruited by corporate headquarters to manage a major group's business evaluation function as part of the restructuring of the strategic planning process: improved declining ROIs by upgrading the pricing structure; saved tens-of-millions of dollars by demonstrating the marginal payback of proposed expenditures.

o Negotiated and closed the leveraged buyout of a $3 million service business formerly owned by the Avery Company: developed a solid business plan which was successfully marketed to major financial institutions with whom I negotiated over a million dollars in financing.

o As owner of a Texas-based venture, turned around sales and operations overcoming most roadblocks except the company's lack of liquidity in a recessionary economy: increased sales 60% in 15 months by upgrading service and promotional programs; restructured cash management; reduced aged receivables 75%; negotiated a 20% reduction in product costs; achieved a 60% increase in productivity.

## EXAMPLE 4: WILLIAM Q. SAMPLE

Results achieved during the past decade with Acme International include:

o Earned multiple promotions up to Executive Vice President of Sales at a U.S. Division of Acme International, one of Europe's largest industrial corporations: created a highly productive sales organization and achieved a fivefold increase in revenue turning the U.S. Division into a $20 million business which now accounts for almost 40% of the subsidiary's global sales.

o In spite of high turnover and chronically unfavorable exchange rates, which adversely impacted the U.S. Division's pricing structure, generated a 500% increase in Acme's customer base through an accelerated client development program which emphasized quality and service to offset the unfavorable pricing.

o In spite of global competition, closed multimillion-dollar clients including Western Electric, AT&T, Boeing, and John Deere: accelerated the AT&T account from zero to $9 million representing half of total sales; generated a ninefold sales increase from the Harvester Division of John Deere; produced an eightfold increase in the Western Electric and Boeing accounts.

o Significantly reduced overhead and logistics expenses and all but eliminated aged receivables and write-offs by creating and enforcing conservative credit policies at Acme; in order to meet scheduled delivery dates through on-time shipments from Europe, also established a first-rate logistics function.

### The Closing Paragraph

The letter should end with an affirmative statement indicating that you would be interested in discussing how you might be able to contribute to the future success of the company.

Examples of closing paragraphs that worked:

I look forward to meeting and discussing how I can help accelerate or turn around your company's revenue and profit growth.

It should be mutually beneficial to meet and assess how I can help accelerate or turn around revenue and profit growth contributing to your company's future success.

I will work hard to achieve bottom-line results and look forward to discussing how I can contribute to your company's future success.

I look forward to discussing how I can help accelerate or turn around the performance of your international operations.

I will work hard to achieve sales objectives and look forward to discussing how I can contribute to your company's future success.

It should be to our mutual benefit to meet and determine how I can contribute to your company's future profitability.

It should be to our mutual benefit to meet and determine how I can help accelerate or turn around company performance, contributing to your future success.

Should we reach a mutually beneficial agreement, I will work hard to help accelerate or turn around your company's international operations and overall operating performance.

I look forward to discussing how I can contribute to your company's future success.

Following are real-life examples of complete cover letters (assembled from the preceding examples) that generated quality interviews and successful career moves up to the senior vice-president level and six-figure salary range.

Note that these examples include, for your optional application, my trademark "headers" which appear on the same line as your name and provide the reader with a brief two- to five-word description of your background/discipline. These headers have been well-received by the marketplace.

# EXAMPLE 1

## JOHN Q. SAMPLE                    Administration/Finance Executive

**123 Any Street, Any City, CA XXXXX (619) 555-1234**

Contact Name                                                  Date
Title
Company
Address
City, State Zip

Dear Mr/Ms. _____:

As a central figure in Acme Corporation's massive restructuring, I applied executive skills in finance, administration, property management, and purchasing to facilitate Acme's turnaround to profitability. I likewise produced multimillion-dollar profits for the ABC Company through productive management of its administration and property management services, receiving accelerated promotions to Director of a $19 million operation.

I am presenting for your review my skills, achievements, and talent for accelerating margins and turning around unprofitable organizations so that we can discuss my joining _____ as a member of your senior management team.

Results achieved to date include:

o Promoted five grade levels during my last four years at ABC Company based on achieving all major P&L goals in directing the $19 million Corporate Administration and Property Management Department.

o As Acme's Corporate Director of Administration & Property Services, generated tens of millions of dollars in cost reductions and cash flow through aggressive property consolidations, upgraded services and procurement, and enforced management accountability.

o Consolidated 29 Acme warehouses down to 4, generating annual savings of $5.8 million; saved $4.6 million by reducing corporate headquarters space 30%; introduced uniform facility standards which reduced total space requirements 20%, generating another $3.4 million in annual cost savings.

o As head of Acme's $230 million purchasing operation, introduced an aggressive multiple-sourcing program which improved the margins of two major product lines by 7% and 9% respectively.

o Productively managed ABC Company's property holdings, achieving 97% occupancy of 800,000 square feet at premium rates; developed a sophisticated model which helped save $7 million on the cost of an out-of-control $40 million building project at ABC.

I look forward to meeting and discussing how I can help accelerate or turn around your company's revenue and profit growth.

Sincerely,

Enclosure:                                          John Q. Sample

## EXAMPLE 2

**DAVID Q. SAMPLE**                    **International Sales/Finance**

**123 Any Street, Any City, CA XXXXX (619) 555-1234**

Contact Name                                        Date
Title
Company
Address
City, State Zip

Dear Mr./Ms. _____:

I have combined a top business degree, global experience, and executive skills in sales, finance, banking, and general management to establish and direct new operations which have generated millions in revenue for well-respected international companies. Bottom-line contributions to profit have been rewarded with accelerated promotions, job security, and a six-figure salary package.

I am bringing to your attention my skills, achievements, strategic brainpower, global network, and talent for exceeding profit goals under negative economic conditions so that we can discuss my joining _____ as a member of your senior sales management team.

Major accomplishments to date include:

o As Vice President of ABC's International Banking Group, produced revenue of $6.5 million through aggressive client development and by saving 90% of the seriously at-risk accounts: accelerated the ROA by focusing on corporate finance, investment banking, and asset sales.

o As Vice President of Corporate Banking at ABC's Southern California headquarters, leveraged my international contacts to market corporate and capital market products generating $5 million in added net income: achieved 250% growth in fees from capital market products.

o Was recruited away and promoted by ABC to start and manage the new International Energy Group: established and directed the lending operation generating over $500 million in new client bookings in only 18 months with an ROA of over 1%.

o As head of Commercial Development in charge of ABC's International Energy Group, initiated and closed several profitable deals including a hard-to-close $600 million project with an international energy company: created and directed a syndicate of major international lenders.

It should be mutually beneficial to meet and assess how I can help accelerate or turn around revenue and profit growth contributing to your company's future success.

                                        Sincerely,


Enclosure:                              David Q. Sample

# EXAMPLE 3

## MATTHEW Q. SAMPLE    Product Management/Strategic Planning/Sales

123 Any Street Address, Any Town, TX  XXXXX  (214) 555-1234

Contact Name                                                                    Date
Title
Company
Street Address
City, State  Zip

Dear Mr./Ms. _____:

I have combined a top school M.B.A. with executive skills in marketing, sales management, product management, strategic planning, and general management to orchestrate a leveraged buyout, head up a $3 million business, strategically reposition troubled operations, and turn around and accelerate profit growth for weak divisions of the Acme Corporation.

I am bringing to your attention my skills, achievements, talent for stimulating sales productivity, and ability to achieve bottom-line results under the most intense pressure so that we can discuss my joining _____ as a member of your senior sales management team.

Results achieved to date include:

o  Upon promotion to Southwestern Sales Director, accelerated sales productivity and major account development achieving a critically needed 35% growth in sales at a pivotal time for the struggling Acme Corporation, which had lost huge market shares due to poor product pricing strategies: achieved highest sales growth and won a major nationwide sales award.

o  As Southeastern Sales Director for a troubled division of Acme, turned around profitability becoming the top-ranked Sales Director in the division: instituted aggressive market expansion, national account programs, and strategic planning increasing revenue from $5 million to $23 million in four years; converted a $3 million loss into a $3 million profit.

o  Based on a track record of achievements in sales management and strategic planning, was recruited by corporate headquarters to manage a major group's business evaluation function as part of the restructuring of the strategic planning process: improved declining ROIs by upgrading the pricing structure; saved tens-of-millions of dollars by demonstrating the marginal payback of proposed expenditures.

o  Negotiated and closed the leveraged buyout of a $3 million service business formerly owned by the Avery Company: developed a solid business plan which was successfully marketed to major financial institutions with whom I negotiated over a million dollars in financing.

o  As owner of a Texas-based venture, turned around sales and operations overcoming most roadblocks except the company's lack of liquidity in a recessionary economy: increased sales 60% in 15 months by upgrading service and promotional programs; restructured cash management; reduced aged receivables 75%; negotiated a 20% reduction in product costs; achieved a 60% increase in productivity.

I will work hard to achieve bottom-line results and look forward to discussing how I can contribute to your company's future success.

Sincerely,


Enclosure:                                                        Matthew Q. Sample

## EXAMPLE 4

**WILLIAM Q. SAMPLE**                      **International Sales Executive**

**123 Any Street, Any Town, NJ  XXXXX  (201) 555-1234**

Contact Name                                            Date
Title
Company
Street Address
City, State  Zip

Dear Mr./Ms. _____:

As Executive Vice President of Sales for the U.S. Division of a European-based corporation, I have applied executive skills in international sales, marketing, client development, and operations to outmaneuver the competition, deal with volatile exchange rates, accelerate growth of the corporate client base, and achieve a fivefold increase in sales—a revenue level which now accounts for 40% of worldwide sales.

I am presenting for your review my skills, achievements, technical degree, global contacts, and talent for creating productive sales forces and achieving aggressive revenue and profit goals so that we can discuss my joining _____ as a member of your senior sales management team.

Results achieved during the past decade with Acme International include:

o  Earned multiple promotions up to Executive Vice-President of Sales at a U.S. Division of Acme International, one of Europe's largest industrial corporations: created a highly productive sales organization and achieved a fivefold increase in revenue turning the U.S. Division into a $20 million business which now accounts for almost 40% of the subsidiary's global sales.

o  In spite of high turnover and chronically unfavorable exchange rates, which adversely impacted the U.S. Division's pricing structure, generated a 500% increase in Acme's customer base through an accelerated client development program which emphasized quality and service to offset the unfavorable pricing.

o  In spite of global competition, closed multimillion-dollar clients including Western Electric, AT&T, Boeing, and John Deere: accelerated the AT&T account from zero to $9 million representing half of total sales; generated a ninefold sales increase from the Harvester Division of John Deere; produced an eightfold increase in the Western Electric and Boeing accounts.

o  Significantly reduced overhead and logistics expenses and all but eliminated aged receivables and write-offs by creating and enforcing conservative credit policies at Acme; in order to meet scheduled delivery dates through on-time shipments from Europe, also established a first-rate logistics function.

I look forward to discussing how I can help accelerate or turn around the performance of your international operations.

Sincerely,

Enclosure:                                              William Q. Sample

# 6

## Market-Tested Sample Resumes and Cover Letters for Executives

### INTRODUCTION

The real-life, market-tested samples in Chapter 6 produced results for executives with 15 to 30-plus years of experience. This chapter offers the following unique features designed to give you the same competitive edge that produced quality interviews and job offers for executives just like you:

1. *Superior Quality Sample Resumes and Cover Letters.* Taken directly from almost 30 real-life client case histories, the market-tested and proven samples in this chapter successfully generated quality interviews and career moves. These samples of unmatched quality enable you to extract, borrow, and adapt key words, phrases, sentences, and paragraphs as you develop your own power package.

2. *A Strong Focus on Packaging Marketable Skills and Achievements.* This workbook subordinates the narrative job descriptions that clutter most resumes. The market has responded favorably to the skills and achievement-oriented resumes featured in the following pages.

3. *An Unparalleled Emphasis on the Marketing Cover Letter.* This workbook treats the cover letter and resume as *coequal* and *inseparable* components of the total marketing package. Based on a frequently heard comment from my management clients, "The cover letter got me the interview," I have no doubts about the letter's importance. Every sample resume in this book has a corresponding cover letter—*no* other book on the market can make this claim.

4. *A Representative Cross Section of Sample Resumes and Letters.* As reflected in the Chapter Index, I have deliberately excluded many highly specialized, often irrelevant, job positions that provide filler for countless resume books. This chapter, instead, presents *eight* major categories and several additional subcategories of mainstream executive-level positions into which most managers fall.

5. *An Intense Focus on Market Response.* Simply stated, the following samples achieved the desired results for veteran managers just like you: They produced positive interviews and job offers in an increasingly tough and selective marketplace, which is, of course, the *ultimate* and *only relevant* judge of quality.

## THE RESUME AND COVER LETTER HEADERS

As discussed earlier, the sample resume and cover letter packages include, for your optional application, my trademark headers which provide the reader with a brief two- to five-word description of your background/discipline. For your convenience and ease in referencing the samples, I have elevated and boxed in these descriptive headers which are cross-referenced in the Index on pages 73 and 74. Should you choose to include the header in your own resume and cover letter package, you will, of course, position it on the same line as your name.

## A WORD ABOUT CLIENT CONFIDENTIALITY

While retaining the full impact and integrity of the real-life marketing packages in this chapter, I have selectively modified and/or otherwise blinded certain confidential information including client names, company names, addresses, specific job titles, employment dates, and other identifying narrative. While education information has also been blinded, colleges and graduate schools of equivalent ranking were substituted where appropriate.

## CHAPTER 6 RESUME INDEX

## WILLIAM Q. SAMPLE (Version 1)

123 Any Street, Any Town, NJ XXXXX (201) 555-1234

Contact Name                                        Date
Title
Company
Street Address
City, State Zip

Dear Mr./Ms. _____:

As Executive Vice President of Sales for the U.S. Division of a European-based corporation, I have applied executive skills in international sales, marketing, client development, and operations to outmaneuver the competition, deal with volatile exchange rates, accelerate growth of the corporate client base, and achieve a fivefold increase in sales—a revenue level which now accounts for 40% of worldwide sales.

I am presenting for your review my skills, achievements, technical degree, global contacts, and talent for creating productive sales forces and achieving aggressive revenue and profit goals so that we can discuss my joining _____ as a member of your senior sales management team.

Results achieved during the past decade with Acme International include:

o Earned multiple promotions up to Executive Vice President of Sales at a U.S. Division of Acme International, one of Europe's largest industrial corporations: created a highly productive sales organization and achieved a fivefold increase in revenue turning the U.S. Division into a $20 million business which now accounts for almost 40% of the subsidiary's global sales.

o In spite of high turnover and chronically unfavorable exchange rates, which adversely impacted the U.S. Division's pricing structure, generated a 500% increase in Acme's customer base through an accelerated client development program which emphasized quality and service to offset the unfavorable pricing.

o In spite of global competition, closed multimillion-dollar clients including Western Electric, AT&T, Boeing, and John Deere: accelerated the AT&T account from zero to $9 million representing half of total sales; generated a ninefold sales increase from the Harvester Division of John Deere; produced an eightfold increase in the Western Electric and Boeing accounts.

o Significantly reduced overhead and logistics expenses and all but eliminated aged receivables and write-offs by creating and enforcing conservative credit policies at Acme; in order to meet scheduled delivery dates through on-time shipments from Europe, also established a first-rate logistics function.

I look forward to discussing how I can help accelerate or turn around the performance of your international operations.

                                           Sincerely,

Enclosure:                                      William Q. Sample

## International Sales Executive

# WILLIAM Q. SAMPLE

123 Any Street Address, Any Town, NJ XXXXX (201) 555-1234

B.S.  Electrical Engineering    International University  Comprehensive Six-Year Program
B.A.  Business Administration  Lehman College          Managerial Studies

International:  Traveled throughout Europe, Asia, South America, and North America
Languages:     Fluent French and Spanish

## CAREER SKILLS/KNOWLEDGE

o Sales/marketing executive
o International sales/markets
o European relations
o Strategic/marketing plans
o Market share strategies
o Major client development
o Competitive maneuvering
o Exchange rate strategies
o Organizational development
o Staff supervision/development

o Operations/materials/engineering
o Purchasing operations
o Cost controls/reductions
o Global distribution/logistics
o Heavy industry clients
o Aircraft engine market
o Engineering operations
o Electrical/systems engineering
o New product design
o Plant operating systems design

## CAREER ACHIEVEMENTS

o Earned multiple promotions up to Executive Vice President of Sales at a U.S. Division of Acme International, one of Europe's largest industrial corporations: created a highly productive sales organization and achieved a fivefold increase in revenue turning the U.S. Division into a $20 million business which now accounts for almost 40% of the subsidiary's global sales.

o In spite of high turnover and chronically unfavorable exchange rates, which adversely impacted the U.S. Division's pricing structure, generated a 500% increase in Acme's customer base through an accelerated client development program which emphasized quality and service to offset the unfavorable pricing.

o In spite of global competition, closed multimillion-dollar clients including Western Electric, AT&T, Boeing, and John Deere: accelerated the AT&T account from zero to $9 million representing half of total sales; generated a ninefold sales increase from the Harvester Division of John Deere; produced an eightfold increase in the Western Electric and Boeing accounts.

o Significantly reduced overhead and logistics expenses and all but eliminated aged receivables and write-offs by creating and enforcing conservative credit policies at Acme; in order to meet scheduled delivery dates through on-time shipments from Europe, also established a first-rate logistics function.

o Earned several promotions up to director within the Engineering Department of a Florida-based division of Essex Corporation: directed high-quality product designs, upgraded operating systems critical to the production process, and effectively troubleshooted the complex power supply systems.

## CAREER EXPERIENCE

## ACME INTERNATIONAL CORPORATION, Any Town, NJ   1984–Present

Executive Vice President of Sales   1987–Present
Direct the Sales Organization with responsibility for direct sales, marketing, strategic planning, client development, import operations, logistics, distribution, and credit.

Vice President of Sales   1984–1987
Directed sales, marketing, strategic planning, and related functions.

## ESSEX CORPORATION, Any Town, FL   1975–1984

Director of Engineering   1980–1984
Earned several promotions based on engineering achievements in directing low-tolerance
design and systems engineering projects. Also successfully planned and executed high-
visibility manufacturing projects.

## MILITARY EXPERIENCE

European Military:  Honorably Discharged


**Affiliations:**       Society of U.S. Engineers; Production Engineers of the Northeast
**Citizenship:**        U.S. Citizen


## REFERENCES AVAILABLE UPON REQUEST

# JOHN A. JONES (Version 1)

**123 Any Street, Any City, WA XXXXX (206) 555-1234**

Contact Name                                          Date
Title
Company
Street Address
City, State Zip

Dear Mr./Ms. _____:

I have combined degrees from Stanford and Wharton with executive skills in sales, marketing, operations, and engineering to build a $20 million company known internationally for its state-of-the-art products, cost-effective production, substantial market shares, and global clients. Achievements were rewarded with growing profits and prestigious awards for delivering vital systems in record time.

I am bringing to your attention my leadership skills, achievements, ability to create cost-effective solutions, and proven talent for accelerating market share and profits to produce financial security for others and myself so that we can discuss my joining _____ as a member of your general management/marketing team.

Results achieved to date include:

o  As founder and chief executive of ABC, Inc., started and built this profitable high-tech electronics company known over 20 years for its innovative products and low-cost volume production: negotiated and executed the lucrative sale of the company to a major corporation.

o  More than doubled ABC's revenue by marketing breakthrough products to over 40 countries and major Fortune 500 corporations: developed damage-proof and modular products; introduced concept of placing electronics into clothing; developed communications systems for space projects, carriers, train systems, executive aircraft, and bank machines.

o  Became one of the world's largest producers of specialized communication devices by focusing on the high volume global market; instituted "people-based" engineering to extend the life of electronic equipment and produce safety-conscious communications for major clients.

o  Turned around out-of-control quality and distribution problems at XYZ Technology increasing on-time shipments from 38% to 95%; also turned around purchasing operations generating $3 million a year in cost reductions while reducing inventory $3 million.

Should we reach mutually agreeable terms, I will work hard to help accelerate or turn around operating performance contributing to your future success.

Sincerely,

Enclosure:                                          John A. Jones

# Sales Executive/General Management

## JOHN A. JONES

**123 Any Street, Any City, WA XXXXX (206) 555-1235**

| | | | |
|---|---|---|---|
| M.B.A. | Management | Wharton | 1974 |
| B.S. | Electrical Engineering | Stanford University | 1972 |
| B.A. | Economics | Stanford University | 1972 |

## CAREER SKILLS/KNOWLEDGE

- International marketing/sales
- General management/finance
- Start-up operations/organization
- Major client development
- Product management
- Competitive maneuvering
- Expansion/turnaround strategies
- Profit/market share growth
- New product marketing/pricing

- Operations/engineering
- Manufacturing/Q.C./materials
- Cost-effective production
- Labor negotiations
- Productivity improvements
- R&D/systems engineering
- New product development
- Cost reduction strategies
- Electronics industry

## CAREER ACHIEVEMENTS

- As founder and chief executive of ABC, Inc., started and built this profitable high-tech electronics company known over 20 years for its innovative products and low-cost volume production: negotiated and executed the lucrative sale of the company to a major corporation.

- Awarded a coveted medal by a foreign government for producing and delivering, in less than 60 days, critically needed communications systems vital to their national defense: crash program cut four months off the schedule.

- More than doubled ABC's revenue by marketing breakthrough products to over 40 countries and major Fortune 500 corporations: developed damage-proof and modular products; introduced concept of placing electronics into clothing; developed communications systems for space projects, carriers, train systems, executive aircraft, and bank machines.

- Became one of the world's largest producers of specialized communication devices by focusing on the high volume global market; instituted "people-based" engineering to extend the life of electronic equipment and produce safety-conscious communications for major clients.

- Turned around out-of-control quality and distribution problems at XYZ Technology increasing on-time shipments from 38% to 95%; also turned around purchasing operations generating $3 million a year in cost reductions while reducing inventory $3 million.

- As Director of Procurement at Acme Company, generated $4 million in annual cost savings and reduced inventory $2 million by resolving serious cost control and material control problems.

## CAREER EXPERIENCE

### ACME COMPANY, Any City, WA    1996–Present

Director of Procurement
Instituted much needed budget systems; upgraded material control, developed off-shore vendors, reduced materials shortages, and stopped downtime; generated cost savings and reduced inventory.

### XYZ TECHNOLOGY CORPORATION, Any Town, WA    1995–1996

Project Director
In a series of manufacturing, technical, and procurement assignments, instituted modern management techniques: improved production quality, cut costs, reduced inventory, and established on-time delivery:

o Upgraded Q.C. operations, policies, and procedures.
o Tightened vendor product quality standards.
o Instituted competitive bidding and second sourcing.
o Introduced Japanese methods of inventory stocking.

### ABC, INCORPORATED, Any Town, WA    1974–1995

Chief Executive and Founder
Founded and managed a high-tech company which grew to over 150 employees:

o Expanded through innovation, systems engineering, and cost-effective manufacturing.
o Oversaw product development from inception through design, engineering, and production.
o Established and monitored marketing and pricing objectives.
o Developed client relations with major corporations and numerous countries.
o Continuously expanded into new markets.
o Redesigned and improved products to reduce costs.
o Established rigid quality control standards.
o Designed a plant layout which dramatically improved assembly productivity.
o Consistently met tight delivery schedules.

## REFERENCES PROVIDED UPON REQUEST

# Marketing Executive/General Management

## THOMAS A. JOHNSON

123 Any Street, Any City, CA XXXXX (619) 555-1234

Contact Name                                                    Date
Title
Company
Street Address
City, State Zip

Dear Mr./Ms. _____ :

I have combined executive skills in marketing, sales, and general management with a first-rate education and military experience to restructure and turn around struggling businesses and accelerate profits and cost controls for Fortune 50 and smaller companies.

Bottom-line results have been rewarded with promotions leading to CEO of a Los Angeles County company which, unfortunately, requires a four-hour commute.

I am presenting for your review my skills, achievements, proven leadership, and no-nonsense ability to get the job done so that we can discuss my joining _____ as a member of your senior sales/marketing management team.

Results achieved to date include:

o As Chief Executive Officer of ABC Energy Company, directed its consolidation and turn-around, streamlining the organization, reducing costs, and doubling pre-tax earnings.

o At ABC, negotiated a separate cost-effective labor agreement for Los Angeles County obtaining substantial wage savings and increased productivity through revised work rules.

o As Marketing Director in charge of retail and wholesale businesses for Avery Energy Company, achieved sales growth of 18% (to $95 million) within a declining total market.

o At a Fortune 100 energy company, earned several major promotions to increasingly responsible Marketing, Sales, Administrative, and Planning positions.

o Promoted to Sales Manager at a Fortune 100 company, achieving sales quota in all major product categories by restructuring the sales area and coordinating over 200 accounts in the San Diego market.

I look forward to a meeting at which we can determine how I can contribute to your company's future success.

                                        Sincerely,


Enclosure:                              Thomas A. Johnson

# Marketing Executive/General Management

## THOMAS A. JOHNSON

123 Any Street, Any City, CA XXXXX (619) 555-1234

B.A.   Duke University   1978

## CAREER SKILLS/KNOWLEDGE

o Marketing/sales executive
o Revenue growth strategies
o Profit maximization
o Competitive strategies
o New account development
o Product strategies
o Sales promotions
o Territory planning
o Dealer recruiting/relations
o Customer relations
o Real estate development
o Site expansion/divestiture

o General management
o Operations
o Turnaround strategies
o Business restructuring
o Leadership skills
o Staff development
o Labor relations
o Contract negotiations
o Administration
o Strategic planning
o Budget management
o Capital planning/control

## CAREER ACHIEVEMENTS

o As Chief Executive Officer of ABC Energy Company, directed its consolidation and turn-around, streamlining the organization, reducing costs, and doubling pre-tax earnings.

o At ABC, negotiated a separate cost-effective labor agreement for Los Angeles County obtaining substantial wage savings and increased productivity through revised work rules.

o As Marketing Director in charge of retail and wholesale businesses for Avery Energy Company, achieved sales growth of 18% (to $95 million) within a declining total market.

o At a Fortune 100 energy company, earned several major promotions to increasingly responsible Marketing, Sales, Administrative, and Planning positions.

o Promoted to Marketing Manager at a Fortune 100 energy company, in charge of preparing five-year plans and evaluating, monitoring, and controlling the $88 million capital budget.

o Promoted to Control Manager at a Fortune 100 company, successfully directing overall administration of the $91 million San Diego District.

o Promoted to Sales Manager at a Fortune 100 company, achieving sales quota in all major product categories by restructuring the sales area and coordinating over 200 accounts in the San Diego market.

o Upon promotion to Site Manager at a Fortune 100 company, researched and added ten highly profitable new business sites and shut down seven unprofitable sites.

## BUSINESS EXPERIENCE

## ACME ENERGY CORPORATION, Any City, CA    2/95–Present

Chief Executive Officer—ABC Energy Company
Doubled subsidiary's net profit contribution to over $1.3 million:

o  Restructured company to streamline operations.
o  Negotiated cost-effective labor agreement for Los Angeles County.
o  Generate new accounts through direct advertising strategy.
o  Increased budget accountability of middle managers.
o  Developed incentives for 86 employees.
o  Improved client relations through better service.
o  Stopped the decline of our existing customer base.
o  Manage multimillion-dollar company assets.

## AVERY ENERGY COMPANY, Any City, CA    9/89–2/95

Marketing Director
Directed growth and cost control of a $90 million operation.

## ESSEX CORPORATION (FORTUNE 100), Any City, CA    8/82–9/89

Marketing Manager    4/87–9/89
Managed capital budget of $88 million: consolidated budgets, presented to management and monitored. Prepared five-year plans and well-received compliance reports for the government.

Control Manager    5/86–4/87
Directed administration for $91 million San Diego District: managed budgeting, controls, facilities, and field support.

Sales Manager    4/84–5/86
Developed staff, restructured territory, and coordinated accounts.

## MILITARY EXPERIENCE    (1978–1982)

o  Attended Officer Candidate School; served on U.S.S. Kennedy
o  Directed 125 service personnel; controlled major logistics operations
o  Awarded multiple performance citations

## COMMUNITY/VOLUNTEER ACTIVITIES

o  Board Member, San Diego County Red Cross and Zoning Commission
o  Vice President & Board Member, San Diego Water Council

## JOHN A. SMITH (Version 1)

**123 Any Street, Any Town, CA XXXXX Home: (619) 555-1234 Office: (619) 555-2345**

Contact Name                                                  Date
Title
Company
Street Address
City, State Zip

Dear Mr./Ms. _____:

I have profitably applied executive skills in sales, marketing, major account development, and finance to exceed revenue targets and play a key role in the start-up and marketing of Asset Management Associates, a division of the $2 billion Acme Corporation which has achieved a 35% ROI through the purchase and sale of real estate worth $200 million. I also played a central role in Acme's entry into both the asset management and financial industries.

I am presenting for your review my skills, achievements, proven leadership, work ethic, and straightforward approach to getting the job done so that we can discuss my joining _____ as a member of your sales/marketing management team.

Results achieved to date include:

o As Director of Sales, played a central role in the start-up, marketing, and general management of Asset Management Associates—a venture which has yielded an on-target 35% return through the purchase and resale of over 2,000 foreclosed properties valued at $200 million: codeveloped the start-up business plan, helped staff the company, and assumed a Director position reporting directly to the President.

o Helped generate third-year profits of $2 million on revenue of $7 million at Asset Management Associates: signed the first major banking client accounting for a 50-house management contract; closed deals which contributed to the company managing 400 properties generating $800,000 in fees; signed a major lender accounting for purchased inventory of over $2 million a month; sold 20 additional accounts yielding 8 management and 12 buy-out clients.

o As Major Account Executive at an Acme Division, exceeded revenue targets by maintaining volume, increasing business, and renegotiating contracts with multimillion-dollar accounts.

o Prior to and during my tenure as a Major Account Executive, directly facilitated Acme's subsequent entry into asset management: at the request of the Chairman, executed a feasibility study which recommended entry into asset management; closed a lucrative deal which represented the company's first asset management client and led to the eventual formation of Asset Management Associates.

o As Director of Investment Acquisition at Asset Management Associates, directed development of a $40 million offering package and formed a syndicate of investors to meet our outside borrowing requirements; previously developed and recommended cancellation of a $200 million public offering.

I look forward to discussing how I can help accelerate or turn around revenue and profit growth, contributing to your future success.

                                                  Sincerely,


Enclosure:                                        John A. Smith

# JOHN A. SMITH

123 Any Street, Any Town, CA XXXXX  Home: (619) 555-1234  Office: (619) 555-2345

| M.B.A. | Finance | University of Maine | 1982 |
| B.A. | Accounting | State University of New York | 1980 |

## CAREER SKILLS/KNOWLEDGE

o Sales/marketing management
o Quota achievement strategies
o Staff supervision/development
o Client/major account development
o Cold-calling/proposals
o Group marketing/seminars/speeches
o Trade show participation
o Marketing materials/brochures
o Closing/customer service
o Asset management/real estate
o Buy-out/resale/ROI strategies
o Balance sheet management

o Financial/treasury management
o Budgeting/capital appropriations
o Consolidations/financial statements
o Auditing operations
o Credit and collections
o Treasury operations
o Cash management/allocation
o Investment strategies
o Borrowing strategies
o Basis point reductions
o Foreign exchange strategies
o Banking relations

## CAREER ACHIEVEMENTS

o As Director of Sales, played a central role in the start-up, marketing, and general management of Asset Management Associates—a venture which has yielded an on-target 35% return through the acquisition and disposition of 2,000 foreclosed properties valued at $200 million: codeveloped the start-up business plan, helped staff the company, and assumed a Director position reporting directly to the President.

o Helped generate third-year profits of $2 million on revenue of $7 million at Asset Management Associates: signed the first major banking client accounting for a 50-house management contract; closed deals which contributed to the company managing 400 properties generating $800,000 in fees; signed a major lender accounting for purchased inventory of over $2 million a month; sold 20 additional accounts yielding 8 management and 12 buy-out clients.

o As a Major Account Executive at an Acme Division, exceeded revenue targets by maintaining volume, increasing business, and renegotiating contracts with multimillion-dollar accounts.

o Prior to and during my tenure as a Major Account Executive, directly facilitated Acme's subsequent entry into asset management: at the request of the Chairman, executed a feasibility study which recommended entry into asset management; closed a lucrative deal which represented the company's first asset management client and led to the eventual formation of Asset Management Associates.

o As Director of Investment Acquisition at Asset Management Associates, directed development of a $40 million offering package and formed a syndicate of investors to meet our outside borrowing requirements; previously developed and recommended cancellation of a $200 million public offering.

o Took the lead in establishing Asset Management Associates first relationship with the FDIC by directly contacting government officials; initiated negotiations for a major purchase from the Resolution Trust Corporation.

o As Treasury Director in charge of treasury operations at a division of Acme, initiated development of financial services which allowed clients to process applications through the mail to bankers with whom we had negotiated contracts: success of the services led to Acme's entry into the financial industry.

# CAREER EXPERIENCE

## ACME CORPORATION, Any City, CA   1990–Present

### ASSET MANAGEMENT ASSOCIATES, Any City, CA   1992–Present

Director of Investment Acquisition   1994–Present
Member of management team responsible for directing business and establishing strategic objectives. While still executing sales responsibilites, directed development of $40 million offering package.

Director of Sales   1993–1994
Developed new business in marketing acquisition and disposition services for foreclosed real estate to savings & loans, banks, the federal government, and other financial institutions.

Director   1992–1993
Member of group formed to assess the need for an Asset Management Company.

### ACME DIVISION, Any City, CA   1990–1992

Major Account Executive   1991–1992
Maintained volume, increased business, and renegotiated contracts with established accounts of Acme.

Treasury Director   1990–1991
Instituted a new method of funding bank accounts which yielded a savings of $3 million a year; instituted a system of billing to clients which reduced receivables by $8 million; stopped a 40% increase in headcount by developing a computerized accounts receivable system during a period of rapid growth; computerized several Cash Management reports which accelerated the reimbursement process thereby reducing excess borrowing by $7 million.

## AVERY INCORPORATED, Any City, CA   1982–1990

Assistant Treasury Manager   1987–1990
Profitably managed a $400 million portfolio of short-term investments; managed the daily cash position; negotiated basis point reductions; established and directed Currency Exchange review process.

Senior Financial Analyst   1984–1987
Reviewed budget submissions from international subsidiaries. Prepared reports with recommended changes that were routinely accepted.

# ADDITIONAL EDUCATION/TRAINING

Professional Courses:       o Professional Marketing Series
                            o The Art of Selling Series
                            o Professional Communications Series

## MATTHEW Q. SAMPLE (Version 1)

**123 Any Street Address, Any Town, TX  XXXXX  (214) 555-1234**

Contact Name                                                    Date
Title
Company
Street Address
City, State  Zip

Dear Mr./Ms. _____:

I have combined a top school M.B.A. with executive skills in marketing, sales management, product management, strategic planning, and general management to orchestrate a lever- aged buyout, head up a $3 million business, strategically reposition troubled operations, and turn around and accelerate profit growth for weak divisions of the Acme Corporation.

I am bringing to your attention my skills, achievements, talent for stimulating sales produc- tivity, and ability to achieve bottom-line results under the most intense pressure so that we can discuss my joining _____ as a member of your senior sales management team.

Results achieved to date include:

o  Upon promotion to Southwestern Sales Director, accelerated sales productivity and major account development achieving a critically needed 35% growth in sales at a pivotal time for the struggling Acme Corporation, which had lost huge market shares due to poor product pricing strategies: achieved highest sales growth and won a major nationwide sales award.

o  As Southeastern Sales Director for a troubled division of Acme, turned around profitability becom- ing the top-ranked Sales Director in the division: instituted aggressive market expansion, national account programs, and strategic planning increasing revenue from $5 million to $23 million in four years; converted a $3 million loss into a $3 million profit.

o  Based on a track record of achievements in sales management and strategic planning, was recruited by corporate headquarters to manage a major group's business evaluation function as part of the restruc- turing of the strategic planning process: improved declining ROIs by upgrading the pricing structure; saved tens-of-millions of dollars by demonstrating the marginal payback of proposed expenditures.

o  Negotiated and closed the leveraged buyout of a $3 million service business formerly owned by the Avery Company: developed a solid business plan which was successfully marketed to major finan- cial institutions with whom I negotiated over a million dollars in financing.

o  As owner of a Texas-based venture, turned around sales and operations overcoming most roadblocks except the company's lack of liquidity in a recessionary economy: increased sales 60% in 15 months by upgrading service and promotional programs; restructured cash management; reduced aged receiv- ables 75%; negotiated a 20% reduction in product costs; achieved a 60% increase in productivity.

I will work hard to achieve bottom-line results and look forward to discussing how I can con- tribute to your company's future success.

Sincerely,


Enclosure:                                                Matthew Q. Sample

## Product Management/Strategic Planning/Sales

# MATTHEW Q. SAMPLE

**123 Any Street, Any Town, TX XXXXX (214) 555-1234**

| M.B.A. | Finance/Marketing | University of Virginia | 1976 |
|--------|-------------------|------------------------|------|
| B.S. | Statistics | UCLA | 1974 |

## CAREER SKILLS/KNOWLEDGE

- o Marketing/sales management
- o Revenue/profit turnaround
- o Product management/market development
- o National accounts programs
- o Sales productivity growth
- o Competitor intelligence systems
- o Business ownership/leveraged buyouts
- o Advertising/promotions
- o Operations turnaround

- o Strategic planning
- o Business plans/market research
- o Market growth/segmentation
- o ROI growth strategies
- o Profit/investment optimization
- o Economic modeling/pricing
- o Supply/demand analysis
- o Finance/controller operations
- o Cash-flow/financing/bank relations

## CAREER ACHIEVEMENTS

o Upon promotion to Southwestern Sales Director, accelerated sales productivity and major account development achieving a critically needed 35% growth in sales at a pivotal time for the struggling Acme Corporation, which had lost huge market shares due to poor product pricing strategies: achieved highest sales growth and won a major nationwide sales award.

o As Southeastern Sales Director for a troubled division of Acme, turned around profitability becoming the top-ranked Sales Director in the division: instituted aggressive market expansion, national account programs, and strategic planning increasing revenue from $5 million to $23 million in four years; converted a $3 million loss into a $3 million profit.

o Upon being promoted to Product Manager at Acme, created a product management system which accelerated the decision-making process for the pricing, promotion, and distribution of products: increased profits 30% through saturation marketing to growth industries.

o Based on a track record of achievements in sales management and strategic planning, was recruited by corporate headquarters to manage a major group's business evaluation function as part of the restructuring of the strategic planning process: improved declining ROIs by upgrading the pricing structure; saved tens-of-millions of dollars by demonstrating the marginal payback of proposed expenditures.

o Upon promotion to Business Planning Director, orchestrated a multibillion-dollar asset reallocation program which helped triple profits within five years: reallocated over a billion dollars of production assets to growth products; proposed a half-billion-dollar plant conversion which was implemented at half the cost of constructing a new plant.

o Negotiated and closed the leveraged buyout of a $3 million service business formerly owned by the Avery Company: developed a solid business plan which was successfully marketed to major financial institutions with whom I negotiated over a million dollars in financing.

o As owner of a Texas-based venture, turned around sales and operations overcoming most roadblocks except the company's lack of liquidity in a recessionary economy: increased sales 60% in 15 months by upgrading service and promotional programs; restructured cash management; reduced aged receivables 75%; negotiated a 20% reduction in product costs; achieved a 60% increase in productivity.

## CAREER EXPERIENCE

## ACME CORPORATION, Any City, TX   1976–1992

Business Planning Director—XYZ Division   1989–1992
Designated to orchestrate the development of corporate strategies and upgrade the planning process.

Business Evaluation Director—ABC Division   1986–1989
Designated to reorganize and turn around strategic planning.

Southwestern Sales Director—ABC Division   1982–1986
Developed and directed a high-producing sales team responsible for national account development.

Product Manager—XYZ Division   1978–1982
Created a product management system which accelerated the decision-making process for the pricing, promotion, and distribution of products.

Southeastern Sales Director—XYZ Division   1977–1978
Implemented a Major Account Program; expanded into growth markets; instituted effective competitor data-gathering procedures; created Division's first comprehensive strategic plan.

Senior Marketing Analyst   1976–1977
Executed comprehensive feasibility studies which resulted in the formation of critically needed account development departments. Developed a well-received business plan for a beleaguered venture.

## ESSEX COMPANY, Any City, TX   1992–1994

Senior Consultant
Determined the feasibility of a client's expansion into major European markets: executed comprehensive product demand and competitive studies as a basis for decision making.

## SERVICE VENTURE, Any City, TX   1994–Present

Founder:  Directed Marketing, Advertising, Sales, Operations, Finance, and Customer Service.

| | |
|---|---|
| **INTERNATIONAL:** | Traveled throughout South America and Europe |
| **LANGUAGES:** | Fluent French, Italian, and Spanish |

## JOHN Q. SAMPLE (Version 1)

**123 Any Street, Any City, CA (619) 555-5678**

Contact Name                                                                    Date
Title
Company
Address
City, State  Zip

Dear Mr./Ms. _____:

As Executive Vice President responsible for directing an $80 million global operation at Prototype Corporation, I have taken the lead in instituting major competitive changes, cost reductions, and productivity improvements which have accelerated the company's competitiveness while increasing profits $20 million annually.

As a central figure in Acme Corporation's massive restructuring, I applied executive skills in finance, administration, real estate, property management, and procurement to facilitate Acme's turnaround to profitability. I likewise produced multimillion-dollar profits for ABC Company through productive management of its administration and property management, receiving accelerated promotions to Director of a $19 million operation.

I am presenting for your review my skills, achievements, ability to recapture the competitive edge, and talent for accelerating profits and turning around out-of-control operations so that we can discuss my joining _____ as a member of your senior management team.

Accomplishments critical to Prototype recapturing its blue-chip profitability:

o As Executive Vice President of Administration, profitably direct an $80 million operation spanning 56 international locations representing over two million square feet: responsibilities executed in directing twelve major departments include the management of $100 million in company assets and the negotiation of $50 million in facility contracts related to properties located worldwide.

o Generated multiyear savings of $50 million and accelerated productivity growth through a major consolidation of Prototype's manufacturing and branch office network: aggressively renegotiated expensive leasehold agreements, eliminated redundant operations, and instituted global efficiencies.

o Consolidated 15 research and administrative sites into 4, generating an annual savings of $5 million through reductions in square footage and rental expense; also directed the successful completion of an important 300,000 square foot research facility which was finished well ahead of schedule and several million dollars under budget.

o Positioned Prototype as a pacesetter in instituting worker accident prevention programs: fostered the company's global reputation for valuing human resources while generating a 50% reduction in insurance premiums.

I look forward to meeting and discussing how I can help accelerate or turn around your company's revenue and profit growth.

Sincerely,

Enclosure:                                                                  John Q. Sample

## JOHN Q. SAMPLE

123 Any Street, Any City, CA  XXXXX  (619) 555-5678

B.S.   Honors   Finance   Georgetown University   1980

### CAREER SKILLS/KNOWLEDGE

o General management
o Finance/administration
o Strategic planning
o Financial planning and analysis
o Procurement operations
o Telecommunications
o Travel/relocation
o Insurance/risk management
o Training/security
o International distribution

o Global property management
o Development/construction
o Occupancy growth strategies
o Premium rate strategies
o Consolidation strategies
o Facilities management
o Lease management/negotiations
o Site selection/space planning
o Budgeting/accountability
o Governmental regulations

### CAREER ACHIEVEMENTS

o As Executive Vice President at Prototype Corporation, profitably direct an $80 million operation spanning 56 international locations representing two million square feet: responsibilities executed in directing twelve major departments include the management of $100 million in company assets and the negotiation of $50 million in facility contracts related to properties located worldwide.

o Generated multiyear savings of $50 million and accelerated productivity growth through a major consolidation of Prototype's manufacturing and branch office network: aggressively renegotiated expensive leasehold agreements, eliminated redundant operations, and instituted global efficiencies.

o Proposed and instituted lucrative outsourcing programs based on competitive benchmarking: improved Prototype's overall competitiveness by redirecting corporate priorities and eliminating costly redundancies, inefficiencies, and excess expenditures.

o Consolidated 15 research and administrative sites into 4, generating an annual savings of $5 million for Prototype through reductions in square footage and rental expense; also directed the successful completion of an important 300,000 square foot research facility which was finished well ahead of schedule and several million dollars under budget.

o Positioned Prototype as a pacesetter in instituting worker accident prevention programs: fostered the company's global reputation for valuing human resources while generating a 50% reduction in insurance premiums.

o Assumed a central role in Prototype's efforts to address and resolve the industry's billion-dollar counterfeiting problem by instituting comprehensive security programs.

o Generated international recognition for Prototype by initiating and instituting cost-effective environmental programs which are recognized by the global business community as the standard against which to measure future programs.

## CAREER EXPERIENCE

### PROTOTYPE CORPORATION, Any Town, CA    4/93–Present

Executive Vice President Administration
Direct Property Management, Travel, Relocation, and Communications. Additional accomplishments:

o  Achieved a 10% reduction in absenteeism by creating healthier employees through the implementation of cost-effective fitness programs.
o  Reopened negotiations with major transportation carriers yielding a million dollar annual savings.
o  Centralized previously decentralized functions generating annual savings of over $500,000.
o  Implemented advanced technologies in teleconferencing: shortened the R&D cycle, improved inquiry response time, and reduced expenses.

### ACME CORPORATION, Any Town, CA    3/88–4/93

Corporate Director of Administration & Property Services
Directed the overall management, planning, site selection, lease negotiations, consolidations, and disposition for property totaling two million square feet. Additionally directed the $230 million purchasing operation and all corporate administrative services. Major accomplishments:

o  Assumed a central role in Acme's turnaround to profitability: generated tens of millions of dollars in cost reductions and cash flow through aggressive property consolidations, upgraded services and procurement, and enforced management accountability.
o  As head of Acme's $230 million purchasing operation, introduced an aggressive multiple-sourcing program which improved the margins of two major product lines by 7% and 9%, respectively.
o  Overcame powerful organizational resistance to produce over $3 million cash and annual savings of $2.1 million by persuading the Chairman to sell off Acme's corporate yacht.

### ABC COMPANY, Any Town, CA    6/80–3/88

Director of Services & Property    3/85–3/88
Earned five promotions during my last four years at ABC Company based on achieving all major profit goals in directing this multimillion-dollar operation. Directed services with a staff of 63 and a budget of $19 million: included property management, purchasing, communications, systems, mail, and office equipment placement and maintenance.

Profitably directed company's real estate holdings, achieving 97% occupancy of 800,000 square feet at premium rates; developed a sophisticated model which helped save $7 million on the cost of an out-of-control $40 million building project.

## REFERENCES PROVIDED UPON REQUEST

## DAVID Q. SAMPLE (Version 1)

123 Any Street, Any City, CA  XXXXX  (619) 555-1234

Contact Name                                                      Date
Title
Company
Address
City, State  Zip

Dear Mr./Ms. _____:

I have combined a top business degree, global experience, and executive skills in finance, banking, sales, and general management to establish and direct new operations which have generated millions in revenue for well-respected international banks. Bottom-line contributions to profit have been rewarded with accelerated promotions, job security, and a six-figure salary package.

I am bringing to your attention my skills, achievements, strategic brainpower, global network, and talent for exceeding profit goals under negative economic conditions so that we can discuss my joining _____ as a member of your senior financial management team.

Results achieved during the past nine years with ABC Bank include:

o  As Vice President of an International Banking Group, produced revenue of $6.5 million through aggressive client development and by saving 90% of the seriously at-risk accounts: accelerated the ROA by focusing on corporate finance, investment banking, and asset sales.

o  As Vice President of Corporate Banking at ABC's Southern California headquarters, leveraged my international contacts to market corporate and capital market products generating $5 million in added net income: achieved 250% growth in fees from capital market products.

o  Was recruited away and promoted by ABC to start and manage the new International Energy Group: established and directed the lending operation generating over $500 million in new client bookings in only 18 months with an ROA of over 1%.

o  As head of Commercial Development in charge of ABC's International Energy Group, initiated and closed several profitable deals including a hard-to-close $600 million project with an international energy company: created and directed a syndicate of major international lenders.

It should be mutually beneficial to meet and assess how I can help accelerate or turn around revenue and profit growth contributing to your company's future success.

Sincerely,

Enclosure:                                          David Q. Sample

# International Financial Executive

## DAVID Q. SAMPLE

123 Any Street, Any City, CA XXXXX (619) 555-1234

M.B.A.   Honors     University of Paris Graduate School of Business     1985

International:     Bilingual French and English; solid knowledge of Mideastern languages; traveled to over 60 nations

Certifications:     Commercial Pilot's License; Black Belt Karate; Championship Skier

## CAREER SKILLS/KNOWLEDGE

o Financial executive
o International banking
o Investment banking
o Corporate/capital markets
o Acquisitions/joint ventures
o Subsidiary recapitalization
o Project financing/syndicates
o Trade financing/foreign exchange

o Marketing/sales executive
o General management
o Start-up operations
o Major client development
o Competitive maneuvering
o Expansion/turnaround strategies
o Revenue/profit growth
o Organizational development

## CAREER ACHIEVEMENTS

o As Vice President of ABC's International Banking Group, produced revenue of $6.5 million through aggressive client development and by saving 90% of the at-risk accounts: accelerated the ROA by focusing on corporate finance, investment banking, and asset sales.

o As Vice President of Corporate Banking at ABC's Southern California headquarters, leveraged my international contacts to market corporate and capital market products generating $5 million in added net income: achieved 250% growth in fees from capital market products.

o Was recruited away and promoted by ABC to start and manage the new International Energy Group: established and directed the lending operation generating over $500 million in new client bookings in only 18 months with an ROA of over 1%.

o As head of Commercial Development in charge of ABC's International Energy Group, initiated and closed several profitable deals including a hard-to-close $600 million project with an international energy company: created and directed a syndicate of major international lenders.

o As Group Officer at Acme International Bank, established and directed operations of a new North American office: achieved and exceeded an aggressive operating plan generating new lending of $300 million and profitability in five months instead of the forecasted ten months.

## CAREER EXPERIENCE

## ABC BANK, Any Town, CA   3/88–Present

INTERNATIONAL BANKING GROUP, Any Town, CA   2/91–Present

Vice President
Responsible for major account development emphasizing high-margin corporate finance and investment banking: acquisitions, recapitalization, and collateralized financing. Upgraded asset quality by addressing and restructuring below-par debt.

CORPORATE BANKING, Any Town, CA   3/88–2/91

Vice President
Created and marketed corporate and capital market products and services to global clients.

## ACME INTERNATIONAL BANK, Any Town, Europe   6/85–3/88

Group Officer (Assistant Vice President), Any Town, British Columbia   4/87–3/88
Managed start-up of a new operation: directed staffing, property selection, facility planning, contract negotiations, and purchasing. Also developed marketing policies and operating procedures.

Officer, Any Town, CA   5/86–4/87
Accelerated global account development quadrupling pre-tax net income to over $4 million.

Officer, Any Town, Europe   6/85–5/86
Established a Credit Group generating over $2 million in fees from new business development.


## REFERENCES PROVIDED UPON REQUEST

## DONALD A. SMITH

**123 Any Street, Any City, NY XXXXX (212) 555-1234**

Contact Name                                                          Date
Title
Company
Street Address
City, State Zip

Dear Mr./Ms. _____:

I have profitably applied skills in general and financial management, treasury, operations, and acquisitions to streamline departments, improve productivity, and increase critically needed cash by 350% at Acme International Corporation.

Based on results achieved during Acme's growth and my contributions during the rapid decline of the energy industry, I have been retained in spite of an unfortunate 85% reduction in staffing.

I would like to discuss the possibility of joining _____ as a member of your financial management team.

Results achieved to date at Acme include:

o As Treasurer, spearheaded a major cost-control and cash-conservation effort which more than quadrupled cash.

o Executed in-depth operational audits of proposed acquisitions: those approved generated over $100 million in revenue; those cancelled included one where the stock value subsequently declined more than 90%.

o Identified and resolved serious product costing problems at the subsidiaries: installed cost systems, corrected inventory records, eliminated marginal products, and increased profits.

o Interacting with subsidiary presidents, coordinated the annual plan review: introduced zero-based budgeting and a disciplined cycle for approving sales, expense, and capital projections.

o Instituted and enforced a capital budgeting and request cycle which accelerated ROIs to 30% and higher.

Once we determine how I can contribute to the future success of your company, I will work hard to achieve bottom-line results.

Sincerely,

Donald A. Smith

Enclosure:

# Treasury/Accounting Management

## DONALD A. SMITH

123 Any Street, Any City, NY XXXXX (212) 555-1234

## ACADEMIC CREDENTIALS

| M.B.A. | Finance | Manhattan College | GPA 3.8 | 1990 |
|--------|---------|-------------------|---------|------|
| B.S. | Mechanical Engineering | Bahrain Institute of Science & Technology | Honors | 1985 |

## CAREER SKILLS/KNOWLEDGE

- o Financial management
- o Treasury operations
- o Acquisition studies
- o Capital budgeting
- o Zero-based budgeting
- o S.E.C. reporting
- o Product line analysis
- o Cost accounting

- o General management
- o Annual and long-range plans
- o Internal consulting
- o Project management
- o Cost reduction strategies
- o Systems design/implementation
- o Excel/Lotus 1-2-3 applications
- o MRP implementation

## CAREER ACHIEVEMENTS AT ACME INTERNATIONAL

o As Treasurer, spearheaded a major cost-control and cash-conservation effort that increased critically needed cash by 350% in eight months.

o Executed in-depth operational audits of proposed acquisitions: those approved generated over $100 million in revenue; those cancelled included one where the stock value subsequently declined more than 90%.

o Interacting with subsidiary presidents, coordinated the annual plan review: introduced zero-based budgeting and a disciplined cycle for approving sales, expense, and capital projections.

o Identified and resolved serious product costing problems at the subsidiaries: installed cost systems, corrected inventory records, eliminated marginal products, and increased profits.

o Streamlined and upgraded departmental systems and procedures, increasing productivity and reducing costs in several areas including manufacturing, engineering, and order entry and billing; initiated MRP implementation improving inventory turns by over 30%.

o Instituted and enforced a capital budgeting and request cycle which accelerated ROIs to 30% and higher.

o Designed and implemented a top management reporting system which became the primary source for identifying problems; reports were based on the subsidiaries' financial and operating reports which were upgraded and standardized.

## CAREER EXPERIENCE

## ACME INTERNATIONAL CORPORATION, Any City, NY    1988–Present

Treasurer    1992–Present
Responsible for cash management, short-term borrowing, bank relations, pension asset management, investments, letters of credit, and foreign exchange. Also coordinate capital budgeting, lease versus buy decisions, and equipment leasing.

Corporate Director of Budgets    1988–1992
Responsibilities executed:

o Directed preparation, review, and consolidation of annual and long-range plans.
o Introduced top management reporting system.
o Evaluated operating results as a basis for corrective actions.
o Troubleshooter and senior consultant to subsidiaries.
o Installed job cost and standard cost systems.
o Directed the $60 million capital expenditure program.
o Executed comprehensive acquisition reviews.
o Audited subsidiaries' operations, systems, and procedures.

Restructured Treasury operations to eliminate duplications, upgrade systems, and reduce costs.

## ENERGY SURVEY OF SAUDI ARABIA, Bahrain, Saudi Arabia    1985–1988

Energy Engineer    1986–1988
Managed 120 employees in directing the turnaround of major energy exploration projects.

## REFERENCES PROVIDED UPON REQUEST

# TIMOTHY A. WILSON

123 Any Street, Any City, CA XXXXX (619) 555-1234

Contact Name                                          Date
Title
Company
Street Address
City, State Zip

Dear Mr./Ms. _____:

As a key player in delivering 75% of Westar Bank's profits, as an early entrant into the multi-million-dollar Japanese aircraft leasing industry, and as a member of core teams which pulled off the lucrative sale of a bankrupt company and closed a $60 million portfolio deal, I have proven my ability to generate bottom-line results.

I am bringing to your attention my skills, achievements, creative energy, and talent for getting the job done. Irrespective of your current staffing, there may well be a "fit" between my skills and background and your business needs, namely:

o **Outstanding** Education (**M.B.A./J.D.**)

o 15 Years of Progressive Experience in Fortune 100, Entrepreneurship, Workouts, Turn-arounds, Start-ups, Consulting, and **Equipment Leasing**

o Multiple and Diverse Skills:

    - **FINANCE** (Corporate; Operations; Leasing)
    - **ACCOUNTING** ("Big 6" Quality)
    - **LEGAL** (Contracts; Taxation)
    - **SYSTEMS** (PC to Mainframe)
    - **PORTFOLIO MANAGEMENT**

o A Proven Track Record of Concrete, Measurable, Bottom-line, **Hands-on,** and **Team-Oriented** Accomplishments

I don't possess a "golden Rolodex" or "smoke & mirror" solutions, but I *can* offer a thorough knowledge of corporate finance, equipment leasing, and asset-based lending as well as a track record of achieving quantifiable results through honest and creative approaches.

Please call at your convenience if you would like to discuss further how I can contribute to your company's future success.

Sincerely yours,

Timothy A. Wilson

## TIMOTHY A. WILSON

123 Any Street, Any City, CA XXXXX (619) 555-1234

### EDUCATION

| | | | |
|---|---|---|---|
| **M.B.A.** | Princeton University | Finance/Marketing | 1984 |
| **J.D.** | University of California | Business/Taxation | 1990 |
| **B.A.** | Princeton University | Economics | 1982 |

### SKILLS THAT ACHIEVE SUCCESS

- o Finance expertise
- o Accounting expertise
- o Complex business/tax issues
- o Legal analysis
- o Staff management
- o PC/systems expertise
- o Strategic planning

- o Lease portfolio evaluation
- o Tax shelter analysis
- o Financing strategies
- o Deal origination/structuring
- o Workouts/turnarounds
- o Start-up ventures
- o Business plan formulation

### CAREER ACHIEVEMENTS

o Negotiated and closed one of the few *true* commercial aircraft *operating* lease transactions for a Japanese owner/lessor.

o Member of four-person team that closed—in 30 days—the sale of residual interests in a 4000 lease, multiple investor portfolio, generating $16.2 million in profit; represented more than 75% of Westar Bank's profits.

o Coexecuted the turnaround and premium price sale of a bankrupt equipment leasing firm with $60 million in assets and $250 million in tax losses; structured and implemented formal profit-planning (cash, tax, and GAAP); modeled and analyzed financing strategies and long-term business growth for equipment leasing.

o Consummated a private placement tax shelter equipment trust by resurrecting "11th hour" negotiations with a major Los Angeles bank and obtaining unsecured note financing for investors.

o Negotiated and closed "the deal that died a dozen deaths": a $60 million portfolio in long-term leases (an L-1011, railroad cars, mining and manufacturing equipment, trucks) originally acquired by the seller as a corporate tax shelter.

o Cofounder of personal computer start-up venture; coauthored business plan that resulted in a successful $1 million IPO.

o Financial member of start-up team for Acme Brands' entry into the soft-drink market: analyzed expansion alternatives, developed pricing strategies, established national bottler distribution network, and helped sell new ideas to senior management.

o Financial manager for $80 million business with multi-plant operations at Acme Brands: coexecuted turnaround strategy and start-up of new packaging technology.

## CAREER EXPERIENCE

**AIRLEASE INTERNATIONAL**                                    12/94–Present
Any City, CA
**VICE PRESIDENT—FINANCE & ADMINISTRATION**
Full responsibility and accountability for all financial, legal, and administrative functions, from in-house CFO duties to structuring investment deals for clients. Promoted the institutional investment opportunity of the 1990s: "Low-Leverage, Short-Term Operating Leasing of Used Commercial Aircraft."

**THE COMLEASE GROUP (WESTAR BANK)**                          12/91–12/94
Any City, CA
**DIRECTOR—FINANCIAL PROJECTS**
Reported to CEO. Responsible for profitability analyses, business reviews, trend and portfolio analysis, pricing, mergers and acquisitions, financial modeling, residual forecasting, and competitive analyses. Renegotiated and managed equity syndications, leveraged leases, tax-oriented deals, and special investments. Net worth doubled in less than two years.

**ABC LEASING SERVICES, INC.**                                4/91–12/91
Any City, CA
**CONSULTANT TO TRUSTEE**
Responsible for analysis and forecasting of business valuation, reorganization alternatives, long-term financing, tax shelter impacts, and accounting issues. Negotiated with several prominent investment groups resulting in a sale price well above the creditors' most optimistic expectations.

**PC VENTURE GROUP, INC.**                                    8/90–4/91
Any City, CA
**COFOUNDER and DIRECTOR OF BUSINESS ANALYSIS**
Start-up venture. Member of three-person team that developed and authored business plan that effected a $1 million IPO. Personal contribution focused on financial projections, ROI/profit analyses, capitalization alternatives, market analysis, and competitive strategies.

**ACME BRANDS CORPORATION**                                   11/84–8/90
Any City, CA
**BUDGET ANALYST TO FINANCIAL MANAGER**
Projects Consultant—Sunset Boulevard Capital Corporation
Financial Manager—Corporate Manufacturing/Operations
Capital Investment Supervisor—Beverage & Breakfast Foods
Financial Associate—Syrup & Pancake Mix
Senior Financial Analyst—Soft-drink Group
EDP/Financial Analyst—Corporate Distribution
Budget Analyst—Corporate Distribution

## OTHER QUALIFICATIONS

o  Admitted to California State Bar
o  Honorable Discharge—U.S. Air Force Finance Corps (2LT)

## DAVID Q. SAMPLE (Version 2)

**123 Any Street, Any City, CA XXXXX (619) 555-1234**

Contact Name                                                    Date
Title
Company
Address
City, State Zip

Dear Mr./Ms. _____:

I have combined a top business degree, global experience, and executive skills in banking, sales, finance, and general management to establish and direct new operations which have generated millions in revenue for well-respected international banks. Bottom-line contributions to profit have been rewarded with accelerated promotions, job security, and a six-figure salary package.

I am bringing to your attention my skills, achievements, strategic brainpower, global network, and talent for exceeding profit goals under negative economic conditions so that we can discuss my joining _____ as a member of your senior management team.

Results achieved during the past nine years with ABC Bank include:

o As Vice President of an International Banking Group, produced revenue of $6.5 million through aggressive client development and by saving 90% of the seriously at-risk accounts: accelerated the ROA by focusing on corporate finance, investment banking, and asset sales.

o As Vice President of Corporate Banking at ABC's Southern California headquarters, leveraged my international contacts to market corporate and capital market products generating $5 million in added net income: achieved 250% growth in fees from capital market products.

o Was recruited away and promoted by ABC to start and manage the new International Energy Group: established and directed the lending operation generating over $500 million in new client bookings in only 18 months with an ROA of over 1%.

o As head of Commercial Development in charge of ABC's International Energy Group, initiated and closed several profitable deals including a hard-to-close $600 million project with an international energy company: created and directed a syndicate of major international lenders.

It should be mutually beneficial to meet and assess how I can help accelerate or turn around revenue and profit growth contributing to your company's future success.

Sincerely,


Enclosure:                                          David Q. Sample

# DAVID Q. SAMPLE

123 Any Street, Any City, CA XXXXX (619) 555-1234

M.B.A.   Honors     University of Paris Graduate School of Business        1985

International:     Bilingual French and English; solid knowledge of Mideastern languages; traveled to over 60 nations

Certifications:     Commercial Pilot's License; Black Belt Karate; Championship Skier

## CAREER SKILLS/KNOWLEDGE

- Banking executive
- International banking
- Investment banking
- Corporate/capital markets
- Acquisitions/joint ventures
- Subsidiary recapitalization
- Project financing/syndicates
- Trade financing/foreign exchange

- Marketing/sales executive
- General management
- Start-up operations
- Major client development
- Competitive maneuvering
- Expansion/turnaround strategies
- Revenue/profit growth
- Organizational development

## CAREER ACHIEVEMENTS

o As Vice President of ABC's International Banking Group, produced revenue of $6.5 million through aggressive client development and by saving 90% of the at-risk accounts: accelerated the ROA by focusing on corporate finance, investment banking, and asset sales.

o As Vice President of Corporate Banking at ABC's Southern California headquarters, leveraged my international contacts to market corporate and capital market products generating $5 million in added net income: achieved 250% growth in fees from capital market products.

o Was recruited away and promoted by ABC to start and manage the new International Energy Group: established and directed the lending operation generating over $500 million in new client bookings in only 18 months with an ROA of over 1%.

o As head of Commercial Development in charge of ABC's International Energy Group, initiated and closed several profitable deals including a hard-to-close $600 million project with an international energy company: created and directed a syndicate of major international lenders.

o As Group Officer at Acme International Bank, established and directed operations of a new North American office: achieved and exceeded an aggressive operating plan generating new lending of $300 million and profitability in five months instead of the forecasted ten months.

# CAREER EXPERIENCE

## ABC BANK, Any Town, CA   3/88–Present

<u>INTERNATIONAL BANKING GROUP, Any Town   2/91–Present</u>

<u>Vice President</u>
Responsible for major account development emphasizing high-margin corporate finance and investment banking: acquisitions, recapitalization, and collateralized financing. Upgraded asset quality by addressing and restructuring below-par debt.

<u>CORPORATE BANKING, Any Town, CA   3/88–2/91</u>

<u>Vice President</u>
Created and marketed corporate and capital market products and services to global clients.

## ACME INTERNATIONAL BANK, Any Town, Europe   6/85–3/88

<u>Group Officer (Assistant Vice President), Any Town, British Columbia   4/87–3/88</u>
Managed start-up of a new operation: directed staffing, property selection, facility planning, contract negotiations, and purchasing. Also developed marketing policies and operating procedures.

<u>Officer, Any Town, CA   5/86–4/87</u>
Accelerated global account development quadrupling pre-tax net income to over $4 million.

<u>Officer, Any Town, Europe   6/85–5/86</u>
Established a Credit Group generating over $2 million in fees from new business development.

# REFERENCES PROVIDED UPON REQUEST

---

## Stock Brokerage Executive

---

# GEORGE A. JOHNSON

---

**123 Any Street, Any City, CA XXXXX (619) 555-1234**

Contact Name                                                    Date
Title
Company
Street Address
City, State Zip

Dear Mr./Ms. _____:

I have profitably applied executive skills in brokerage management, sales, marketing, and client development to become a top five producer, Western Region Vice President, and a top earner with XYZ Securities. I have consistently demonstrated my talent for directing brokerage operations which generate tens-of-millions of dollars in fees exceeding even the most aggressive revenue targets.

I am presenting for your review my skills, bottom-line achievements, and accelerated experience so that we can initiate discussions about my joining _____ as a member of your senior brokerage management team.

Results achieved by applying my diverse skills include:

o Based on my nationwide ranking, productive management of the San Diego Branch, and turnaround of the Northern Los Angeles Branch, was promoted to Regional Vice President of XYZ Securities at age 29.

o At XYZ, generate as much as $4,000,000 monthly in "new" money; personally generate as much as $800,000 monthly.

o At Acme Inc., more than doubled the dollar volume generated by 15 high-dollar accounts.

o Consistently ranked among the top five sales producers at ABC Products, Inc.

I look forward to a face-to-face meeting at which we can determine how I can contribute to your company's future success.

                                                    Sincerely,


Enclosure:                                          George A. Johnson

---

| Stock Brokerage Executive |
| --- |

# GEORGE A. JOHNSON

123 Any Street, Any City, CA XXXXX (619) 555-1234

## BROKERAGE INDUSTRY EXPERIENCE

### XYZ SECURITIES, INC., Any City, CA   6/95–Present

Western Region Vice President   6/96–Present
Responsible for Northern Los Angeles:

o Based on top five nationwide ranking, successful management of the San Diego Branch, and turnaround of the Northern Los Angeles Branch, was promoted to Western Region Vice President at age 29.
o Generate up to $4,000,000 monthly in "new" money; personally generate as much as $800,000 monthly, servicing over 2,000 accounts.

## BROKERAGE/MANAGEMENT SKILLS

| | |
| --- | --- |
| o Regional executive | o Staff recruiting |
| o New account development | o Staff development |
| o Account management | o Advertising |
| o Underwriting | o NASD/banking rules |

## SALES EXPERIENCE

### ABC PRODUCTS, INC., Any Town, CA   4/93–6/95

Sales Representative
Ranked among the top five producers.

### AVERY COMPANY, INC., Any Town, CA   4/92–4/93

Sales Representative
Produced a 100% increase in the territory customer base.

### ACME, INC., Any Town, CA   6/90–4/92

Account Representative
More than doubled the dollar volume generated by fifteen high-dollar accounts.

## EDUCATION/CREDENTIALS

| B.A. | Business Administration | University of San Diego | 1990 |
| --- | --- | --- | --- |

**Honor/Athletics:**  o Graduated top quarter; varsity team captain
  o Named a Top Athlete in U.S. Colleges (1989)
**Certification:**  o Registered Broker Principal (NASD)
  o Registered Full Service Broker Representative (NASD)

# MARK A. WILSON

**123 Any Street, Any City, WA XXXXX (206) 555-1234**

Contact Name                                                            Date
Title
Company
Street Address
City, State  Zip

Dear Mr./Ms. _____:

As Division Manager of Acme Corporation's Leasing Subsidiary, directed its turnaround and major contribution to profits in an otherwise disappointing period for the company. Achieved this by instituting a lucrative remarketing program, upgrading financial controls, and turning around out-of-control reporting.

I am presenting for your review my skills, achievements, leasing industry expertise, and talent for generating bottom-line results within problem operations so that we can discuss my joining _____ as a member of your management team.

Results achieved to date include:

o Instituted Acme's lucrative remarketing program for off-lease equipment generating substantial rentals from the over $4 million in equipment leased to date under the program.

o Investigated and uncovered several million dollars of off-lease equipment that had never been returned to inventory recovering $700,000 in fees for Acme.

o Restructured and turned around Acme's third-party leasing portfolio, upgrading the accounting and administrative controls and creating an accurate database of all equipment.

o As Program Director at ABC Computer Leasing, introduced critically needed administrative and accounting controls for an affiliated leasing company; thoroughly analyzed the affiliate's portfolio of leases, loans, sale/leasebacks, and remarketing agreements.

o One of five key veteran managers remaining after the bankruptcy of XYZ Leasing Services, a nationwide company with revenues of $200 million; comanaged its turnaround and better-than-forecasted $30 million sale.

I look forward to discussing how I can contribute to your company's future success.

Sincerely,


Enclosure:                                              Mark A. Wilson

# Leasing Industry Management

## MARK A. WILSON

123 Any Street, Any City, WA XXXXX (206) 555-1234

B.B.A.   Accounting   University of Seattle   1986

Certified Public Accountant

## CAREER SKILLS/KNOWLEDGE

o Leasing industry expertise
o Lease financing cycle
o Division management
o P&L responsibility
o Marketing/sales
o MIS operations
o Personnel/payroll
o Staff supervision/development
o Information security

o Finance/accounting
o Controller operations
o Treasury operations
o Portfolio management
o Banking relations
o Audit operations
o General accounting
o Budgeting/controls
o Collections/taxes

## CAREER ACHIEVEMENTS

o As Division Manager of Acme Corporation's Leasing Subsidiary, directed its turnaround and major contribution to profits in an otherwise disappointing period for the corporation.

o Instituted Acme's lucrative remarketing program for off-lease equipment generating substantial rentals from the over $4 million in equipment leased to date under the program.

o Investigated and uncovered several million dollars of off-lease equipment that had never been returned to inventory recovering $700,000 in fees for Acme.

o Restructured and turned around Acme's third-party leasing portfolio, upgrading the accounting and administrative controls and creating an accurate database of all equipment.

o As Program Director at ABC Computer Leasing, introduced critically needed administrative and accounting controls for an affiliated leasing company; thoroughly analyzed the affiliate's portfolio of leases, loans, sale/leasebacks, and remarketing agreements.

o Instituted critically needed Equity Tracking System upgrading and streamlining the calculation and distribution of residual rents to ABC Computer Leasing's equity investors.

o One of five key veteran managers remaining after the bankruptcy of XYZ Leasing Services, a nationwide company with revenues of $200 million; comanaged its turnaround and better-than-forecasted $30 million sale.

# CAREER EXPERIENCE

## ACME CORPORATION, INC., Any Town, WA    2/95–Present

Division Manager
Responsibilities executed for the Acme Leasing Subsidiary:

o  Achieved targeted P&L goals; instituted remarketing program.
o  Direct senior staff: Controller, Systems Director, and Operations and Credit Managers.
o  Upgraded financial and operational controls and reporting.
o  Negotiate, screen, and approve all contracts.
o  Upgraded relations with banks.
o  Reduced aged receivables; upgraded inventory control.
o  Eliminated aged backlog of customer inquiries.

## ABC COMPUTER LEASING COMPANY, Any Town, WA    3/94–2/95

Program Director
Audited portfolio of affiliated leasing company from its inception through current status; instituted Equity Tracking System; assisted in transition to new database system.

## XYZ LEASING SERVICES, INC., Any Town, WA    6/86–3/94

Treasurer    2/91–3/94
Responsibilities executed:

o  Upgraded portfolio management increasing return on $40 million cash.
o  Developed relations with major northwestern banks.
o  Gained approval for post-bankruptcy exception request.
o  Managed Personnel, Payroll, and Collections Departments.

Executed a major systems database project critical to the $30 million sale of the company.

Controller    3/89–2/91
Responsibilities executed:

o  Recruited, trained, and supervised several staff accountants.
o  Directed the Bookkeeping Department.
o  Directed general ledger accounting; prepared consolidations.
o  Managed in-depth operational reviews; initiated corrective actions.
o  Supervised tax area; reduced equipment property taxes.

Instituted effective post-bankruptcy financial controls returning critically needed credibility to XYZ.

**REFERENCES PROVIDED UPON REQUEST**

---

**Asset Management Executive**

---

## JOHN A. SMITH (Version 2)

---

**123 Any Street, Any Town, CA XXXXX  Home: (619) 555-1234  Office: (619) 555-2345**

Contact Name                                                    Date
Title
Company
Street Address
City, State  Zip

Dear Mr./Ms. _____:

I have profitably applied executive skills in asset management, marketing, finance, real estate, and treasury to play a key role in the start-up and marketing of Asset Management Associates, a division of the $2 billion Acme Corporation which has achieved a 35% ROI through the acquisition and disposition of foreclosed real estate worth $200 million. I also played a central role in Acme Corporation's entry into both the asset management and financial industries.

I am presenting for your review my skills, achievements, proven leadership, work ethic, and straight-forward approach to getting the job done so that we can discuss my joining _____ as a member of your Asset Management Team.

Results achieved to date include:

o As Director of Sales, played a central role in the start-up, marketing, and general management of Asset Management Associates—a venture which has yielded an on-target 35% return through the purchase and resale of over 2,000 foreclosed properties valued at $200 million: codeveloped the start-up business plan, helped staff the company, and assumed a Director position reporting directly to the President.

o Helped generate third-year profits of $2 million on revenue of $7 million at Asset Management Associates: signed the first major banking client accounting for a 50-house management contract; closed deals which contributed to the company managing 400 properties generating $800,000 in fees; signed a major lender accounting for purchased inventory of over $2 million a month; sold 20 additional accounts yielding 8 management and 12 buy-out clients.

o Prior to and during my tenure as a Major Account Executive, directly facilitated Acme's subsequent entry into asset management: at the request of the Chairman, executed a feasibility study which recommended entry into asset management; closed a lucrative deal which represented the company's first asset management client and led to the eventual formation of Asset Management Associates.

o Took the lead in establishing Asset Management Associates' first relationship with the FDIC by directly contacting government officials; initiated negotiations for a major purchase from the Resolution Trust Corporation.

o As Treasury Director in charge of treasury operations at a division of Acme, initiated development of financial services which allowed clients to process applications through the mail to bankers with whom we had negotiated contracts: success of the services led to Acme's entry into the financial industry.

I look forward to discussing how I can help accelerate or turn around revenue and profit growth, contributing to your future success.

Sincerely,

Enclosure:                                                      John A. Smith

# Asset Management/Executive

## JOHN A. SMITH

123 Any Street, Any Town, CA XXXXX Home: (619) 555-1234 Office: (619) 555-2345

| M.B.A. | Finance | University of Maine | 1982 |
| B.A. | Accounting | State University of New York | 1980 |

## CAREER SKILLS/KNOWLEDGE

o Asset management/marketing
o Sales/marketing management
o Balance sheet management
o Real estate foreclosures
o Collections/work-outs
o Buy-out negotiations
o Resale/ROI target strategies
o Real estate management
o Mortgage services
o Cold-calling/client development
o Proposals/presentations/closing

o Financial/treasury management
o Treasury operations
o Cash management/allocation
o Investment strategies
o Borrowing strategies
o Basis point reductions
o Foreign exchange strategies
o Banking relations
o Budgeting/capital appropriations
o Consolidations/financial statements
o Auditing/credit and collections

## CAREER ACHIEVEMENTS

o As Director of Sales, played a central role in the start-up, marketing, and general management of Asset Management Associates—a venture which has yielded an on-target 35% return through the acquisition and disposition of 2,000 foreclosed properties valued at $200 million: codeveloped the start-up business plan, helped staff the company, and assumed a Director position reporting directly to the President.

o Helped generate third-year profits of $2 million on revenue of $7 million at Asset Management Associates: signed the first major banking client accounting for a 50-house management contract; closed deals which contributed to the company managing 400 properties generating $800,000 in fees; signed a major lender accounting for purchased inventory of over $2 million a month; sold 20 additional accounts yielding 8 management and 12 buy-out clients.

o Prior to and during my tenure as a Major Account Executive, directly facilitated Acme's subsequent entry into asset management: at the request of the Chairman, executed a feasibility study which recommended entry into asset management; closed a lucrative deal which represented the company's first asset management client and led to the eventual formation of Asset Management Associates.

o As Director of Investment Acquisition at Asset Management Associates, directed development of a $40 million offering package and formed a syndicate of investors to meet our outside borrowing requirements; previously developed and recommended cancellation of a $200 million public offering.

o Took the lead in establishing Asset Management Associates' first relationship with the FDIC by directly contacting government officials; initiated negotiations for a major purchase from the Resolution Trust Corporation.

o As a Major Account Executive at an Acme Division, exceeded revenue targets by maintaining volume, increasing business, and renegotiating contracts with multimillion-dollar accounts.

o As Treasury Director in charge of treasury operations at a division of Acme, initiated development of financial services which allowed clients to process applications through the mail to bankers with whom we had negotiated contracts: success of the services led to Acme's entry into the financial industry.

## CAREER EXPERIENCE

## ACME CORPORATION, Any City, CA   1990–Present

## ASSET MANAGEMENT ASSOCIATES, Any City, CA   1992–Present

Director of Investment Acquisition   1994–Present
Member of management team responsible for directing business and establishing strategic objectives. While still executing sales responsibilities, directed development of $40 million offering package.

Director of Sales   1993–1994
Developed new business in marketing acquisition and disposition services for foreclosed real estate to savings and loans, banks, the federal government, and other financial institutions.

Director   1992–1993
Member of group formed to assess the need for an Asset Management Company.

## ACME DIVISION, Any City, CA   1990–1992

Major Account Executive   1991–1992
Maintained volume, increased business, and renegotiated contracts with established accounts of Acme.

Treasury Director   1990–1991
Instituted a new method of funding bank accounts which yielded a savings of $3 million a year; instituted a system of billing to clients which reduced receivables by $8 million; stopped a 40% increase in headcount by developing a computerized accounts receivable system during a period of rapid growth; computerized several Cash Management reports which accelerated the reimbursement process thereby reducing excess borrowing by $7 million.

## AVERY INCORPORATED, Any City, CA   1982–1990

Assistant Treasury Manager   1987–1990
Profitably managed a $400 million portfolio of short-term investments; managed the daily cash position; negotiated basis point reductions; established and directed Currency Exchange review process.

Senior Financial Analyst   1984–1987
Reviewed budget submissions from international subsidiaries. Prepared reports with recommended changes that were routinely accepted.

## ADDITIONAL EDUCATION/TRAINING

Professional Courses:        o Professional Marketing Series
                             o The Art of Selling Series
                             o Professional Communications Series

# Property Management/Development Executive

## JOHN Q. SAMPLE (Version 2)

**123 Any Street, Any City, CA XXXXX (619) 555-1234**

Contact Name                                                  Date
Title
Company
Address
City, State Zip

Dear Mr./Ms. _____:

As a central figure in Acme Corporation's massive restructuring, I applied executive skills in property management, property development, administration, and purchasing to facilitate Acme's turnaround to profitability. I likewise produced multimillion-dollar profits for the ABC Company through productive management of its property management services and administration, receiving accelerated promotions to Director of a $19 million operation.

I am presenting for your review my skills, achievements, and talent for accelerating margins and turning around unprofitable organizations so that we can discuss my joining _____ as a member of your senior management team.

Results achieved to date include:

o As Acme's Corporate Director of Property Services & Administration, generated tens of millions of dollars in cost reductions and cash flow through aggressive property consolidations, up-graded services and procurement, and enforced management accountability.

o Promoted five grade levels during my last four years at ABC Company based on achieving all major P&L goals in directing the $19 million Corporate Property Management and Administration Department.

o Consolidated 29 Acme warehouses down to 4, generating annual savings of $5.8 million; saved $4.6 million by reducing corporate headquarters space 30%; introduced uniform facility standards which reduced total space requirements 20%, generating another $3.4 million in annual cost savings.

o Productively managed ABC Company's property holdings, achieving 97% occupancy of 800,000 square feet at premium rates; developed a sophisticated model which helped save $7 million on the cost of an out-of-control $40 million building project at ABC.

o As head of Acme's $230 million purchasing operation, introduced an aggressive multiple-sourcing program which improved the margins of two major product lines by 7% and 9%, respectively.

I look forward to meeting and discussing how I can help accelerate or turn around your company's revenue and profit growth.

                                                  Sincerely,

Enclosure:                                        John Q. Sample

---
## Property Management/Development Executive
---

## JOHN Q. SAMPLE
---

**123 Any Street, Any City, CA XXXXX (619) 555-1234**

B.S. Honors Finance Georgetown University 1980

### CAREER SKILLS/KNOWLEDGE

o Property management
o Development/construction
o Occupancy growth strategies
o Premium rate strategies
o Consolidation strategies
o Lease management/negotiations
o Site selection/space planning
o Budgeting/accountability
o Government regulations
o Environmental guidelines

o Finance/administration management
o General management
o Strategic/operational planning
o General/administrative services
o Financial planning and analysis
o Procurement operations
o Facilities/telecommunications
o Training operations
o Logistics services
o Global transportation

### CAREER ACHIEVEMENTS

o As Corporate Director of Property Services & Administration, assumed a central role in Acme's turnaround to profitability: generated tens of millions of dollars in cost reductions and cash flow through aggressive property consolidations, upgraded services and procurement, and enforced management accountability.

o Promoted five grade levels during my last four years at ABC Company based on achieving all major P&L goals in directing the $19 million Corporate Property Management and Administration Department.

o Consolidated 29 Acme warehouses down to 4, generating annual savings of $5.8 million; saved $4.6 million by reducing corporate headquarters space 30%; introduced uniform facility standards which reduced total space requirements 20%, generating another $3.4 million in annual cost savings.

o Productively managed ABC Company's property holdings, achieving 97% occupancy of 800,000 square feet at premium rates; developed a sophisticated model which helped save $7 million on the cost of an out-of-control $40 million building project at ABC.

o As head of Acme's $230 million purchasing operation, introduced an aggressive multiple-sourcing program which improved the margins of two major product lines by 7% and 9%, respectively.

o Overcame powerful organizational resistance to produce over $3 million cash and annual savings of $2.1 million by persuading the Chairman to sell off Acme's corporate yacht.

o Generated annual cost savings of over $800,000 by installing a Novell network and upgrading ABC Company's distribution, travel, and other corporate services.

## CAREER EXPERIENCE

## ACME CORPORATION, Any Town, CA   3/88–Present

Corporate Director of Property Services & Administration
Direct the overall management, planning, site selection, lease negotiations, consolidations, and disposition for property totaling two million square feet. Additionally direct the $230 million purchasing operation and all corporate administrative services.

## ABC COMPANY, Any Town, CA   6/80–3/88

Director of Property & Services   3/85–3/88
Directed services with a staff of 63 and a budget of $19 million: included property management, purchasing, communications, systems, mail, and office equipment placement and maintenance. Reviewed and approved all facilities and construction contracts. Audited almost $100 million in operating expense budgets.

Manager of Administration   2/83–3/85
Developed policies and procedures, negotiated property transactions, and created a model which turned around a $40 million building project.

Senior Facilities Consultant   8/81–2/83
Developed well-received proposals that resulted in the creation of a $12 million Facilities Group.

Senior Consultant   6/80–8/81
Introduced the much needed zero-based budgeting concept to seven major operations.

## REFERENCES PROVIDED UPON REQUEST

## JANET A. JONES

**123 Any Street, Any City, CA  XXXXX  (619) 555-1234**

Contact Name                                         Date
Title
Company
Address
City, State  Zip

Dear Mr./Ms. _____:

As Vice President in charge of XYZ Corporation's real estate referral service, I expanded the network from 21 to 264 firms, turned this money-losing operation into a highly profitable one, and referred $550 million in real estate deals to XYZ Realty.

I am presenting for your review my skills, achievements, and ability to motivate personnel and generate bottom-line results so that we can discuss my joining _____ as a member of your senior management team.

Additional results achieved by aggressively applying my diverse skills include:

o  Initiated research and identified serious economic problems with the Warranty Sales Plan; based on my recommendation, XYZ discontinued the program thereby preventing major losses.

o  As Director of Relocation Services at XYZ, cost effectively managed the move of transferees involved in corporate relocations at General Electric, MCI, and TWA.

o  During six years with ABC Realty, Inc., ranked as a top producer selling as much as $3 million in modestly priced real estate annually.

o  Recognized at Annual Meeting for "Outstanding Service to XYZ."

I look forward to meeting you, at which time we can determine how I can contribute to your company's future success.

Sincerely,


Enclosure:                                           Janet A. Jones

# JANET A. JONES

123 Any Street, Any City, CA  XXXXX  (619) 555-1234

## REAL ESTATE ACHIEVEMENTS

o  As Vice President of XYZ Corporation's real estate referral service, developed and executed a marketing plan which expanded the network from 21 to 264 firms in four years.

o  Turned around XYZ from a money-losing operation into a highly profitable one generating $2.5 million in fees annually; referred $550 million in real estate deals to XYZ Realty.

o  Recognized at Annual Meeting for "Outstanding Service to XYZ."

o  Initiated research and identified serious economic problems with the Warranty Sales Plan; based on my recommendation, XYZ discontinued the program thereby preventing major losses.

o  As Director of Relocation Services at XYZ, cost effectively managed the move of transferees involved in corporate relocations at General Electric, MCI, and TWA.

o  During six years with ABC Realty, Inc., ranked as a top producer selling as much as $3 million in modestly priced real estate annually.

o  Developed a homesale program for XYZ to generate additional revenues, currently not captured.

## REAL ESTATE EXPERIENCE

### XYZ CORPORATION, Any City, CA   5/89–Present

Vice President   5/94–Present
Develop, expand, and direct overall operations of a full-service referral network:

o  Member of the advisory board responsible for developing policies and programs for recruitment, marketing, and productivity.
o  Manage development of Relocation Directors and Referral Coordinators; selected as lead instructor at regional meetings.
o  In charge of the National Convention: develop all programs and select and contract for featured speakers.
o  Member of Planning Committee for Employee Relocations Council's Conference.

Director of Relocation Services   5/89–5/94
In charge of developing and upgrading staffs in company-owned firms nationwide; also developed new revenue-generating programs.

### ABC REALTY, INC., Any City, CA   5/83–5/89

Sales Associate: Consistently achieved Million-Dollar-Club status.

## REFERENCES PROVIDED UPON REQUEST

## JOHN A. CUMMINGS

123 Any Street, Any City, CA XXXXX (213) 555-1234

Contact Name                                    Date
Title
Company
Street Address
City, State Zip

Dear Mr./Ms. _____:

I have applied executive skills in advertising, marketing, new product introductions, and acquisitions to generate multimillion-dollar billings and accelerate the revenue and profit growth of major Fortune 500 clients. Results have been rewarded with stock options and accelerated promotions up to vice president from Richard Smith, president of Prestigious Advertising, Inc.

I am bringing to your attention my skills, achievements, and proven ability to accelerate billings so that we can discuss my joining _____ as a member of your senior management team.

Results achieved at Prestigious Advertising, Inc. include:

o Singlehandedly developed the long-range corporate strategy and business plan for the development and acquisition of new products by the ABC affiliate of XYZ; profitably integrated the Essex Baking Company, a several hundred million dollar acquisition, into ABC.

o Initiated and executed aggressive new product introductions by the QRS Division of Acme, Inc.: codirected product development, packaging, market positioning, advertising, and testing; over a dozen high-profit-potential products were put into various stages of development.

o After winning key toy and game accounts of Acme, Inc., comanaged their new product acquisitions and development; coexecuted start-up of the multimillion-dollar Dimensions account.

o After recommending that senior management "kill" the frozen product lines of the Smith Division of Acme, Inc., presented a ten-part proposal that helped save the division; codirected a major new product introduction generating second-year sales of $80,000,000.

o Member of the core team which created, produced, and launched a highly successful cereal campaign featuring what turned into a well-known and nationally popular character; achieved highest persuasion and recall scores and sales gains of over 60% for Acme.

I know that an exploratory meeting to determine how I can, likewise, contribute to your company's future success will be to our mutual benefit.

Sincerely,

Enclosure:                                      John A. Cummings

## Advertising Industry Executive

# JOHN A. CUMMINGS

123 Any Street, Any City, CA XXXXX (213) 555-1234

B.A.   English    University of Massachusetts    1982

## CAREER SKILLS/KNOWLEDGE

o Advertising executive
o Account management
o Business reviews
o Media/copy expertise
o Market positioning
o Commercial production
o Product testing
o Roll-out strategies
o Oral/written presentations
o Staff supervision
o Budget management/control

o Marketing executive
o New business development
o New product introduction
o P&L responsibility
o Acquisitions/mergers
o Business plan development
o Marketing strategies
o Competitive analyses
o Pricing/margin strategies
o Financial analyses
o International marketing

## BUSINESS ACHIEVEMENTS AT PRESTIGIOUS ADVERTISING, INC.

o As Vice President, developed the long-range corporate strategy and business plan for the development and acquisition of new products by the ABC affiliate of XYZ; profitably integrated the Essex Baking Company, a several hundred million dollar acquisition, into ABC.

o Initiated and executed aggressive new product introductions by the QRS Division of Acme, Inc.: codirected product development, packaging, market positioning, advertising, and testing; over a dozen high-profit-potential products were put into various stages of development.

o After winning key toy and game accounts of Acme, Inc., comanaged their new product acquisitions and development; coexecuted start-up of the multimillion-dollar Dimensions account.

o Member of the core team which created, produced, and launched a highly successful cereal campaign featuring what turned into a well-known and nationally popular character; achieved highest persuasion and recall scores and sales gains of over 60% for Acme.

o After recommending that senior management "kill" the frozen product lines of the Smith Division of Acme, Inc., presented a ten-part proposal that helped save the division.

o At a critical strategy meeting of the New Business Division of Acme, candidly assessed a proposed soft drink line as competitively inferior, causing senior management to "kill" it.

o Promoted to Senior Account Executive on the Acme account responsible for management of a main brand and introduction of a major new product; totally redesigned the new product packaging and codirected the overall project generating second-year sales of $80,000,000.

## CAREER EXPERIENCE

### PRESTIGIOUS ADVERTISING, INC., Any City, CA   9/90–Present

<u>Vice President, Account Supervisor</u>
Responsibilities executed for major international clients:

o Coordinated long-range strategic planning and business plan development.
o Integral member of new and established products business development team.
o Conducted in-depth product feasibility studies as a basis for marketing decisions.
o Formulated market share growth strategies.
o Established product priorities.
o Established and monitored development schedules.
o Planned for acquisitions and mergers.
o Integrated acquisitions into client's corporate structure.
o Planned and implemented advertising campaigns.

### ANOTHER ADVERTISING FIRM, Any City, CA   7/85–9/90

<u>Account Executive</u>
Achieved brand share growth, in spite of aggressive competition, for major clients including Major Brand A (Product 1, Product 2, Product 3) and Major Brand B (Product 1, Product 2, Product 3). Prepared corporate annual report for the CEO and Chairman.

### ANOTHER ADVERTISING FIRM, Any City, CA   6/82–7/85

<u>Account Executive</u>
Sole Account Executive assigned to the multimillion-dollar Major Consumer Products Company account. Selected by the President of the Agency to be an on-site representative to a Fortune 50 Corporation.

## REFERENCES AVAILABLE UPON REQUEST

---

## Broadcast Industry/Sales Executive

---

## JOHN A. DRAKE

---

**123 Any Street, Any Town, CA XXXXX (619) 555-1234**

Contact Name                                                        Date
Title
Company
Address
City, State  Zip

Dear Mr./Ms. _____:

I have formulated and executed expert sales, marketing, broadcasting, and product strategies to outmaneuver the competition, sell at premium rates, accelerate billings, and exceed revenue targets for the National Broadcasting Company during the past several years. I routinely generate millions in advertising revenue and a high six-figure income.

I am bringing to your attention my skills, achievements, and special talent for penetrating and selling even the toughest decision makers to that we can discuss my joining _____ as a member of your Senior Sales Management Team.

Results achieved during the last 13 years with NBC include:

o Earn a six-figure income by selling and servicing an expanding base of corporate clients for NBC Channel 6 in Los Angeles: generated four-year billings in excess of $60 million ranking as the number two biller the last two years.

o Ranked among the top Account Managers at NBC's Regional Sales Office in Los Angeles; achieved this by penetrating agencies and advertisers to reach decision makers to whom I sold a high percentage of available commercial time at premium prices.

o Developed and sold lucrative entertainment packages and created several well-received programming ideas for telecast over NBC-owned stations, generating millions in advertising revenue.

o Promoted to NBC's Regional Sales Office in Los Angeles in less than two years instead of the normal four to five year cycle.

o Accelerated NBC's Regional Sales Office in Miami from fourth place to second place in billings.

It should be to our mutual benefit to meet and determine how I can help accelerate or turn around sales, thereby contributing to your company's future success.

Sincerely,


Enclosure:                                                      John A. Drake


---

---

## JOHN A. DRAKE

123 Any Street, Any Town, CA XXXXX (619) 555-1234

B.A.   University of Iowa    Self-financed     1977

### CAREER SKILLS/KNOWLEDGE

- Broadcast industry sales
- Station operations
- Advertiser relations
- Program development
- Automotive advertising expert
- Market share strategies
- Premium rate strategies

- Sales/marketing
- Decision-maker contact
- Market penetration
- Competitive strategies
- Long-range planning
- Staff training/development
- Systems planning

### SALES/MARKETING ACHIEVEMENTS

- Earn a high six-figure income by selling and servicing an expanding base of corporate clients for NBC Channel 6 in Los Angeles: generated four-year billings in excess of $60 million ranking as the number two biller the last two years.

- Ranked among the top Account Managers at NBC's Regional Sales Office in Los Angeles; achieved this by penetrating agencies and advertisers to reach decision makers to whom I sold a high percentage of available commercial time at premium prices.

- Developed and sold lucrative entertainment packages and created several well-received programming ideas for telecast over NBC owned stations generating millions in advertising revenue.

- Promoted to NBC's Regional Sales Office in Los Angeles in less than two years instead of the normal four to five year cycle.

- Accelerated NBC's Regional Sales Office in Miami from fourth place to second place in billings.

- Achieved market shares of 35% plus for BBD&O by outmaneuvering the competition and charging premium rates.

- Ranked as a top producer for Acme Television in Atlanta: achieved market shares of 30% through effective marketing of special programming to major client corporations.

- Promoted to Miami Office Manager for Acme Television after productively representing 83 outlets.

## CAREER EXPERIENCE

### NATIONAL BROADCASTING COMPANY, Los Angeles, CA   6/84–Present

Executive Account Manager   3/91–Present
Responsibilities executed at the Los Angeles owned station:

o  Maintain and accelerate base of corporate clients.
o  Create rate cards; review and sign off exceptions.
o  Head of Productivity Group formed to improve overall sales productivity.

Executive Account Manager   11/87–3/91
Responsibilities executed at the Regional Sales Office in Los Angeles:

o  Optimized commercial time usage and revenue generated per spot.
o  Developed entertainment packages and created programming.
o  Marketed special programming to major corporate clients.
o  Trained and developed new sales recruits.

Account Manager   6/84–11/87
At the Regional Sales Office in Miami, exceeded billing targets and elevated our national ranking.

### BBD&O, Miami, FL   2/81–6/84

Account Manager
Consistently exceeded billing targets.

### ACME TELEVISION, Miami/Atlanta   1/79–2/81

Sales Manager/Account Manager
Represented some 83 outlets.

### CAPITAL CITIES BROADCASTING, Dallas, TX   6/77–1/79

Account Manager
Produced commercials, accelerated the client base, and exceeded revenue targets.

### REFERENCES PROVIDED UPON REQUEST

## JEFFREY A. CUMMINGS

**123 Any Street, Any City, WA XXXXX (609) 555-1234**

Contact Name                                                  Date
Title
Company
Street Address
City, State  Zip

Dear Mr./Ms. _____:

Having developed and applied a command of Executive Hotel Management and the technical and organizational facets of hotel operations, I have proven my ability to achieve bottom-line results. My accelerated experience combined with academic credentials from the top-ranked universities for executive hotel management has prepared me to assume a general management role.

I am very interested in exploring the possibility of joining _____ as a member of your senior management team.

Results achieved by applying the managerial/technical skills detailed on the attached resume include:

o As General Manager, elevated the occupancy rate at a major 1,000 acre hotel and resort from an unsatisfactorily low level to over 90%; significantly improved profit margins.

o Significantly improved our all-important rating by reorganizing and modernizing all departments of the 1,000 acre hotel and resort including the 1,000 seat restaurant, separate celebrity nightclub, villas, theatres, and beach facilities.

o Successfully marketed and expanded lucrative convention operations as General Manager of a top-ranked European hotel.

o As General Manager of a major hotel, developed and directed a separate operation devoted to servicing/catering a major international airline: won this contract in a major "bidding war."

I know that I can achieve similar results for your company. I feel it will be to our mutual benefit to meet and talk face-to-face. You may contact me at the above number to set up an appointment. I look forward to our meeting.

                                                        Sincerely,


Enclosure:                                              Jeffrey A. Cummings

# JEFFREY A. CUMMINGS

123 Any Street, Any City, WA XXXXX (609) 555-1234

U.S. Citizen

## ACADEMIC CREDENTIALS

| | |
|---|---|
| GRADUATE DEGREE 1980 | PRESTIGIOUS INTERNATIONAL INSTITUTE, Europe<br>School for Executive Hotel Management<br>High academic standards; selective; premier institution.<br>Honors graduate. |
| COLLEGE DEGREE 1978 | SCHOOL OF HOTEL PROFESSIONS, Europe<br>Highly respected academic training; selective; prestigious. Honors graduate. |
| COLLEGE DEGREE 1976 | UNIVERSITY OF LONDON<br>Major: English Literature. Honors Graduate |
| Internships: | Summers during college at major International Hotels |
| Professional Seminars: | Attended and, in some cases, organized comprehensive training seminars for hotel executives conducted by major institutions: Major U.S. University; European-based Law School; European Center for Productivity |
| Languages: | Fluent in English, French, and German |

## HOTEL MANAGEMENT/TECHNICAL SKILLS

o Executive hotel management
o Full P&L responsibility
o Hotel marketing/sales
o Public relations
o Food and beverage management
o Classical French preparation
o Menu composition
o Personnel selection/training
o Banquet management
o Catering: inside/outside
o Special catering
o Hasidic Kosher/other ethnic cuisines
o Wine expertise

o Trainer/educator
o Executive consultant
o Operational planning
o Organization and staffing
o Procurement/product selection
o Layout/construction
o Interior decoration
o Inventory control/storage
o Interaction with public officials
o Hotel operations law
o Tourist/convention management
o Negotiations with travel organizations
o Hotel computer applications

## EUROPEAN CAREER EXPERIENCE

### MAJOR BEACH RESORT HOTEL, Europe    1989–1991

General Manager
Managed 1,000 acre hotel and resort: 1,000 seat restaurant; nightclub with name celebrities; separate villas; theatres; beach resort facilities and sports; other facilities. Major achievements:

o  Occupancy rate climbed significantly to over 90%.
o  Reorganized and modernized all departments.
o  Significantly improved profits and critical rating.

Reason for leaving: to move permanently to the United States

### EUROPEAN PALACE HOTEL, Europe    1986–1989

General Manager
Managed top-rated operations: marketing, promotion, and public relations; food and beverage; major conventions including NATO, International Athletic Medicine Association; reservations strategy; negotiations with travel organizations; support services including engineering, housekeeping, and security. Major achievements:

o  Marketed/expanded lucrative convention operations; new clients included International Auto Exhibition and several governmental functions negotiated in talks with high officials.
o  Developed/directed separate operation to service/cater a major international airline: won this contract in a major "bidding war."
o  Named benefactor of a local prestigious hotel school.

### HOTEL CONSULTING CORP., Europe    1983–1986

Senior Consultant—Hotel Specialist
Promoted to this position. One of 10 consultants selected to perform key assignments including: reorganization of highly rated hotels; architectural design—maximizing productivity and service; market research studies for developing menus and defining service needs; floor plan layouts, design of hotel machinery and technical specifications; purchasing equipment and materials; supervision of construction; development of policies/procedures.

### EUROPEAN CRUISE LINE, Europe    1980–1983

Director of Hotel Services
Promoted to position. Managed hospitality services on large cruise ships. Recipes and menus developed earned accolades.

## AMERICAN CAREER EXPERIENCE

### NORTHWEST EXECUTIVE HOTEL, Any City, WA    1994–Present

Director of Catering/Executive Maitre d'
Market catering services to corporate clients; plan, schedule, and coordinate execution of banquets.

### TOP OF THE HILL RESTAURANT, Any City, WA    1993–1994

Executive Maitre d'
In charge of banquet operations for this prestigious restaurant and caterer; emphasized negotiations with customers, planning, and overall supervision. Successfully managed over 200 wedding receptions and several corporate/social functions.

### PORT OF CALL RESTAURANT, Any City, WA    1992–1993

Manager
Upon returning from Europe, was asked by a major lending institution to manage the turnaround of this troubled operation. Converted this low-rated local operation into a profitable, first-class restaurant.

### ESSEX INN, Any City, WA    1991–1992

Food and Beverage Director
In charge of: major banquets; marketing/sales; procurement; entertainment lounge; and overall management of personnel. Received excellent feedback from senior management and customers.

## REFERENCES PROVIDED UPON REQUEST

# LEONARD A. SMITH

**123 Any Street, Any City, WA XXXXX (206) 555-1234**

Contact Name                                           Date
Title
Company
Street Address
City, State  Zip

Dear Mr./Ms. _____:

I have applied executive skills in systems operations, project management, systems development, and manufacturing to implement multimillion-dollar systems, turn around out-of-control projects, accelerate productivity, and reduce costs for Fortune 500 companies. This has been rewarded with multiple promotions and a reputation for getting the job done.

I am bringing to your attention my skills, achievements, ability to produce under crisis management conditions, and talent for completing projects on time and under budget so that we can discuss my joining _____ as a member of your Systems/Manufacturing Management Team.

Results achieved to date include:

o As Project Director at Acme Corporation, brought critically needed cooperation and discipline to the Essex Manufacturing System, a $5 million MRPII project: instituted project planning, status reporting, and accountability; chaired status meeting; and upgraded relations between Systems and Manufacturing.

o As MIS Director at XYZ Corporation, installed Purchasing, Receiving, and Payables systems: reduced purchase order cycle from four weeks to one, elevated receiving accuracy from 55% to 97%, increased staff productivity 25%, and saved over $100,000 annually in overpayments.

o Promoted to MIS Director at XYZ after implementing the on-line Bill of Material and Inventory Control systems which turned around inventory accuracy from 65% up to 95%.

o Resolved serious vendor delivery problems and increased user involvement to successfully install the IBM 4000 Series and VSE and VM systems software at XYZ; also turned around the out-of-control computer operations.

o Converted ABC, Inc.'s obsolete systems, installing CICS and DL/1 in three months instead of the projected ten; installed Bill of Material and Parts Control systems which helped reduce obsolete inventory by 60%.

I look forward to discussing how I can, likewise, contribute to your company's future success.

Sincerely,


Enclosure:                                           Leonard A. Smith

# LEONARD A. SMITH

123 Any Street, Any City, WA XXXXX (206) 555-1234

| | | | |
|---|---|---|---|
| M.B.A. | Computer Science | Washington State University | 1980 |
| B.S. | Computer Science | Washington State University | 1978 |

Member: American Production and Inventory Control Society (APICS)

## CAREER SKILLS

- o MIS management
- o Project management
- o Systems development
- o Planning/budgeting
- o Design/specifications
- o Staff supervision/training
- o User relations/training
- o Testing/implementation
- o Major conversions
- o Turnaround strategies

- o Manufacturing operations
- o Customer support/service
- o Production systems
- o MRP implementation
- o Bill of material
- o Inventory control
- o Quality control
- o Purchasing/receiving systems
- o Service management systems
- o Financial/sales systems

## CAREER ACHIEVEMENTS

o As Project Director at Acme Corporation, brought critically needed cooperation and discipline to the Essex Manufacturing System, a $5 million MRPII project: instituted project planning, status reporting, and accountability; chaired status meetings; and upgraded relations between Systems and Manufacturing.

o Led the troubleshooting and resolution of project-threatening problems with vendor software packages on which the above system is based, identifying and correcting 400 major "bugs."

o As MIS Director at XYZ Corporation, installed Purchasing, Receiving, and Payables systems: reduced purchase order cycle from four weeks to one, elevated receiving accuracy from 55% to 97%, increased staff productivity 25%, and saved over $100,000 annually in overpayments.

o Promoted to MIS Director at XYZ after implementing the on-line Bill of Material and Inventory Control systems which turned around inventory accuracy from 65% up to 95%.

o Resolved serious vendor delivery problems and increased user involvement to successfully install the IBM 4000 Series and VSE and VM systems software at XYZ; also turned around the out-of-control computer operations.

o Converted ABC, Inc.'s obsolete systems, installing CICS and DL/1 in only three months versus the projected ten months by developing a conversion program to change the 150 programs.

o Installed ABC's Bill of Material and Parts Control systems which helped reduce obsolete inventory 60% from $4 million down to $1.6 million.

o Implemented, in record time, a comprehensive Service Control system upgrading the management of ABC's $70 million service business.

# CAREER EXPERIENCE

## ACME CORPORATION, Any Town, WA  6/93–Present

Project Director
Total responsibility for the implementation and support of the Essex Manufacturing System:

o Direct and train the professional staff.
o Interact closely with manufacturing to resolve design issues.
o Coordinate with the software vendor on the next release.

## XYZ CORPORATION, Any Town, CA  5/88–6/93

MIS Director
Responsible for budgeting, planning, and staff management and training. Implemented several systems including Procurement/Receiving, Bill of Material, Inventory Control, and Accounts Payable. Instituted Systems Control software to manage systems changes, problems, and networking. Saved well over $100,000 annually by instituting key production cost reports.

## ABC, INC., Any Town, CA  5/84–5/88

Senior Analyst
Led the conversion from batch mode to on-line, accelerating the number of computer terminals from only a few to 125; implemented data retrieval system on time-sharing giving users access to key reports within hours instead of days. Initiated and executed feasibility study which led to the cost-saving cancellation of a major systems project.

## AVERY COMPANY, Any Town, CA  5/80–5/84

Systems Analyst
Promoted based on the on-time and under-budget implementation of critically-needed financial systems and reporting.

# SYSTEMS ENVIRONMENTS

| | |
|---|---|
| o CICS | o 308X |
| o IDMS | o 4341 |
| o DL/1 | o 3090 |
| o IMS | o 303X |
| o AS | o MVS |
| o VSAM | o VSE |
| o PROFS | o VM |

# REFERENCES PROVIDED UPON REQUEST

## WILLIAM A. JONES (Version 1)

123 Any Street, Any Town, CA XXXXX  Home: (619) 555-1234  Work: (619) 555-2345

Contact Name                                                                Date
Title
Company
Address
City, State  Zip

Dear Mr./Ms. _____:

I have applied expert skills in training, development, systems implementation, operations, materials management, and MRP to train and upgrade staffs, teach major quality improvement programs, turn around out-of-control operations, resolve serious inventory problems, implement critically needed MRP systems, and generate crucial project funding for Fortune 500 and smaller companies. Results achieved have been rewarded with promotions and major cross-divisional job offers.

I am bringing to your attention my skills, achievements, talent for teaching complex subject matter, and dedication to producing the best so that we can discuss my joining _____ as a member of your Training Management Team.

Results achieved to date include:

o As Materials Director at ABC Corporation, turned around out-of-control inventory problems within 15 months reducing inventory by 40%: implemented a critically needed IBM-based MRP system in only six months; created a critically needed Master Scheduling function; restructured and upgraded the previously ineffective Excess and Obsolescence process.

o As Director of Production Systems, took the initiative at a critical time for the beleaguered XYZ Company by initiating and executing a military funded study designed to justify and solicit multimillion-dollar military funding for XYZ's MRP II implementation: study led to funding approval.

o As Manager of P&IC at XYZ, accelerated inventory turn rates without impacting product lead times and was selected as an Instructor for the complex Quality Improvement Process: while executing my full-time responsibilities, worked several hours a week overtime to teach this ground-breaking course which impacted every department.

o Chosen from several candidates to direct and execute a high-profile corporate assignment aimed at providing project leadership for the planning and start-up of the Acme MRP II Manufacturing System at XYZ's Systems Division: developed a detailed, 24-month plan and organized a 200-person implementation team earning praise and a major job offer.

I will work hard to achieve bottom-line results and look forward to discussing how I can contribute to your company's future success.

Sincerely,

Enclosure:                                                      William A. Jones

## Systems Training/Manufacturing/MRP

# WILLIAM A. JONES

123 Any Street, Any Town, CA XXXXX  Home: (619) 555-1234  Work: (619) 555-2345

B.A.  Honors  Pace University  Scholarship Recipient  1980

Certifications:  o American Production and Inventory Control Society
o Certified in Production and Inventory Management

## CAREER SKILLS/KNOWLEDGE

o Training/development
o Systems consulting
o Quality improvement instructor
o Systems implementation
o Manufacturing systems
o Design/specifications
o Testing/debugging
o Alpha/Beta site testing
o Government guidelines
o Vendor/user relations

o Operations/materials management
o MRP systems expertise
o IBM/Acme MRP systems
o Commercial versions
o Production and inventory control
o Made/engineered to order/stock
o Master scheduling/forecasting/planning
o Excess/obsolescence control
o Procurement/distribution operations
o Service operations

## CAREER ACHIEVEMENTS

o As Materials Director at ABC Corporation, turned around out-of-control inventory problems within 15 months reducing inventory by 40%: implemented a critically needed IBM-based MRP system in only six months; created a critically needed Master Scheduling function; restructured and upgraded the previously ineffective Excess and Obsolescence process.

o As Director of Production Systems, took the initiative at a critical time for the beleaguered XYZ Company by initiating and executing a military funded study designed to justify and solicit multi-million-dollar military funding for XYZ's MRP II implementation: study led to funding approval.

o As Manager of P&IC at XYZ, accelerated inventory turn rates without impacting product lead times and was selected as an Instructor for the complex Quality Improvement Process: while executing my full-time responsibilities, worked several hours a week overtime to teach this ground-breaking course which impacted every department.

o Chosen from several candidates to direct and execute a high-profile corporate assignment aimed at providing project leadership for the planning and start-up of the Acme MRP II Manufacturing System at XYZ's Systems Division: developed a detailed, 24-month plan and organized a 200-person implementation team earning praise and a major job offer.

o As Project Director for the implementation of the Acme MRP Manufacturing System at XYZ's Printer Division, directed and forced vendor's cooperation in executing design modifications, testing, and debugging of all modules including BOM, INVENTORY, MRP, PURCHASING, and all interfaces to shop floor control, data collection, and accounting: with minimal interruption to business, loaded over 70,000 part numbers and 50,000 bills of material.

o As Materials Manager within a multi-warehousing environment at XYZ, implemented a critically needed on-line order entry system including a time-phased requirements module; planned and directed the on-schedule relocation of a 100,000 sq. ft. warehouse.

# CAREER EXPERIENCE

## ABC CORPORATION, Any City, CA   4/92–Present

Materials Director
Implemented IBM-based MRP system in only a few months; established Master Scheduling function; formalized the Excess and Obsolescence process.

## XYZ COMPANY, VARIOUS DIVISIONS   5/86–4/92

## ESSEX DIVISION, Any City, CA   3/91–4/92

Director of Production Systems
Adviser for implementation of the multimillion-dollar Acme MRP II Manufacturing System. Coordinated and controlled all system changes.

## AVERY PRINTER DIVISION, Any City, CA   5/86–3/91

Project Director   1/89–3/91
Projected managed implementation of Acme Integrated Manufacturing System.

Project Consultant   2/88–1/89
Executed this critical corporate assignment: provided project leadership for the implementation planning of the Acme MRP implementation.

Manager P&IC   3/87–2/88
Managed master scheduling, forecasting, and inventory. As an Instructor for the Quality Improvement Process, assumed a central role in instituting this ground-breaking program.

Materials Manager   5/86–3/87
Responsible for customer order through shipping process for parts sales in excess of $80 million: managed procurement, inventory, warehousing, and transportation.

## SMART PRODUCTS COMPANY, Any City, CA   6/80–5/86

Manager of Production Control   6/83–5/86
Promoted to this position becoming the youngest supervisor in the company; responsible for the planning, master scheduling, and expediting functions; was chosen for a corporate task force which developed the standards for material control.

Master Scheduling Supervisor   8/81–6/83
Worked long hours to bring a lucrative product into production.

Supervisor   6/80–8/81
Redesigned Bill of Material; instituted uniform methods and procedures.

# REFERENCES AVAILABLE UPON REQUEST

## JOHN A. JONES (Version 2)

**123 Any Street, Any City, WA XXXXX (206) 555-1235**

Contact Name                                                     Date
Title
Company
Street Address
City, State Zip

Dear Mr./Ms. _____:

I have combined degrees from Stanford and Wharton with executive skills in operations, manufacturing, engineering, and sales to build a $20 million company known internationally for its state-of-the-art products, cost-effective production, substantial market shares, and global clients. Achievements were rewarded with growing profits and prestigious awards for delivering vital systems in record time.

I am bringing to your attention my leadership skills, achievements, ability to create cost-effective solutions, and proven talent for accelerating market share and profits to produce financial security for others and myself so that we can discuss my joining _____
as a member of your general management/operations/engineering team.

Results achieved to date include:

o As founder and chief executive of ABC, Inc., started and built this profitable high-tech electronics company known over 20 years for its innovative products and low-cost volume production: negotiated and executed the lucrative sale of the company to a major corporation.

o More than doubled ABC's revenue by marketing breakthrough products to over 40 countries and major Fortune 500 corporations: developed damage-proof and modular products; introduced concept of placing electronics into clothing; developed communications systems for space projects, carriers, train systems, executive aircraft, and bank machines.

o Became one of the world's largest producers of specialized communication devices by focusing on the high volume global market; instituted "people-based" engineering to extend the life of electronic equipment and produce safety-conscious communications for major clients.

o Turned around out-of-control quality and distributions problems at XYZ Technology increasing on-time shipments from 38% to 95%; also turned around purchasing operations generating $3 million a year in cost reductions while reducing inventory $3 million.

Should we reach mutually agreeable terms, I will work hard to help accelerate or turn around operating performance contributing to your future success.

Sincerely,

Enclosure:                                                       John A. Jones

## JOHN A. JONES

123 Any Street, Any City, WA XXXXX (206) 555-1235

| | | | |
|---|---|---|---|
| M.B.A. | Management | Wharton | 1974 |
| B.S. | Electrical Engineering | Stanford University | 1972 |
| B.A. | Economics | Stanford University | 1972 |

### CAREER SKILLS/KNOWLEDGE

o Operations/engineering
o Manufacturing/Q.C./materials
o Cost-effective production
o Labor negotiations
o Productivity improvements
o R&D/systems engineering
o New product development
o Cost reduction strategies
o Electronics industry

o International marketing/sales
o General management/finance
o Start-up operations/organization
o Major client development
o Product management
o Competitive maneuvering
o Expansion/turnaround strategies
o Profit/market share growth
o New product marketing/pricing

### CAREER ACHIEVEMENTS

o As founder and chief executive of ABC, Inc., started and built this profitable high-tech electronics company known over 20 years for its innovative products and low-cost volume production: negotiated and executed the lucrative sale of the company to a major corporation.

o Awarded a coveted medal by a foreign government for producing and delivering, in less than 60 days, critically needed communications systems vital to their national defense: crash program cut four months off the schedule.

o More than doubled ABC's revenue by marketing breakthrough products to over 40 countries and major Fortune 500 corporations: developed damage-proof and modular products; introduced concept of placing electronics into clothing; developed communications systems for space projects, carriers, train systems, executive aircraft, and bank machines.

o Became one of the world's largest producers of specialized communication devices by focusing on the high volume global market; instituted "people-based" engineering to extend the life of electronic equipment and produce safety-conscious communications for major clients.

o Turned around out-of-control quality and distribution problems at XYZ Technology increasing on-time shipments from 38% to 95%; also turned around purchasing operations generating $3 million a year in cost reductions while reducing inventory $3 million.

o As Director of Procurement at Acme Company, generated $4 million in annual cost savings and reduced inventory $2 million by resolving serious cost control and material control problems.

## CAREER EXPERIENCE

### ACME COMPANY, Any City, WA    1996–Present

Director of Procurement
Instituted much needed budget systems; upgraded material control, developed off-shore vendors, reduced materials shortages, and stopped downtime; generated cost savings and reduced inventory.

### XYZ TECHNOLOGY CORPORATION, Any Town, WA    1995–1996

Project Director
In a series of manufacturing, technical, and procurement assignments, instituted modern management techniques: improved production quality, cut costs, reduced inventory, and established on-time delivery:

o Upgraded Q.C. operations, policies, and procedures.
o Tightened vendor product quality standards.
o Instituted competitive bidding and second sourcing.
o Introduced Japanese methods of inventory stocking.

### ABC, INCORPORATED, Any Town, WA    1974–1995

Chief Executive and Founder
Founded and managed a high-tech company which grew to over 150 employees:

o Expanded through innovation, systems engineering, and cost-effective manufacturing.
o Oversaw product development from inception through design, engineering, and production.
o Established and monitored marketing and pricing objectives.
o Developed client relations with major corporations and numerous countries.
o Continuously expanded into new markets.
o Redesigned and improved products to reduce costs.
o Established rigid quality control standards.
o Designed a plant layout which dramatically improved assembly productivity.
o Consistently met tight delivery schedules.

## REFERENCES PROVIDED UPON REQUEST

## PATRICK A. WILSON

123 Any Street, Any City, CA XXXXX (619) 555-1234

Contact Name                                                                    Date
Title
Company
Street Address
City, State Zip

Dear Mr./Ms. _____:

I have applied proficient skills in project management, engineering, product development, client relations, and marketing to develop state-of-the-art systems, execute complex communications studies, turn around out-of-control projects, and generate lucrative accounts for Fortune 500 companies. This has been rewarded with promotions and a reputation for getting the job done.

I am bringing to your attention my skills, achievements, talent for motivating teams, and ability to produce results under intense pressure and out-of-control conditions so that we can discuss my joining _____ as a member of your Project Management Team.

Results achieved to date include:

o As Project Director on a critical $300 million program, directed the development of complex state-of-the-art systems at Acme: sub-systems under my control are among the very few within the total project that are under control and on schedule.

o Turned around relations between Acme Industries and a major client who had stopped payments toward a $300 million project: was singled out by the client for helping Acme to pass a critical Demonstration Review which led to resumption of monthly progress payments.

o As a Project Director at ABC, Inc., generated satisfied clients and substantial revenue by expediting installation of multimillion-dollar space projects for XYZ Company, MCA, and CBS; established productive client rapport and had reputation for delivering on-time projects.

o Played a central role in XYZ Company's efforts to penetrate the closed Asian markets: presented well-received studies to Korea's Ministry of Telecommunications and Osaka Telegraph and Telephone, paving the way for several hundred million dollar deals.

o Upon promotion to Director of ABC's $2 million Space Engineering Unit, stimulated revenue growth, turned around eroding morale, upgraded staff performance, and improved productivity.

It should be to our mutual benefit to meet and determine how I can contribute to your company's bottom-line success.

Sincerely,

Enclosure:                                                                  Patrick A. Wilson

## PATRICK A. WILSON

123 Any Street, Any City, CA XXXXX (619) 555-1234

B.S.    Electrical Engineering    University of Texas    1982

### CAREER SKILLS/KNOWLEDGE

- o Project management
- o Product development
- o Communications studies
- o Engineering/administration
- o Planning/scheduling
- o Team motivation
- o Subcontractor relations
- o Cost control/reductions
- o Design/specifications/prototypes
- o Testing/release/support

- o Sales/account management
- o Program management
- o Client development/relations
- o Revenue growth strategies
- o Profit growth strategies
- o Deal-making/negotiating
- o Turnaround strategies
- o Staff supervision/development
- o Productivity improvements
- o International markets

### CAREER ACHIEVEMENTS

o As Project Director on a critical $300 million program, directed the development of complex state-of-the-art systems at Acme: sub-systems under my control are among the very few within the total project that are under control and on schedule.

o Turned around relations between Acme Industries and a major client who had stopped payments toward a $300 million project: was singled out by the client for helping Acme to pass a critical Demonstration Review which led to resumption of monthly progress payments.

o As a Project Director at ABC, Inc., generated satisfied clients and substantial revenue by expediting installation of multimillion-dollar space projects for XYZ Company, MCA, and CBS; established productive client rapport and had reputation for delivering on-time projects.

o Played a central role in XYZ Company's efforts to penetrate the closed Asian markets: presented well-received studies to Korea's Ministry of Telecommunications and Osaka Telegraph and Telephone, paving the way for several hundred million dollar deals.

o Upon promotion to Director of ABC's $2.0 million Space Engineering Unit, stimulated revenue growth, turned around eroding morale, upgraded staff performance, and improved productivity.

o Played a pivotal role in ABC's landing the lucrative XYZ Company and MCA accounts: convinced MCA to leave a competitor and turned around negative relations with XYZ.

o Built a reputation at ABC for accomplishing the impossible, receiving numerous accolades from executives at XYZ Company and Essex Communications where one executive voiced his opinion that "Pat is one of the finest Project Managers in the world."

## BUSINESS EXPERIENCE

### ACME INDUSTRIES, Any Town, CA   2/94–Present

Project Director
Manage client relations and overall planning, scheduling, and staffing for a state-of-the-art system development contract. Direct staff of 50 in executing hardware design, fabrication, and testing.

### ABC, INC., Any Town, CA   3/91–2/94

Director—Space Engineering Unit   9/92–2/94
General management responsibility for this engineering services and market research firm:

o Directed staff of 45 sales, marketing, and product management personnel.
o Provided engineering services, interacting with major clients on proposals, price negotiations, and technical issues.
o Delivered critical presentations to Asian clients.

Project Director   3/91–9/92
Primary liaison to XYZ Communications, Essex Communication, MCA, and CBS:

o Established excellent rapport with clientele.
o Conducted complex frequency interference studies of station sites.
o Performed frequency coordination of remote stations, prepared site report, and analyzed field-measurement data.

### RIGOR SERVICES COMPANY, Any Town, OR   11/89–3/91

Engineer
Under contract to provide a Mideastern Air Force with on-the-job instruction in F-16 systems troubleshooting.

### AVERY COMPANY, Any Town, OH   6/88–11/89

Engineer
Completed rigorous company training at a government facility: managed group on overseas assignment providing technical support for the F-14. Based on results achieved, was requested to stay past the normal pull-out date; such requests are almost never made by the government.

## MILITARY CREDENTIALS

Underwater Operations   6/82–6/88
Graduate of the rigorous Nuclear Training Program: ranked near the top of the class and completed long-term assignment aboard a nuclear-powered submarine; substituted for the First Officer; was consulted on major operational decisions.

**INTERNATIONAL TRAVEL:**   Traveled throughout Europe and Asia.

## WILLIAM Q. SAMPLE (Version 2)

123 Any Street, Any Town, NJ XXXXX (201) 555-1234

Contact Name                                                    Date
Title
Company
Street Address
City, State Zip

Dear Mr./Ms. _____:

As Executive Vice President for the U.S. Division of a European-based corporation, I have applied executive skills in operations, materials, engineering, and sales to outmaneuver the competition, deal with volatile exchange rates, accelerate growth of the corporate client base, and achieve a fivefold increase in sales—a revenue level which now accounts for 40% of worldwide sales.

I am presenting for your review my skills, achievements, technical degree, global contacts, and talent for creating productive organizations and achieving aggressive revenue and profit goals so that we can discuss my joining _____ as a member of your senior operations team.

Results achieved to date include:

o  Earned multiple promotions up to Executive Vice President at a U.S. Division of Acme International, one of Europe's largest industrial corporations: created a highly productive sales organization and achieved a fivefold increase in revenue turning the U.S. Division into a $20 million business which now accounts for almost 40% of the subsidiary's global sales.

o  In spite of global competition, closed multimillion-dollar clients including Western Electric, AT&T, Boeing, and John Deere: accelerated the AT&T account from zero to $9 million representing half of total sales; generated a ninefold sales increase from the Harvester Division of John Deere; produced an eightfold increase in the Western Electric and Boeing accounts.

o  Significantly reduced overhead and logistics expenses and all but eliminated aged receivables and write-offs by creating and enforcing conservative credit policies at Acme; in order to meet scheduled delivery dates through on-time shipments from Europe, also established a first-rate logistics function.

o  Earned several promotions up to director within the Engineering Department of a Florida-based division of Essex Corporation: directed high-quality product designs, upgraded operating systems critical to the production process, and effectively troubleshooted the complex power supply systems.

I look forward to discussing how I can help accelerate or turn around the performance of your international operations.

                                                    Sincerely,

Enclosure:                                          William Q. Sample

# International Operations Executive

## WILLIAM Q. SAMPLE

123 Any Street Address, Any Town, NJ XXXXX (201) 555-1234

B.S. Electrical Engineering    International University   Comprehensive Six-Year Program
B.A. Business Administration   Lehman College            Managerial Studies

International:          Traveled throughout Europe, Asia, South America, and North America
Languages:             Fluent French and Spanish

## CAREER SKILLS/KNOWLEDGE

- o Operations/materials/engineering
- o Purchasing operations
- o Cost controls/reductions
- o Global distribution/logistics
- o Heavy industry clients
- o Aircraft engine market
- o Engineering operations
- o Electrical/systems engineering
- o New product design
- o Plant operating systems design
- o Sales/marketing executive
- o International sales/markets
- o European relations
- o Strategic/marketing plans
- o Market share strategies
- o Major client development
- o Competitive maneuvering
- o Exchange rate strategies
- o Organizational development
- o Staff supervision/development

## CAREER ACHIEVEMENTS

o Earned multiple promotions up to Executive Vice President at a U.S. Division of Acme International, one of Europe's largest industrial corporations: created a highly productive sales organization and achieved a fivefold increase in revenue turning the U.S. Division into a $20 million business which now accounts for almost 40% of the subsidiary's global sales.

o In spite of high turnover and chronically unfavorable exchange rates, which adversely impacted the U.S. Division's pricing structure, generated a 500% increase in Acme's customer base through an accelerated client development program which emphasized quality and service to offset the unfavorable pricing.

o In spite of global competition, closed multimillion-dollar clients including Western Electric, AT&T, Boeing, and John Deere: accelerated the AT&T account from zero to $9 million representing half of total sales; generated a ninefold sales increase from the Harvester Division of John Deere; produced an eightfold increase in the Western Electric and Boeing accounts.

o Significantly reduced overhead and logistics expenses and all but eliminated aged receivables and write-offs by creating and enforcing conservative credit policies at Acme; in order to meet scheduled delivery dates through on-time shipments from Europe, also established a first-rate logistics function.

o Earned several promotions up to director within the Engineering Department of a Florida-based division of Essex Corporation: directed high-quality product designs, upgraded operating systems critical to the production process, and effectively troubleshooted the complex power supply systems.

## CAREER EXPERIENCE

### ACME INTERNATIONAL CORPORATION, Any Town, NJ   1984–Present

Executive Vice President   1987–Present
Direct sales, marketing, strategic planning, client development, import operations, logistics, distribution, and credit.

Vice President of Sales   1984–1987
Directed sales, marketing, strategic planning, and related functions.

### ESSEX CORPORATION, Any Town, FL   1975–1984

Director of Engineering   1980–1984
Earned several promotions based on engineering achievements in directing low-tolerance design and systems engineering projects. Also successfully planned and executed high-visibility manufacturing projects.

## MILITARY EXPERIENCE

European Military:   Honorably Discharged

**Affiliations:**      Society of U.S. Engineers; Production Engineers of the Northeast
**Citizenship:**       U.S. Citizen

## REFERENCES AVAILABLE UPON REQUEST

# Materials Management Executive

## WILLIAM A. JONES (Version 2)

123 Any Street, Any Town, CA XXXXX  Home: (619) 555-1234  Office: (619) 555-2345

Contact Name                                                        Date
Title
Company
Address
City, State  Zip

Dear Mr./Ms. _____:

I have applied executive skills in materials management, operations, systems implementation, MRP, procurement, and distribution to turn around out-of-control operations, address and resolve serious inventory problems, implement critically needed MRP systems, institute major quality improvement programs, and generate critically needed project funding for Fortune 500 and smaller companies. Results achieved have been rewarded with promotions and major cross-divisional job offers.

I am bringing to your attention my skills, achievements, talent for generating bottom-line results, and dedication to producing the best so that we can discuss my joining _____ as a member of your Materials/Operations Management Team.

Results achieved to date include:

o  As Materials Director at ABC Corporation, turned around out-of-control inventory problems within 15 months reducing inventory by 40%: implemented a critically needed IBM-based MRP system in only six months; created a critically needed Master Scheduling function; restructured and upgraded the previously ineffective Excess and Obsolescence process.

o  As Director of Production Systems, took the initiative at a critical time for the beleaguered XYZ Company by initiating and executing a military funded study designed to justify and solicit multimillion-dollar military funding for XYZ's MRP II implementation: study led to funding approval.

o  As Project Director for the implementation of the Acme MRP Manufacturing System at XYZ's Printer Division, directed and forced vendor's cooperation in executing design modifications, testing, and debugging of all modules including BOM, INVENTORY, MRP, PURCHASING and all interfaces to shop floor control, data collection, and accounting: loaded over 70,000 part numbers and 50,000 bills of material.

o  Chosen from several candidates to direct and execute a high-profile corporate assignment aimed at providing project leadership for the planning and start-up of the Acme MRP II Manufacturing System at XYZ's Systems Division: developed a detailed 24-month plan and organized a 200-person project team earning praise and a major job offer.

I will work hard to achieve bottom-line results and look forward to discussing how I can contribute to your company's future success.

Sincerely,

Enclosure:

William A. Jones

# WILLIAM A. JONES

123 Any Street, Any Town, CA XXXXX Home: (619) 555-1234 Work: (619) 555-2345

| | | | | |
|---|---|---|---|---|
| B.A. | Honors | Pace University | Scholarship Recipient | 1980 |

Certifications:  o American Production and Inventory Control Society
                            o Certified in Production and Inventory Management

## CAREER SKILLS/KNOWLEDGE

o Operations/materials management
o MRP systems expertise
o IBM/Acme MRP systems
o Commercial versions
o Production and inventory control
o Made/engineered to order/stock
o Master scheduling/forecasting/planning
o Excess/obsolescence control
o Procurement/distribution operations
o Service operations

o Systems implementation
o Manufacturing systems
o Design/specifications
o Testing/debugging
o Alpha/Beta site testing
o Government guidelines
o Vendor/user relations
o Training/development
o Quality improvement instructor
o IBM mainframes/DEC minis

## CAREER ACHIEVEMENTS

o As Materials Director at ABC Corporation, turned around out-of-control inventory problems within 15 months reducing inventory by 40% implemented a critically needed IBM-based MRP system in only six months; created a critically needed Master Scheduling function; restructured and upgraded the previously ineffective Excess and Obsolescence process.

o As Director of Production Systems, took the initiative at a critical time for the beleaguered XYZ Company by initiating and executing a military funded study designed to justify and solicit multimillion-dollar military funding for XYZ's MRP II implementation: study led to funding approval.

o As Project Director for the implementation of the Acme Manufacturing System at XYZ's Printer Division, directed and forced vendor's cooperation in executing design modifications, testing, and debugging of all modules including BOM, INVENTORY, MRP, PURCHASING and all interfaces to shop floor control, data collection, and accounting: with minimal interruption to business, loaded over 70,000 part numbers and 50,000 bills of material.

o Chosen from several candidates to direct and execute a high-profile corporate assignment aimed at providing project leadership for the planning and start-up of the Acme MRP II Manufacturing System at XYZ's Systems Division: developed a detailed, 24-month plan and organized a 200-person implementation team earning praise and a major job offer.

o As Manager of P&IC at XYZ, accelerated inventory turn rates without impacting product lead times and was selected as an Instructor for the complex Quality Improvement Process: while executing my full-time responsibilities, worked several hours a week overtime to teach this ground-breaking course which impacted every department.

o As Materials Manager within a multi-warehousing environment at XYZ, implemented a critically needed on-line order entry system including a time-phased requirements module; planned and directed the on-schedule relocation of a 100,000 sq. ft. warehouse.

## CAREER EXPERIENCE

## ABC CORPORATION, Any City, CA   4/92–Present

Materials Director
Implemented IBM-based MRP system in only a few months; established Master Scheduling function; formalized the Excess and Obsolescence process.

## XYZ COMPANY, VARIOUS DIVISIONS   5/86–4/92

## ESSEX DIVISION, Any City, CA   3/91–4/92

Director of Production Systems
Advisor for implementation of the multimillion-dollar Acme MRP II Manufacturing System. Coordinated and controlled all system changes.

## AVERY PRINTER DIVISION, Any City, CA   5/86–3/91

Project Director   1/89–3/91
Projected managed implementation of Acme Integrated Manufacturing System.

Project Consultant   2/88–1/89
Executed this critical corporate assignment: provided project leadership for the implementation planning of the Acme MRP implementation.

Manager P&IC   3/87–2/88
Managed master scheduling, forecasting, and inventory. As an Instructor for the Quality Improvement Process, assumed a central role in instituting this ground-breaking program.

Materials Manager   5/86–3/87
Responsible for customer order through shipping process for parts sales in excess of $80 million: managed procurement, inventory, warehousing, and transportation.

## SMART PRODUCTS COMPANY, Any City, CA   6/80–5/86

Manager of Production Control   6/83–5/86
Promoted to this position becoming the youngest supervisor in the company; responsible for the planning, master scheduling, and expediting functions; was chosen for a corporate task force which developed the standards for material control.

Master Scheduling Supervisor   8/81–6/83
Worked long hours to bring a lucrative product into production.

Supervisor   6/80–8/81
Redesigned Bill of Material; instituted uniform methods and procedures.

## REFERENCES AVAILABLE UPON REQUEST

## JENNIFER A. SMITH

**123 Any Street, Any City, WA  XXXXX  (206) 555-1234**

Contact Name                                                                    Date
Title
Company
Address
City, State  Zip

Dear Mr./Ms. _____:

I have applied proven skills in HR management, recruiting, redeployment, training, and systems to turn around HR operations, achieve challenging hiring objectives, and institute critically needed systems and training for Fortune 500 corporations. Bottom-line achievements have been rewarded with bonuses and several promotions.

I am bringing to your attention my skills, achievements, high energy, talent for improving job candidate quality, and track record of cost reductions so that we can discuss my joining _____ as a member of your HR Management Team.

Results achieved to date include:

o As HR Director at the Essex Company, upgraded Human Resources for over 3,000 employees: filled over 500 openings annually improving candidate quality while cutting the recruiting cycle in half; reduced excessive benefits operating costs; instituted critically needed cross-training; computerized previously manual systems; directed the upgrade of policies and procedures.

o As HR Manager at ABC Corporation, project managed the start-up of a new headquarters: coordinated the logistics and successfully recruited and hired over 400 employees in only seven months; also directed and accelerated the productivity of the administrative support staff.

o Directed Acme Development Center's Human Resources start-up and operation: achieved first-year staffing goals in less than nine months and instituted comprehensive employee relations programs.

o Turned around Acme's Personnel Redeployment Program achieving over a 90% placement rate through well-received seminars and workshops.

o Directed the highly successful implementation of Acme's critically needed $12 million Human Resource, Benefits, and Payroll system.

I look forward to discussing how I can, likewise, contribute to your company's future success.

Sincerely,


Enclosure:                                                                    Jennifer A. Smith

# JENNIFER A. SMITH

123 Any Street, Any City, WA XXXXX (206) 555-1234

B.A. Honors Communications Smith College GPA 3.7/4.0 1980

## CAREER SKILLS/KNOWLEDGE

o Human resources professional
o Recruiting techniques
o Training and development
o Outplacement counseling
o Seminar/workshop development
o Video role playing/feedback
o Payroll/benefits administration
o Performance appraisal/merit guidelines
o Communications/public relations

o Systems implementation
o Systems consulting/design
o Installation troubleshooter
o User training/support
o Computer-based training
o Micro/mainframe applications
o Excel/LOTUS 1-2-3 applications
o Administration
o Staff supervision

## CAREER ACHIEVEMENTS

o As HR Director at the Essex Company, upgraded Human Resources for over 3,000 employees: filled over 500 openings annually improving candidate quality while cutting the recruiting cycle in half; reduced excessive benefits operating costs; instituted critically needed cross-training; computerized previously manual systems; directed the upgrade of policies and procedures.

o As HR Manager at ABC Corporation, project managed the start-up of a new headquarters: coordinated the logistics and successfully recruited and hired over 400 employees in only seven months; also directed and accelerated the productivity of the administrative support staff.

o Directed Acme Development Center's Human Resources start-up and operation: achieved first-year staffing goals in less than nine months and instituted comprehensive employee relations programs.

o Turned around Acme's Personnel Redeployment Program achieving over a 90% placement rate through well-received seminars and workshops.

o Directed the highly successful implementation of Acme's critically needed $12 million Human Resource, Benefits, and Payroll system.

o Created and executed job search and redeployment workshops for the homeless in Seattle.

## CAREER EXPERIENCE

### ESSEX COMPANY, Any Town, WA    7/94–Present

HR Director
Directed recruiting, managed multimillion-dollar benefits plan, computerized operations, instituted aggressive cost-reduction programs, and upgraded policies and procedures.

## ABC CORPORATION, Any Town, WA    2/89–7/94

HR Manager
Project managed the logistics and staffing of a new headquarters.

## ACME, INC., Any Town, WA    3/84–2/89

Corporate Benefits Administration    1/88–2/89
Performed benefits evaluations and upgraded several outdated HR manuals.

Corporate HR Systems Analyst    12/86–1/88
Project managed the implementation of a major HR system designed to support in excess of
200,000 employees.

Personnel Redeployment    3/85–12/86
Executed well-received Redeployment Programs.

HR Administrator    3/84–3/85
Recruited and hired all staff for the Development Center; established Communications and
Benefits Groups; also developed EEO Plans and authored several policies and procedures.

## AVERY SERVICE CORPORATION, Any Town, WA    6/80–3/84

HR Administrator
Accelerated cost reduction programs; upgraded and assisted in the administration of relocations, recruiting, terminations, payroll, benefits, and employee orientations.

## VOLUNTEER ACTIVITIES

o  Created job search seminars for the homeless
o  Provided support of the learning disabled
o  Taught reading skills to adults

## REFERENCES PROVIDED UPON REQUEST

## MARTHA A. JONES

**123 Any Street, Any City, CA XXXXX (213) 555-1234**

Contact Name                                              Date
Title
Company
Street Address
City, State Zip

Dear Mr./Ms. _____:

I have applied executive skills in training and development, marketing and management to start up and direct training departments, develop highly marketable training programs, accelerate staff productivity, and turn around the strategic and business planning process for major Fortune 500 corporations.

I am bringing to your attention my skills, achievements, creative energy, and proven talent for satisfying tough clients and achieving bottom-line results so that we can discuss my joining _____ as a member of your Training Management Team.

Results achieved to date include:

o Recruited as the first-ever training director for Acme, Inc.: overcame strong resistance and negativism to establish and direct a cost-effective Training Department offering 80 programs and training over 5000 employees in less than two years.

o As head of training at Acme, initiated and implemented the first-ever senior management business planning and team-building meetings: led to the first team-developed and team-supported business plans and MBOs in the company's history.

o Introduced widely accepted management, technical, and basic skills training programs at Acme: included state-of-the-art systems training as well as proposal development training designed to improve proposal accuracy while cutting the completion time in half.

o As Training Director at XYZ Company, started and managed the Training Department offering 70 management, sales, technical, and basic skills programs—trained over 2,000 people.

o Founded and managed a successful Training Consulting Company, marketing to and servicing major corporate clients including Apple Computer and W.R. Grace: created and produced training programs which were marketed and sold internationally by client companies.

I look forward to discussing how I can contribute to your company's future success.

Sincerely,

Enclosure:                                              Martha A. Jones

## MARTHA A. JONES

123 Any Street, Any City, CA XXXXX (213) 555-1234

### CAREER SKILLS/KNOWLEDGE

o Training professional
o Training department management
o Training seminar development
o Management development
o Strategic planning workshops
o Marketing/technical training
o Trainer instruction
o Basic skills training

o Sales/marketing
o Networking strategies
o Business development
o Independent consultant
o Platform skills
o HR operations
o Redeployment planning
o Counseling/development

### CAREER ACHIEVEMENTS

o Recruited as the first-ever training director for Acme, Inc.: overcame strong resistance and negativism to establish and direct a cost-effective Training Department offering 80 programs and training over 5000 employees in less than two years.

o As head of training at Acme, initiated and implemented the first-ever senior management business planning and team-building meetings: led to the first team-developed and team-supported business plans and MBOs in the company's history.

o Introduced widely accepted management, technical, and basic skills training programs at Acme: included state-of-the-art systems training as well as proposal development training designed to improve proposal accuracy while cutting the completion time in half.

o Improved communication between Acme's upper and middle management by introducing successful Executive Communication Meetings offering open and productive dialogue between the senior level executives and middle management.

o As Acme's representative on the Productivity Council, comanaged the Annual Productivity Conferences held to honor the best performing employees.

o As Training Director at XYZ Company, started and managed the Training Department offering 70 management, sales, technical, and basic skills programs—trained over 2,000 people.

o Codirected start-up of a training company: developed and sold state-of-the-art techniques for supervisory level and shop-floor training; trained and managed staff of 40 professionals.

o Founded and managed a successful Training Consulting Company, marketing to and servicing major corporate clients including Apple Computer and W.R. Grace: created and produced training programs which were marketed and sold internationally by client companies.

## CAREER EXPERIENCE

### ACME, INC., Any Town, CA    6/92–Present

Training Director
Responsibilities executed in support of the company's aggressive growth strategy include:

o  Design and implement comprehensive needs evaluation systems.
o  Develop and coordinate comprehensive employee development programs.
o  Direct the training of all instructors.
o  Select and hire outside training resources.
o  Coordinate and audit the Educational Aid Program.

### XYZ COMPANY, Any Town, CA    3/88–6/92

Training Director
Started and directed Training Department: created, purchased, and instituted 70 programs covering Management Development, Redeployment Planning, Marketing, Technical Training, and Shop-Floor Training.

### TRAINING CONSULTING COMPANY, Any Town, CA    12/84–3/88

Founder
Completed major training projects for Fortune 500 clients: designed and produced sales training programs sold nationwide; designed and executed Management Development Workshops; designed and executed Minorities in Management Workshops.

### ABC, INC., Any Town, CA    6/80–12/84

Training & Development Manager
Played a central role in the start-up of this firm which authors and publishes custom and standardized management training programs: designed and implemented a wide selection of training programs; recruited and trained staff of professionals.

## EDUCATION

B.A.    University of Vienna         1980

## PROFESSIONAL AFFILIATIONS

o  Member: Board of Directors, Any Town, CA Girl Scouts of America
o  Advisor, California Education Group
o  Member, American Society for Training and Development

## REFERENCES AVAILABLE UPON REQUEST

## MATTHEW Q. SAMPLE (Version 2)   Strategic Planning/Sales/General Management

123 Any Street Address, Any Town, TX  XXXXX  (214) 555-1234

Contact Name                                                          Date
Title
Company
Street Address
City, State  Zip

Dear Mr./Ms. _____:

I have combined a top school M.B.A. with executive skills in strategic planning, marketing, sales management, and general management to orchestrate a leveraged buyout, head up a $3 million business, strategically reposition troubled operations, and turn around and accelerate profit growth for weak divisions of the Acme Corporation.

I am bringing to your attention my skills, achievements, talent for stimulating sales productivity, and ability to achieve bottom-line results under the most intense pressure so that we can discuss my joining _____ as a member of your senior planning management team.

Results achieved to date include:

o As Southeastern Sales Director for a troubled division of Acme, turned around profitability becoming the top-ranked Sales Director in the division: instituted aggressive market expansion, national account programs, and strategic planning increasing revenue from $5 million to $23 million in four years; converted a $3 million loss into a $3 million profit.

o Upon promotion to Southwestern Sales Director, accelerated sales productivity and major account development achieving a critically needed 35% growth in sales at a pivotal time for the struggling Acme Corporation, which had lost huge market shares due to poor product pricing strategies: achieved highest sales growth and won a major nationwide sales award.

o Based on a track record of achievements in sales management and strategic planning, was recruited by corporate headquarters to manage a major group's business evaluation function as part of the restructuring of the strategic planning process: improved declining ROIs by upgrading the pricing structure; saved tens-of-millions of dollars by demonstrating the marginal payback of proposed expenditures.

o Negotiated and closed the leveraged buyout of a $3 million service business formerly owned by the Avery Company: developed a solid business plan which was successfully marketed to major financial institutions with whom I negotiated over a million dollars in financing.

o As owner of a Texas-based venture, turned around sales and operations overcoming most roadblocks except the company's lack of liquidity in a recessionary economy: increased sales 60% in 15 months by upgrading service and promotional programs; restructured cash management; reduced aged receivables 75%; negotiated a 20% reduction in product costs; achieved a 60% increase in productivity.

I will work hard to achieve bottom-line results and look forward to discussing how I can contribute to your company's future success.

                                                          Sincerely,


Enclosure:                                                Matthew Q. Sample

## MATTHEW Q. SAMPLE    Strategic Planning/Sales/General Management

123 Any Street, Any Town, TX  XXXXX  (214) 555-1234

### CAREER SKILLS/KNOWLEDGE

o Strategic planning
o Business plans/market research
o Market growth/segmentation
o ROI growth strategies
o Profit/investment optimization
o Economic modeling/pricing
o Supply/demand analysis
o Finance/controller operations
o Cash-flow/financing/bank relations

o Marketing/sales management
o Revenue/profit turnaround
o Product management
o National accounts programs
o Sales productivity growth
o Competitor intelligence systems
o Business ownership/leveraged buyouts
o Advertising/promotions
o Operations turnaround

### CAREER ACHIEVEMENTS

o As Southeastern Sales Director for a troubled division of Acme, turned around profitability becoming the top-ranked Sales Director in the division: instituted aggressive market expansion, national account programs, and strategic planning increasing revenue from $5 million to $23 million in four years; converted a $3 million loss into a $3 million profit.

o Upon promotion to Southwestern Sales Director, accelerated sales productivity and major account development achieving a critically needed 35% growth in sales at a pivotal time for the struggling Acme Corporation, which had lost huge market shares due to poor product pricing strategies: achieved highest sales growth and won a major nationwide sales award.

o Based on a track record of achievements in sales management and strategic planning, was recruited by corporate headquarters to manage a major group's business evaluation function as part of the restructuring of the strategic planning process: improved declining ROIs by upgrading the pricing structure; saved tens-of-millions of dollars by demonstrating the marginal payback of proposed expenditures.

o Upon promotion to Business Planning Director, orchestrated a multibillion-dollar asset reallocation program which helped triple profits within five years: reallocated over a billion dollars of production assets to growth products; proposed a half-billion-dollar plant conversion which was implemented at half the cost of constructing a new plant.

o Upon being promoted to Product Manager at Acme, created a product management system which accelerated the decision-making process for the pricing, promotion, and distribution of products: increased profits 30% through saturation marketing to growth industries.

o Negotiated and closed the leveraged buyout of a $3 million service business formerly owned by the Avery Company: developed a solid business plan which was successfully marketed to major financial institutions with whom I negotiated over a million dollars in financing.

o As owner of a Texas-based venture, turned around sales and operations overcoming most roadblocks except the company's lack of liquidity in a recessionary economy: increased sales 60% in 15 months by upgrading service and promotional programs; restructured cash management; reduced aged receivables 75%; negotiated a 20% reduction in product costs; achieved a 60% increase in productivity.

## CAREER EXPERIENCE

### ACME CORPORATION, Any City, TX   1976–1992

Business Planning Director—XYZ Division   1989–1992
Designated to orchestrate the development of corporate strategies and upgrade the planning process.

Business Evaluation Director—ABC Division   1986–1989
Designated to reorganize and turn around strategic planning.

Southwestern Sales Director—ABC Division   1982–1986
Developed and directed a high-producing sales team responsible for national account development.

Product Manager—XYZ Division   1978–1982
Created a product management system which accelerated the decision-making process for the pricing, promotion, and distribution of products.

Southeastern Sales Director—XYZ Division   1977–1978
Implemented a Major Account Program; expanded into growth markets; instituted effective competitor data-gathering procedures; created Division's first comprehensive strategic plan.

Senior Marketing Analyst   1976–1977
Executed comprehensive feasibility studies which resulted in the formation of critically needed account development departments. Developed a well-received business plan for a beleaguered venture.

### ESSEX COMPANY, Any City, TX   1992–1994

Senior Consultant
Determined the feasibility of a client's expansion into major European markets: executed comprehensive product demand and competitive studies as a basis for decision-making.

### SERVICE VENTURE, Any City, TX   1994–Present

Founder:  Directed Marketing, Advertising, Sales, Operations, Finance, and Customer Service.

## EDUCATION

| M.B.A. | Finance/Marketing | University of Virginia | 1976 |
| B.S. | Statistics | UCLA | 1974 |

**INTERNATIONAL:**   Traveled throughout South America and Europe
**LANGUAGES:**   Fluent French, Italian, and Spanish

## DAVID A. WILSON                          Senior Financial Advisor

123 Any Street, Any City, NJ  XXXXX  (201) 555-1234

Contact Name                                    Date
Title
Company
Street Address
City, State  Zip

Dear Mr./Ms. _____:

I have combined degrees from Stanford and Rutgers with dual careers as a Financial Advisor and Educator to develop expertise in world economics, generate millions in profits for clients, build a loyal client base, teach internationally, and produce Merit Scholars.

I am bringing to your attention my skills, achievements, and special talent for producing financial security for others and myself so that we can discuss my joining _____ as a member of your financial advisory team.

Results achieved to date include:

o  As a Registered Broker for Shearson, generated six-figure gross commissions, expanded the customer base to 200 clients, and provided well-researched advice to satisfied customers.

o  Based on in-depth research and prudent risk versus reward advice to Shearson clients, recommended several winning stocks which soared as much as 400%; clients continued to seek advice years after I returned to teaching.

o  As a well-respected Independent Financial Advisor, created a Risk Avoidance System which has effectively reduced investment risks while producing substantial economic returns for clients.

o  Was recruited by a private academy as department chairperson: upgraded the curriculum and faculty, expedited the accreditation process, and produced a record number of Merit Scholars.

o  Awarded Aristotle Foundation Award for "Excellence in Teaching Econometric Theory."

I feel it will be to our mutual benefit to meet and discuss how I can contribute to your company's future success.

                                    Sincerely,


Enclosure:                          David A. Wilson

## DAVID A. WILSON                                    Senior Financial Advisor

**123 Any Street, Any City, NJ XXXXX  (201) 555-1234**

| M.A. | History | Stanford University | 1974 |
| B.A. | Economics | Rutgers University | 1972 |

Fulbright Grant: Summer study in France

## CAREER SKILLS/KNOWLEDGE

o Finance/economics
o Financial services
o Senior investment advisor
o Registered broker
o Stock/bond investments
o Options strategies
o Insurance annuities
o Banking industry/operations
o New account development
o Competitive analyses
o Published author
o International/multilingual

o Educator
o Department chairman
o Educational consulting
o Upgrading standards
o Curriculum development
o Faculty evaluation
o Workshop development
o Accreditation expertise
o Staff supervision
o Student motivation
o Counselor/coach
o International studies

## CAREER ACHIEVEMENTS

o As a Registered Broker for Shearson, generated six-figure gross commissions, expanded the customer base to 200 clients, and provided well-researched advice to satisfied customers.

o Based on in-depth research and prudent risk versus reward advice to Shearson clients, recommended several winning stocks which soared as much as 400%; clients continued to seek advice years after I returned to teaching.

o As a well-respected Independent Financial Advisor, created a Risk Avoidance System which has effectively reduced investment risks while producing substantial economic returns for clients.

o Was recruited by a private academy as department chairperson: upgraded the curriculum and faculty, expedited the accreditation process, and produced a record number of Merit Scholars.

o At a private academy, introduced programs which activated student involvement in community and government affairs: included exposure to low-income communities.

o Selected for prestigious teaching assignment at the Global School in the Mideast where I was faculty chairperson and taught an international curriculum.

o Awarded Aristotle Foundation Award for "Excellence in Teaching Econometric Theory."

## CAREER EXPERIENCE

### A PRIVATE ACADEMY, Any Town, NJ   1995–Present

Chairperson - Economics Department
Responsibilities executed:

o  Develop and implement coherent curriculum.
o  Recruit, train, and evaluate faculty.
o  Teach Economics, History, and Sociology.
o  Expedited the accreditation process.

### SHEARSON LEHMAN BROTHERS, Any City, NJ   1993–1995

Broker
Increased client base through cold-calling and networking; communicated quality advice to clients based on detailed research and management interviews.

### A TOP-RATED SUBURBAN HIGH SCHOOL, Any Town, NJ   1989–1993

Teacher
Instituted seminars to upgrade faculty; taught Social Studies, History, and Economics; introduced course in Value Systems Clarification.

### AN INTERNATIONAL SCHOOL IN MIDEAST, Any Town, Mideast   1987–1989

Faculty Chairman
Taught international curriculum of Economics, History, and Sociology.

### ANOTHER TOP-RATED SUBURBAN HIGH SCHOOL, Any Town, NJ   1984–1987

Department Chairman
Created new curriculum; supervised and upgraded faculty; initiated programs between different socioeconomic communities.

### ANOTHER TOP-RATED SUBURBAN HIGH SCHOOL, Any Town, NY   1974–1984

Teacher
Introduced Economics course study; taught History. Coached championship soccer team.

## ADDITIONAL EDUCATION/LICENSES

Post Masters:    30 credits earned from major universities including Columbia
Licenses:        Series 7 & 63 Brokerage; NJ State Insurance License

# 7

## Market-Tested Sample Resumes and Cover Letters for Managers and Professionals

**INTRODUCTION**

The real-life, market-tested samples in Chapter 7 produced results for upper-middle managers, professionals, and technical specialists with 10 to 25-plus years of experience. This chapter, like the previous one, offers the following unique features designed to give you the same competitive edge that produced quality interviews and job offers for managers just like you:

1. *Superior Quality Sample Resumes and Cover Letters.* Taken directly from almost 30 real-life client case histories, these market-tested and proven resumes and letters are samples of unmatched quality from which to extract, borrow, and adapt key words, phrases, sentences, and paragraphs as you develop your own power package.

2. *A Strong Focus on Packaging Marketable Skills and Achievements.* This workbook subordinates the narrative job descriptions that clutter most resumes. The market has responded

favorably to the skills and achievement-oriented resumes featured in this chapter.

3. *An Unparalleled Emphasis on the Marketing Cover Letter.* This workbook treats the cover letter and resume as *coequal* and *inseparable* components of the total marketing package. A frequently heard comment from my management clients, "The cover letter got me the interview," underscores the importance of the letter. Every sample resume in this book has a corresponding cover letter—*no* other book on the market can make this claim.

4. *A Representative Cross Section of Sample Resumes and Letters.* As reflected in the Chapter Index, I have deliberately excluded many highly specialized, often irrelevant, job positions that provide filler for countless resume books. This chapter, instead, presents *seven* major categories and several additional subcategories of mainstream positions into which most managers fall.

5. *An Intense Focus on Market Response.* Simply stated, the following samples achieved the desired results for veteran managers just like you: They produced positive interviews and job offers in an increasingly tough and selective marketplace, which is, of course, the *ultimate* and *only relevant* judge of quality.

## THE RESUME AND COVER LETTER HEADERS

As discussed earlier, the sample resume and cover letter packages include, for your optional application, my trademark headers that provide the reader with a brief two- to five-word description of your background/discipline. For your convenience and ease in referencing the samples, I have elevated and boxed in these descriptive headers which are cross-referenced in the Index on pages 160 and 161. Should you choose to include the header in your own resume and cover letter package, you will, of course, position it on the same line as your name.

## A WORD ABOUT CLIENT CONFIDENTIALITY

While retaining the full impact and integrity of the real-life marketing packages in this chapter, I have selectively modified and/or otherwise blinded certain confidential information including client names, company names, addresses, specific job titles, employment dates, and other identifying narrative. While education information has also been blinded, colleges and graduate schools of equivalent ranking were substituted where appropriate.

## CHAPTER 7 RESUME INDEX

## IAN A. SMITH

**123 Any Street, Any City, CA XXXXX (619) 555-1234**

Contact Name                                               Date
Title
Company
Address
City, State, Zip

Dear Mr./Ms. _____:

I have formulated and executed expert sales and marketing strategies to outmaneuver the competition, penetrate new markets, and generate record sales in the Los Angeles market-place during the past decade with a subsidiary of Acme Industries. This has been rewarded with six-figure incomes and number one national ranking.

I am bringing to your attention my skills, achievements, and special talent for identifying, penetrating, and selling even the toughest decision makers so that we can discuss my joining _____ as a member of your senior management team.

Results achieved to date include:

o  As Director of Sales for ABC, Inc., a subsidiary of Acme Industries, generated a record $10 million in sales and up to a six-figure annual income during the past 10 years: consistently ranked in the top 10% nationally including three years at number one.

o  As a major revenue-producer for ABC, contributed to the company's pivotal milestones over the past decade: included a tripling of gross revenues over six years from $20 million to $60 million; a 600% growth in the value of the stock; and the acquisition of the company.

o  Developed and turned around ABC's untapped Los Angeles market during the past 11 years, setting sales records by instituting a cohesive, focused marketing strategy to identify lucrative markets, penetrate key decision makers, and build a loyal client base.

o  In a major marketing coup, initiated and closed a half million dollar order selling high-tech processing equipment to all 300 XYZ branches in a market where such multibranch deals for our product line are nearly impossible to close.

It should be to our mutual benefit to meet and determine how I can help accelerate or turn around sales, contributing to your company's future success.

Sincerely,

Enclosure:                                               Ian A. Smith

# Sales/Marketing Management

## IAN A. SMITH

123 Any Street, Any City, CA XXXXX (619) 555-1234

B.A.   Communications/Psychology   Ohio State University   1980

### CAREER SKILLS/KNOWLEDGE

o Sales/marketing management
o Revenue growth strategies
o Competitive maneuvering
o Market identification/penetration
o Decision-maker relations
o Client development
o Expert closer

o Profit growth strategies
o Expert communicator
o Negotiating skills
o Staff supervision/development
o Operations
o Customer service
o Installation/training

### CAREER ACHIEVEMENTS

o As Director of Sales for ABC, Inc., a subsidiary of Acme Industries, generated a record $10 million in sales and up to a six-figure annual income during the past decade: consistently ranked in the top 10% nationally including three years at number one.

o As a major revenue-producer for ABC, contributed to the company's pivotal milestones over the past decade: included a tripling of gross revenues over six years from $20 million to $60 million; a 600% growth in the value of the stock; and the acquisition of the company.

o Developed and turned around ABC's untapped Los Angeles market during the past 11 years, setting sales records by instituting a cohesive, focused marketing strategy to identify lucrative markets, penetrate key decision makers, and build a loyal client base.

o In a major marketing coup, initiated and closed a half million dollar order selling high-tech processing equipment to all 300 XYZ branches in a market where such multibranch deals for our product line are nearly impossible to close.

### CAREER EXPERIENCE

#### ACME INDUSTRIES, ABC, INC., SUBSIDIARY, Any Town, CA   1986–Present

Director of Sales
Market sophisticated processing systems to Fortune 500 clients:

o Train, develop, and direct the sales force.
o Emphasize client relations, new account development, and sales force productivity.
o Create innovative and effective presentations; conceptualize productive selling programs.

## <u>ESSEX CORPORATION, Any Town, Ohio  1984–1986</u>

<u>Regional Manager</u>
Consulted with and advised financial industry executives regarding the disposition and settlement of defaulted loans: reduced company's loss factor on reclaimed properties from as high as 60% down to only 25% through aggressive resale strategies and negotiations.

## <u>AVERY SERVICE COMPANY, Any Town, Ohio  1980–1984</u>

<u>General Sales Manager    1983–1984</u>
Responsible for direct sales, production, and customer service for this business which marketed data processing services to the Fortune 1000: achieved quota, managed and trained employees, and implemented records data processing systems for major financial institutions.

## REFERENCES PROVIDED UPON REQUEST

## DAVID Q. SAMPLE

**123 Any Street, Any City, CA  XXXXX  (619) 555-1234**

Contact Name                                                     Date
Title
Company
Address
City, State  Zip

Dear Mr./Ms. _____:

I have combined a top business degree, global experience, and executive skills in sales, finance, banking, and general management to establish and direct new operations which have generated millions in revenue for well-respected international companies. Bottom-line contributions to profit have been rewarded with accelerated promotions, job security, and a six-figure salary package.

I am bringing to your attention my skills, achievements, strategic brainpower, global network, and talent for exceeding profit goals under negative economic conditions so that we can discuss my joining _____ as a member of your senior sales management team.

Major accomplishments to date include:

o As Vice President of ABC's International Banking Group, produced revenue of $6.5 million through aggressive client development and by saving 90% of the seriously at-risk accounts: accelerated the ROA by focusing on corporate finance, investment banking, and asset sales.

o As Vice President of Corporate Banking at ABC's Southern California headquarters, leveraged my international contacts to market corporate and capital market products generating $5 million in added net income: achieved 250% growth in fees from capital market products.

o Was recruited away and promoted by ABC to start and manage the new International Energy Group: established and directed the lending operation generating over $500 million in new client bookings in only 18 months with an ROA of over 1%.

o As head of Commercial Development in charge of ABC's International Energy Group, initiated and closed several profitable deals including a hard-to-close $600 million project with an international energy company: created and directed a syndicate of major international lenders.

It should be mutually beneficial to meet and assess how I can help accelerate or turn around revenue and profit growth contributing to your company's future success.

Sincerely,

Enclosure:                                              David Q. Sample

# DAVID Q. SAMPLE

123 Any Street, Any City, CA XXXXX (619) 555-1234

M.B.A.  Honors    University of Paris Graduate School of Business    1985

International:    Bilingual French and English; solid knowledge of Mideastern languages; traveled to over 60 nations

Certifications:    Commercial Pilot's License; Black Belt Karate; Championship Skier

## CAREER SKILLS/KNOWLEDGE

o Marketing/sales executive
o General management
o Start-up operations
o Major client development
o Competitive maneuvering
o Expansion/turnaround strategies
o Revenue/profit growth
o Organizational development

o Financial executive
o International banking
o Investment banking
o Corporate/capital markets
o Acquisitions/joint ventures
o Subsidiary recapitalization
o Project financing/syndicates
o Trade financing/foreign exchange

## CAREER ACHIEVEMENTS

o As Vice President of ABC's International Banking Group, produced revenue of $6.5 million through aggressive client development and by saving 90% of the at-risk accounts: accelerated the ROA by focusing on corporate finance, investment banking, and asset sales.

o As Vice President of Corporate Banking at ABC's Southern California headquarters, leveraged my international contacts to market corporate and capital market products generating $5 million in added net income: achieved 250% growth in fees from capital market products.

o Was recruited away and promoted by ABC to start and manage the new International Energy Group: established and directed the lending operation generating over $500 million in new client bookings in only 18 months with an ROA of over 1%.

o As head of Commercial Development in charge of ABC's International Energy Group, initiated and closed several profitable deals including a hard-to-close $600 million project with an international energy company: created and directed a syndicate of major international lenders.

o As Group Officer at Acme International Bank, established and directed operations of a new North American office: achieved and exceeded an aggressive operating plan generating new lending of $300 million and profitability in five months instead of the forecasted ten months.

## CAREER EXPERIENCE

### ABC BANK, Any Town, CA   3/88–Present

INTERNATIONAL BANKING GROUP, Any Town, CA   2/91–Present

Vice President
Responsible for major account development emphasizing high-margin corporate finance and investment banking: acquisitions, recapitalization, and collateralized financing. Upgraded asset quality by addressing and restructuring below-par debt.

CORPORATE BANKING, Any Town, CA   3/88–2/91

Vice President
Created and marketed corporate and capital market products and services to global clients.

### ACME INTERNATIONAL BANK, Any Town, Europe   6/85–3/88

Group Officer (Assistant Vice President), Any Town, British Columbia   4/87–3/88
Managed start-up of a new operation: directed staffing, property selection, facility planning, contract negotiations, and purchasing. Also developed marketing policies and operating procedures.

Officer, Any Town, CA   5/86–4/87
Accelerated global account development quadrupling pre-tax net income to over $4 million.

Officer, Any Town, Europe   6/85–5/86
Established a Credit Group generating over $2 million in fees from new business development.

## REFERENCES PROVIDED UPON REQUEST

## PATRICK A. WILSON

**123 Any Street, Any City, CA XXXXX (619) 555-1234**

Contact Name                                                         Date
Title
Company
Street Address
City, State  Zip

Dear Mr./Ms. _____:

I have profitably applied skills in sales, client relations, program management, engineering, and product development to generate lucrative accounts, turn around client relations, open up closed markets, and develop state-of-the-art systems for Fortune 500 companies. This has been rewarded with multiple promotions and a reputation for getting the job done.

I am bringing to your attention my skills, achievements, and ability to produce results under intense pressure and out-of-control conditions so that we can discuss my joining _____ as a member of your Sales or Program Management Team.

Results achieved to date include:

o As a Project Director at ABC, Inc., generated satisfied clients and substantial revenue by expediting installation of multimillion-dollar space projects for XYZ Company, MCA, and CBS; established productive client rapport and had reputation for delivering on-time projects.

o Played a pivotal role in ABC's landing the lucrative XYZ Company and MCA accounts: convinced MCA to leave a competitor and turned around negative relations with XYZ.

o Played a central role in XYZ Company's efforts to penetrate the closed Asian markets: presented well-received studies to Korea's Ministry of Telecommunications and Osaka Telegraph and Telephone, paving the way for several hundred million dollar deals.

o Turned around relations between Acme Industries and a major client who had stopped payments toward a $300 million project: was singled out by the client for helping Acme to pass a critical Demonstration Review which led to resumption of monthly progress payments.

o As Project Director on a critical $300 million program, directed the development of complex state-of-the-art systems at Acme: sub-systems under my control are among the very few within the total project that are under control and on schedule.

It should be to our mutual benefit to meet and determine how I can contribute to your company's bottom-line success.

Sincerely,


Enclosure:                                                      Patrick A. Wilson

# Technical/Systems Sales

## PATRICK A. WILSON

123 Any Street, Any City, CA XXXXX (619) 555-1234

B.S.   Electrical Engineering    University of Texas    1982

### CAREER SKILLS/KNOWLEDGE

o Sales/account management
o Program management
o Client development/relations
o Revenue growth strategies
o Profit growth strategies
o Deal-making/negotiating
o Turnaround strategies
o Staff supervision/development
o Productivity improvements
o International markets

o Project management
o Product development
o Communications studies
o Engineering/administration
o Planning/scheduling
o Team motivation
o Subcontractor relations
o Cost control/reductions
o Design/specifications/prototypes
o Testing/release/support

### CAREER ACHIEVEMENTS

o As a Project Director at ABC, Inc., generated satisfied clients and substantial revenue by expediting installation of multimillion-dollar space projects for XYZ Company, MCA, and CBS; established productive client rapport and had reputation for delivering on-time projects.

o Played a pivotal role in ABC's landing the lucrative XYZ Company and MCA accounts: convinced MCA to leave a competitor and turned around negative relations with XYZ.

o Played a central role in XYZ Company's efforts to penetrate the closed Asian markets: presented well-received studies to Korea's Ministry of Telecommunications and Osaka Telegraph and Telephone, paving the way for several hundred million dollar deals.

o Turned around relations between Acme Industries and a major client who had stopped payments toward a $300 million project: was singled out by the client for helping Acme to pass a critical Demonstration Review which led to resumption of monthly progress payments.

o As Project Director on a critical $300 million program, directed the development of complex state-of-the-art systems at Acme: sub-systems under my control are among the very few within the total project that are under control and on schedule.

o Upon promotion to Director of ABC's $2 million Space Engineering Unit, stimulated revenue growth, turned around eroding morale, upgraded staff performance, and improved productivity.

o Built a reputation at ABC for accomplishing the impossible, receiving numerous accolades from executives at XYZ Company and Essex Communication where one executive voiced his opinion that "Pat is one of the finest Project Managers in the world."

## BUSINESS EXPERIENCE

### ACME INDUSTRIES, Any Town, CA   2/94–Present

Project Director
Manage client relations and overall planning, scheduling, and staffing for a state-of-the-art system development contract. Direct staff of 50 in executing hardware design, fabrication, and testing.

### ABC, INC., Any Town, CA   3/91–2/94

Director—Space Engineering Unit   9/92–2/94
General management responsibility for this engineering services and market research firm:

o  Directed staff of 45 sales, marketing, and product management personnel.
o  Provided engineering services, interacting with major clients on proposals, price negotiations, and technical issues.
o  Delivered critical presentations to Asian clients.

Project Director   3/91–9/92
Primary liaison to XYZ Communications, Essex Communication, MCA, and CBS:

o  Established excellent rapport with clientele.
o  Conducted complex frequency interference studies of station sites.
o  Performed frequency coordination of remote stations, prepared site reports, and analyzed field-measurement data.

### RIGOR SERVICES COMPANY, Any Town, OR   11/89–3/91

Engineer
Under contract to provide a Mideastern Air Force with on-the-job instruction in F-16 systems troubleshooting.

### AVERY COMPANY, Any Town, OH   6/88–11/89

Engineer
Completed rigorous company training at a government facility: managed group on overseas assignment providing technical support for the F-14. Based on results achieved, was requested to stay past the normal pull-out date; such requests are almost never made by the government.

## MILITARY CREDENTIALS

Underwater Operations   6/82–6/88
Graduate of the rigorous Nuclear Training Program: ranked near the top of the class and completed long-term assignment aboard a nuclear-powered submarine; substituted for the First Officer; was consulted on major operational decisions.

INTERNATIONAL TRAVEL: Traveled throughout Europe and Asia.

## DENNIS A. CUMMINGS

**123 Any Street, Any City, IL XXXXX (312) 555-1234**

Contact Name                                                          Date
Title
Company
Street Address
City, State  Zip

Dear Mr./Ms. _____:

I have applied proficient skills in product management, marketing, sales, strategic planning, and technical service to help generate over $25,000,000 in revenue for two Fortune 50 corporations during the past 14 years.

I am bringing to your attention my skills, achievements, and talent for improving sales and profits so that we can discuss my joining _____ as a member of your Product Management/Marketing/Sales Team.

Results achieved to date include:

o Product managed XYZ's introduction of major custom product features that ultimately generated $14 million annually.

o Initiated and pushed through major changes to XYZ's product color mix, upstaging the competition with new colors that generated $3 million in added revenue the first two years.

o Directed XYZ's on-schedule implementation of Monitored Service, a program critical to XYZ's future competitiveness.

o Researched, introduced, and marketed the first "residential" specialty feature product that produced $4 million over five years: executed Marketing and Distribution Plan that was rated by key managers as one of the most comprehensive plans ever completed at XYZ.

o Earned multiple promotions at ABC Corporation based on results achieved in sales and technical service: achieved sales quota and managed a field staff that exceeded aggressive service objectives.

A 30-minute exploratory discussion to determine how I can contribute to your future success should be to our mutual benefit.

Sincerely,

Enclosure:                                                    Dennis A. Cummings

# DENNIS A. CUMMINGS

123 Any Street, Any City, IL  XXXXX  (312) 555-1234

## CAREER SKILLS/KNOWLEDGE

o Product management
o Strategic planning
o New product research
o Competitive strategies/pricing
o Product introduction
o Organizational restructuring
o Business start-up

o Marketing/sales
o Revenue growth strategies
o Direct sales
o Presentations/public speaking
o Technical service management
o Staff supervision/training
o Negotiating skills

## CAREER ACHIEVEMENTS

o Product managed XYZ's introduction of major custom product features that ultimately generated $14 million annually; developed marketing plans for all operating companies and overcame strong internal resistance.

o Directed XYZ's on-schedule implementation of Monitored Service, a program critical to future competitiveness.

o Initiated and pushed through major changes to XYZ's product color mix, upstaging the competition with new colors that generated $3 million in added revenue the first two years.

o Product managed XYZ's introduction of mobile and voice messaging products that generate over $4 million a year: evaluated feasibility, determined profitability, established distribution channels, and negotiated vendor contracts.

o Researched, introduced, and marketed the first "residential" specialty feature product that produced $4 million over five years: executed Marketing and Distribution Plan that was rated by key managers as one of the most comprehensive plans ever completed at XYZ.

o Earned multiple promotions at ABC Corporation based on results achieved in sales and technical service: achieved sales quota and managed a field staff that exceeded aggressive service objectives.

## CAREER EXPERIENCE

### XYZ CORPORATION, Any City, IL    11/87–Present

Senior Product Manager   6/92–Present
Direct the nationwide implementation of Monitored Service:

o Chair program teams at headquarters and operating companies.
o Prepared short- and long-term implementation plans.
o Ensure implementation of monitoring rating and billing systems.

Product Manager   7/89–6/92
Responsibilities executed to introduce mobile and voice messaging products for resale nationwide:

o Directed headquarters and interdepartmental product teams.
o Established profitability objectives and distribution channels.
o Provided financial and operational requirements for budgeting and strategic planning.

Manager—Forecasting and Pricing   11/87–7/89
Responsibilities executed:

o Developed pricing policy and methodologies for new services.
o Helped plan and implement successful restructing of headquarters and operating companies.

## ABC CORPORATION, Any Town, IL   11/82–11/87

Sales Representative   11/84–11/87
Achieved 100% of the annual sales quota in only eight months.

Field Manager   11/82–11/84
Supervised and trained staff; developed and executed operating plans; managed territories. Named Field Manager of the Quarter.

Reason for leaving: Recruited by an XYZ Department Director.

## MILITARY EXPERIENCE   (10/78–10/82)

U.S. Army: Earned multiple promotions and was recommended for Officer Candidate School based on achievements as a Technical Trainer and Mechanical Technician.

## TRAINING/VOLUNTEER ACTIVITIES

o Guest speaker in Product Management and Marketing: several colleges including Minnesota State and Drake University
o Instructor: XYZ Management Skills Development Program
o Instructor: ABC's Volunteer Education Program
o Vice Chairman: Chicago Human Relations Commission
o Executive Board: United Way

## EDUCATION

B.A.   Ohio State University      1978

## REFERENCES PROVIDED UPON REQUEST

# MARY A. JOHNSON

**123 Any Street, Any City, NJ XXXXX (201) 555-1234**

Contact Name                                                                    Date
Title
Company
Street Address
City, State  Zip

Dear Mr./Ms. _____ :

Having developed and applied strong skills in market research from the design state through analysis and report preparation, I have proven my ability to achieve bottom-line results. I would like to bring my skills, experience, and motivation to your attention.

I am interested in exploring the possibility of joining _____ as a member of your Market Research Team.

Results achieved by applying the market research skills outlined in the attached resume include:

o Completed a well-received year-long research study for the credit card division of a major financial services corporation; resulted in major changes in their strategy for promoting credit card use in discount retail outlets.

o At ABC Company, performed a major product comparison research study which was rated excellent; a rating not often given to studies at ABC.

o Prevented serious customer relations problems for a major southwestern bank by identifying the specific negative impacts of closing down local branches; resulted in specific actions to reduce the negative perceptions of customers displaced by the branch consolidations.

o Conducted a research study which outlined the most effective strategy for introducing a new banking package that merged credit card, checking, savings, and money market accounts into a single compact statement—the strategy worked well.

o At ABC, performed a spokesperson research study for a well-known specialty product; resulted in retaining the current celebrity spokesperson, as study results confirmed the correctness of the original selection.

I feel it will be to our mutual benefit to meet and talk face-to-face. You may contact me at the above number to set up an appointment. I look forward to our meeting.

Sincerely,

Enclosure:                                                                    Mary A. Johnson

# MARY A. JOHNSON

123 Any Street, Any City, NJ XXXXX (201) 555-1234

## EDUCATION

| | | | |
|---|---|---|---|
| M.B.A. | Marketing | New York University<br>Graduate School of Business | 1988 |
| B.A. | Psychology | College of New Rochelle | 1980 |

## MARKET RESEARCH SKILLS

o Questionnaire development
o Attribute lists
o Features definition
o Product/service characteristics
o Questionnaire validation
o Client interaction
o Pretest for bid costing
o Response precoding
o Field staff interaction

o Develop/write table shells
o Establish/design tab plan
o Data collection/validation
o Topline analysis
o Analysis of marginals
o Closed-end data analysis
o Open-end data analysis
o Presentation of results
o Draft/final reports

## MARKET RESEARCH ACHIEVEMENTS

o Completed a well-received year-long research study for the credit card division of a major financial services corporation; resulted in major changes in their strategy for promoting credit card use in discount retail outlets.

o Prevented serious customer relations problems for a major southwestern bank by identifying the specific negative impacts of closing down local branches; resulted in specific actions to reduce the negative perceptions of customers displaced by the branch consolidations.

o At ABC Company, attention to detail resulted in my uncovering the specific reasons causing a new version of a well-known consumer product to score poorly with institutional buyers.

o At ABC Company, performed a major product comparison research study which was rated excellent; a rating not often given to studies at ABC.

o Conducted a research study which outlined the most effective strategy for introducing a new banking package that merged credit card, checking, savings, and money market accounts into a single compact statement—the strategy worked well.

o Significantly upgraded the image of a discount line of widgets through a creative visual marketing campaign showing the widgets in upscale settings.

o At ABC, performed a spokesperson research study for a well-known specialty product; resulted in retaining the current celebrity spokesperson, as study results confirmed the correctness of the original selection.

## CAREER EXPERIENCE

### ABC COMPANY, Any Town, NJ   7/89–Present

Senior Project Director
Conducted market research studies for major consumer product and financial services industry clients.

### XYZ, INCORPORATED, Any Town, NJ   3/87–7/89

Senior Project Director
Conducted research projects as a member of the in-house market research staff of this manufacturer of consumer products.

### ACME RESEARCH ASSOCIATES, INC., Any Town, NJ   6/82–3/87

Project Coordinator—Custom Market Research Services
Promoted to this position. Received in-depth training in key aspects of primary consumer market research, learning and experiencing all the steps in conducting a research study from the design state through analysis and report preparation.

Applied skills to produce studies which had bottom-line impact in marketing of our products.

### AVERY SERVICE COMPANY, Any Town, NJ   8/80–6/82

Research Analyst
Performed quantitative and administrative functions for this supplier of audit information to Fortune 500 consumer products companies. Prepared weekly posting sheets and sent to field auditors; pulled summary posting sheets when returned; compiled data and performed analytical steps to get monthly calculations; and assisted in report writing.

## REFERENCES PROVIDED UPON REQUEST

## ALEXIS A. JONES

**123 Any Street, Any Town, PA  XXXXX  (215) 555-1234**

Contact Name                                                                   Date
Title
Company
Address
City, State  Zip

Dear Ms./Mr. _____:

I have applied skills in sales, marketing, administration, customer service, and systems to accelerate profits, strengthen sales networks, turn around weak operations, and help a Fortune 100 company be selected for an international performance award. By directing the turnaround of administrative operations at Acme Business Services, assumed a leadership role in helping the subsidiary to become certified for a prestigious Productivity Award.

I am bringing to your attention my skills, achievements, work ethic, standards of excellence, and talent for achieving bottom-line results so that we can discuss my joining _____ as a member of your administrative management team.

Results achieved to date at Acme Company, Inc. include:

o Upon earning a multilevel promotion to Manager of Administration at Acme Business Services, a $20 million subsidiary, upgraded and turned around administrative operations contributing to the subsidiary being certified for a National Productivity Award.

o As Manager of Administration, took the lead in winning several Outstanding Group of the Month Awards—represented the first such awards in over six years: achieved this by significantly improving customer satisfaction, profit contribution, expense control, productivity, billing, inventory control, and systems support.

o Accelerated year-to-date profit performance to 110% of target and top-20 national ranking by reducing expenses and improving productivity: included a half million dollar contribution to profits generated by creating and installing a tracking system to recover outstanding charges.

o As the focal point for customer satisfaction at Acme, turned around a drastic decline in customer satisfaction by creating and enforcing customer service follow-up procedures to expedite corrective actions: within one quarter, customer satisfaction levels accelerated to 95% from a low of 55%.

o Selected for newly created Sales Coordinator position acting as liaison between Acme and its Mid-Atlantic sales agents: introduced critically needed performance reporting systems and controls contributing to Region's top ranking; identified poor performing agents and uncovered gross inefficiencies generating a 60% turnover and a more profitable sales network.

I will work hard to achieve results and look forward to discussing how I can contribute to your company's future success.

                                                                   Sincerely,


Enclosure:                                                         Alexis A. Jones

## ALEXIS A. JONES

123 Any Street, Any Town, PA XXXXX (215) 555-1234

| | | | | |
|---|---|---|---|---|
| M.B.A. | Systems | New York University | GPA 3.8/4.0 | 1986 |
| B.S. | Marketing | Lehman College | Self-financed | 1984 |

### CAREER SKILLS/KNOWLEDGE

o Marketing support/sales productivity
o Client development/relations
o Revenue/profit growth strategies
o Proposals/pricing/closing
o Customer service/satisfaction turnaround
o Administration/controller operations
o Department set-up/turnaround
o Budgeting/cost reductions
o Staff development/productivity growth

o Management information systems
o Systems consulting
o Sales/service support
o Systems/workstation installation
o Systems implementation/training
o IBM PC applications
o Novell network
o Excel/Lotus 1-2-3 expertise
o Graphics/PowerPoint

### CAREER ACHIEVEMENTS AT ACME COMPANY, INC.

o Upon earning a multilevel promotion to Manager of Administration at Acme Business Services, a $20 million subsidiary, upgraded and turned around administrative operations contributing to the subsidiary being certified for a National Productivity Award.

o As Manager of Administration, took the lead in winning several Outstanding Group of the Month Awards—represented the first such awards in over six years: achieved this by significantly improving customer satisfaction, profit contribution, expense control, productivity, billing, inventory control, and systems support.

o Accelerated year-to-date profit performace to 110% of target and top-20 national ranking by reducing expenses and improving productivity: included a half million dollar contribution to profits generated by creating and installing a tracking system to recover outstanding charges.

o As the focal point for customer satisfaction at Acme, turned around a drastic decline in customer satisfaction by creating and enforcing customer service follow-up procedures to expedite corrective actions: within one quarter, customer satisfaction levels accelerated to 95% from a low of 55%.

o Instituted much needed cross-training while computerizing what had been manually run administrative operations: selected, installed, and troubleshooted several workstations; instituted thorough systems training to maximize productivity of newly installed systems.

o Accelerated productivity by implementing productivity-improving processes that helped the administrative staff to win multiple Leader of Customer Satisfaction awards.

o Selected for newly-created Sales Coordinator position acting as liaison between Acme and its Mid-Atlantic sales agents: introduced critically needed performance reporting systems and controls contributing to Region's top ranking; identified poor performing agents and uncovered gross inefficiencies generating a 60% turnover and a more profitable sales network.

## CAREER EXPERIENCE

## ACME COMPANY, INC., Any City, PA    10/90–Present

Manager of Administration    10/94–Present
Responsibilities include: staff development, systems implementation, customer service, cost control, billing, credit, collection, procurement, accounts payable, cash management, inventory control, and reporting.

Systems Analyst    6/93–10/94
Troubleshot network crashes; installed workstations, processed sales manager compensation including the in-depth auditing of adjustments and exceptions. Ranked as one of the top analysts in the nation.

Sales Coordinator    11/91–6/93
Managed sales systems for a network of sales agents:

o  Assumed a leadership role in managing all aspects of the business.
o  Developed forecasts and upgraded reporting.
o  Formulated strategies for sales promotions.
o  Developed sales proposals.
o  Managed expenditures and inventory.
o  Performed expense analysis; provided pricing input.

Service Analyst    10/90–11/91
Computerized key reports generating more timely and accurate data for management decision-making. The newly automated reports became the standard for the entire corporation.

## MAJOR RETAILER, Any City, PA    6/86–10/90

Department Manager
Achieved 300% of plan by profitably directing 20 Departments with a staff of 30 and $2.5 million in inventory; established and directed profitable holiday and special promotion shops producing a 200% increase in sales.

## SYSTEMS TRAINING

Systems Seminar; Accelerated Administrator Training; Administrator Training; Lotus 1-2-3; Listing; Graphics; Tables

## REFERENCES PROVIDED UPON REQUEST

## NANCY A. CUMMINGS

**123 Any Street, Any City, MA  XXXXX  (617) 555-1234**

Contact Name                                                    Date
Title
Company
Street Address
City, State  Zip

Dear Mr./Ms. _____:

I have profitably applied skills and experience in retailing, store ownership, operations, buying, inventory management, and promotions to start up the first International Merchandise store in the Northeast Region and generate revenue and profit growth as high as 50%.

I am presenting for your review my skills, achievements, and talent for increasing profits even in a declining market so that we can discuss my joining _____ as a member of your Regional/Corporate Staff.

Results achieved to date include:

o Own and manage an International Merchandise franchise outlet: direct operations, attend international buyer shows in major metropolitan areas, and manage the product mix to eliminate slow-moving lines.

o By selecting popular products, instituting aggressive sales, and developing a top staff, made our International Merchandise store profitable from the first year.

o As Outlet Manager at Acme Retailing, Inc., reduced staff turnover and instituted aggressive promotions and inventory management to increase sales in spite of a recessional market.

o As Sales Supervisor at XYZ Corporation, more than quadrupled sales over a seven-year period; contributed to a successful stock offering.

o Generated 50% sales growth in the Domestics Department of a major retailer by upgrading customer relations and identifying and selling off slow-moving merchandise.

A 30-minute discussion to determine how I can contribute to your company's future success might well be to our mutual benefit.

                                                    Sincerely,


Enclosure:                                          Nancy A. Cummings

# Retail Sales Management

## NANCY A. CUMMINGS

123 Any Street, Any City, MA  XXXXX  (617) 555-1234

B.A.   Business/Psychology    Brunswick College    GPA 3.8    1980

Graduate Courses:    Business & Organizational Psychology

### CAREER SKILLS/KNOWLEDGE

- Retail management
- Franchise ownership
- Store operations
- Buying expertise
- Sales promotion strategies
- Cash-flow management

- Marketing/sales
- Telemarketing/cold-calling
- Client presentations
- Closing the sale
- Customer training/service
- Computer applications

### CAREER ACHIEVEMENTS

- Own and manage an International Merchandise franchise outlet: direct operations, attend international buyer shows in major metropolitan areas, and manage the product mix to eliminate slow-moving lines.

- By selecting popular products, instituting aggressive sales and developing a top staff, made our International Merchandise store profitable from the first year.

- As Outlet Manager at Acme Retailing, Inc., reduced staff turnover and instituted aggressive promotions and inventory management to increase sales in spite of a recessional market.

- Generated 50% sales growth in the Domestics Department of a major retailer by upgrading customer relations and identifying and selling off slow-moving merchandise.

- As Sales Supervisor at XYZ Corporation, more than quadrupled sales over a seven-year period; contributed to a successful stock offering.

### CAREER EXPERIENCE

#### INTERNATIONAL MERCHANDISE STORE, Any Town, MA    8/93–Present

Owner/Manager
Started and operate this high-end specialty store:

- Executed demographic study to select site location.
- Set up the store and direct overall operations.
- Hired and trained the manager and support staff.
- Execute product mix changes and aggressive promotions.

## ACME RETAILING, INC., Any Town, MA   6/89–8/93

Outlet Manager
Managed operations for the Any Town store:

o  Hired and trained staff.
o  Directed weekly promotions.
o  Set up computerized registers.
o  Coordinated customer relations.
o  Interacted with region management.

## AVERY RETAILING, INC., Any Town, MA   11/88–6/89

Department Manager
Responsibilities executed:

o  Hired, trained, and supervised staff ranging up to 50 people.
o  Specified goods to be purchased based on sales analysis.
o  Coordinated customer relations and inventory control.
o  Designed and set up window and in-store displays.
o  Managed and reported cash.

## ESSEX ECOLOGICAL PROGRAM, Any Town, MA   9/87–11/88

Coordinator
Project managed well-received program which introduced students to the world of ecology.

## XYZ CORPORATION, Any Town, MA   6/80–9/87

Sales Supervisor
Telemarketed and cold-called to sell sophisticated and expensive high-tech equipment to corporations. Also directed support staff responsible for order processing, customer relations, and receivables.

**REFERENCES PROVIDED UPON REQUEST**

# JOHN Q. SAMPLE

123 Any Street, Any City, CA XXXXX (619) 555-1234

Contact Name                                                    Date
Title
Company
Address
City, State  Zip

Dear Mr./Ms. _____:

As a central figure in Acme Corporation's massive restructuring, I applied executive skills in finance, administration, property management, and purchasing to facilitate Acme's turn-around to profitability. I likewise produced multimillion-dollar profits for the ABC Company through productive management of its administration and property management services, receiving accelerated promotions to Director of a $19 million operation.

I am presenting for your review my skills, achievements, and talent for accelerating margins and turning around unprofitable organizations so that we can discuss my joining _____ as a member of your senior management team.

Results achieved to date include:

o Promoted five grade levels during my last four years at ABC Company based on achieving all major P&L goals in directing the $19 million Corporate Administration and Property Management Department.

o As Acme's Corporate Director of Administration & Property Services, generated tens of millions of dollars in cost reductions and cash flow through aggressive property consolidations, up-graded services and procurement, and enforced management accountability.

o Consolidated 29 Acme warehouses down to 4, generating annual savings of $5.8 million; saved $4.6 million by reducing corporate headquarters space 30%; introduced uniform facility standards which reduced total space requirements 20%, generating another $3.4 million in annual cost savings.

o As head of Acme's $230 million purchasing operation, introduced an aggressive multiple-sourcing program which improved the margins of two major product lines by 7% and 9%, respectively.

o Productively managed ABC Company's property holdings, achieving 97% occupancy of 800,000 square feet at premium rates; developed a sophisticated model which helped save $7 million on the cost of an out-of-control $40 million building project at ABC.

I look forward to meeting and discussing how I can help accelerate or turn around your company's revenue and profit growth.

Sincerely,

Enclosure:                                              John Q. Sample

## Administration/Finance Executive

# JOHN Q. SAMPLE

**123 Any Street, Any City, CA XXXXX  (619) 555-1234**

B.S.    Honors    Finance    Georgetown University    1980

## CAREER SKILLS/KNOWLEDGE

o Finance/administration management
o General management
o Strategic/operational planning
o General/administrative services
o Financial planning & analysis
o Procurement operations
o Facilities/telecommunications
o Training operations
o Logistics services
o Global transportation

o Property management
o Development/construction
o Occupancy growth strategies
o Premium rate strategies
o Consolidation strategies
o Lease management/negotiations
o Site selection/space planning
o Budgeting/accountability
o Government regulations
o Environmental guidelines

## CAREER ACHIEVEMENTS

o As Corporate Director of Administration & Property Services, assumed a central role in Acme's turnaround to profitability: generated tens of millions of dollars in cost reductions and cash flow through aggressive property consolidations, upgraded services and procurement, and enforced management accountability.

o Promoted five grade levels during my last four years at ABC Company based on achieving all major P&L goals in directing the $19 million Corporate Administration and Property Management Department.

o Consolidated 29 Acme warehouses down to 4, generating annual savings of $5.8 million; saved $4.6 million by reducing corporate headquarters space 30%; introduced uniform facility standards which reduced total space requirements 20%, generating another $3.4 million in annual cost savings.

o As head of Acme's $230 million purchasing operation, introduced an aggressive multiple-sourcing program which improved the margins of two major product lines by 7% and 9%, respectively.

o Overcame powerful organizational resistance to produce over $3 million cash and annual savings of $2.1 million by persuading the Chairman to sell off Acme's corporate yacht.

o Generated annual cost savings of over $800,000 by installing a Novell network and upgrading ABC Company's distribution, travel, and other corporate services.

o Productively managed ABC Company's property holdings, achieving 97% occupancy of 800,000 square feet at premium rates; developed a sophisticated model which helped save $7 million on the cost of an out-of-control $40 million building project at ABC.

## CAREER EXPERIENCE

### ACME CORPORATION, Any Town, CA   3/88–Present

Corporate Director of Administration & Property Services
Direct the overall management, planning, site selection, lease negotiations, consolidations, and disposition for property totaling two million square feet. Additionally direct the $230 million purchasing operation and all corporate administrative services.

### ABC COMPANY, Any Town, CA   6/80–3/88

Director of Services & Property   3/85–3/88
Directed services with a staff of 63 and a budget of $19 million: included property management, purchasing, communications, systems, mail, and office equipment placement and maintenance. Reviewed and approved all facilities and construction contracts. Audited almost $100 million in operating expense budgets.

Manager of Administration   2/83–3/85
Developed policies and procedures, negotiated property transactions, and created a model which turned around a $40 million building project.

Senior Facilities Consultant   8/81–2/83
Developed well-received proposals that resulted in the creation of a $12 million Facilities Group.

Senior Consultant   6/80–8/81
Introduced the much needed zero-based budgeting concept to seven major operations.

## REFERENCES PROVIDED UPON REQUEST

## MARK A. WILSON

**123 Any Street, Any City, WA XXXXX (206) 555-1234**

Contact Name                                                           Date
Title
Company
Street Address
City, State  Zip

Dear Mr./Ms. _____:

As Treasurer of XYZ Leasing Services, Inc., I played a central role in returning critically needed financial credibility to this out-of-control company. As Division Manager of Acme Corporation's Leasing Subsidiary, I directed its turnaround and major contribution to profits in an otherwise disappointing period for the company.

I am presenting for your review my skills, achievements, ability to turn around treasury operations, and talent for generating bottom-line results within problem organizations so that we can discuss my joining _____ as a member of your financial management team.

Results achieved to date include:

o As one of five key veteran managers remaining after the bankruptcy of XYZ Leasing Services, a nationwide company with revenues of $200 million, was promoted to Treasurer: codirected the company's turnaround and better-than-forecasted $30 million sale.

o As Treasurer and Controller of XYZ Leasing Services, instituted effective post-bankruptcy financial controls returning critically needed credibility to XYZ; also executed a major systems database project critical to the $30 million sale of the company.

o As Division Manager, instituted Acme Corporation's lucrative remarketing program for off-lease equipment generating substantial rentals from the over $4 million in equipment leased to date under the program.

o Investigated and uncovered several million dollars of off-lease equipment that had never been returned to inventory recovering $700,000 in fees for Acme.

o Restructured and turned around Acme's third-party leasing portfolio, upgrading the accounting and administrative controls and creating an accurate database of all equipment.

I look forward to discussing how I can contribute to your company's future success.

Sincerely,


Enclosure:                                                             Mark A. Wilson

# MARK A. WILSON

123 Any Street, Any City, WA XXXXX (206) 555-1234

B.B.A.   Accounting   University of Seattle   1986

Certified Public Accountant

## CAREER SKILLS/KNOWLEDGE

o Treasury operations
o Portfolio management
o Banking relations
o Finance/accounting
o Controller operations
o Audit operations
o General accounting
o Budgeting/controls
o Collections/taxes

o Leasing industry expertise
o Lease financing cycle
o Division management
o P&L responsibility
o Marketing/sales
o MIS operations
o Personnel/payroll
o Staff supervision/development
o Information security

## CAREER ACHIEVEMENTS

o As one of five key veteran managers remaining after the bankruptcy of XYZ Leasing Services, a nationwide company with revenues of $200 million, was promoted to Treasurer: codirected the company's turnaround and better-than-forecasted $30 million sale.

o As Treasurer and Controller of XYZ Leasing Services, instituted effective post-bankruptcy financial controls returning critically needed credibility to XYZ; also executed a major systems database project critical to the $30 million sale of the company.

o As Division Manager of Acme Corporation's Leasing Subsidiary, directed its turnaround and major contribution to profits in an otherwise disappointing period for the corporation.

o Instituted Acme's lucrative remarketing program for off-lease equipment generating substantial rentals from the over $4 million in equipment leased to date under the program.

o Investigated and uncovered several million dollars of off-lease equipment that had never been returned to inventory recovering $700,000 in fees for Acme.

o Restructured and turned around Acme's third-party leasing portfolio, upgrading the accounting and administrative controls and creating an accurate database of all equipment.

o As Program Director at ABC Computer Leasing, introduced critically needed administrative and accounting controls for an affiliated leasing company; thoroughly analyzed the affiliate's portfolio of leases, loans, sale/leasebacks, and remarketing agreements.

# CAREER EXPERIENCE

## ACME CORPORATION, INC., Any Town, WA    2/95–Present

Division Manager
Responsibilities executed for the Acme Leasing Subsidiary:

o Achieved targeted P&L goals; instituted remarketing program.
o Direct senior staff: Controller, Systems Director, and Operations and Credit Managers.
o Upgraded financial and operational controls and reporting.
o Negotiate, screen, and approve all contracts.
o Upgraded relations with banks.
o Reduced aged receivables; upgraded inventory control.
o Eliminated aged backlog of customer inquiries.

## ABC COMPUTER LEASING COMPANY, Any Town, WA    3/94–2/95

Program Director
Audited portfolio of affiliated leasing company from its inception through current status; instituted Equity Tracking System; assisted in transition to new database system.

## XYZ LEASING SERVICES, INC., Any Town, WA    6/86–3/94

Treasurer    2/91–3/94
Responsibilities executed:

o Upgraded portfolio management increasing return on $40 million cash.
o Developed relations with major northwestern banks.
o Gained approval for post-bankruptcy exception request.
o Managed Personnel, Payroll, and Collections Departments.

Controller    3/89–2/91
Responsibilities executed:

o Recruited, trained, and supervised several staff accountants.
o Directed the Bookkeeping Department.
o Directed general ledger accounting; prepared consolidations.
o Managed in-depth operational reviews; initiated corrective actions.
o Supervised tax area; reduced equipment property taxes.

## REFERENCES PROVIDED UPON REQUEST

## SAMUEL A. JONES (Version 1)

123 Any Street, Any Town, CA  XXXXX  (619) 555-1234

Contact Name                                                                       Date
Title
Company
Address
City, State  Zip

Dear Mr./Ms. _____:

I have combined in-depth knowledge of Eastern Europe with skills in finance, administration, sales, manufacturing, banking, credit, and management to resolve serious cash shortages, achieve critical cost savings, and accelerate productivity as Director of Finance of an Eastern European operation. Achievements resulted in multiple management promotions in spite of my unwillingness to join the Communist Party.

I am bringing to your attention my skills, achievements, ability to achieve bottom-line results under negative conditions, and talent for executing tough projects including my escape from Eastern Europe so that we can discuss my joining _____ as a member of your International Finance Team.

Major achievements to date include:

o  Earned promotion to the much-sought-after position of Director of Finance at a major European operation, the largest such operation in the country, in spite of my negative attitude toward joining the Communist Party: assumed total responsibility for the review and approval of expense outlays for the operation; reduced the multimillion-dollar expense budget 35% while improving overall productivity.

o  Upon promotion to Financial Analyst at a European factory, researched and prepared well-conceived financial plans that exceeded cost-reduction targets without sacrificing operational effectiveness; took the lead in negotiating with banks to meet weekly payrolls in the face of critical cash-flow problems.

o  Earned rarely achieved first-year promotion within the Cost Department of a European manufacturer based on producing quality multimillion-dollar cost studies: assumed ever-increasing responsibilities with multimillion-dollar signing authority.

o  Over a four-year period, planned and executed my escape from the Communist Regime: completed a physical training program; maneuvered access to a waterfront complex; escaped across an inlet and posed as a West German citizen to get to West Germany where the United States granted asylum.

o  As a Partner in a San Diego firm, purchase, restore, and successfully market antique furniture; as a Sales Representative for an upscale American business, acted as Assistant Manager and consistently exceeded sales quotas selling $50,000 worth of product in a three-week period: nurtured a loyal client base right up to the unfortunate closing of the business.

I look forward to discussing how I can contribute to your international revenue and profit growth.

Sincerely,


Enclosure:                                                              Samuel A. Jones

# SAMUEL A. JONES

**123 Any Street, Any City, CA  XXXXX  (619) 555-1234**

B.S.  Finance/Economics  Finance Institute  1981

Honors:          Chosen to attend selective Institute
                 Recipient of major scholarship; Graduated with honors
Citizenship:     U.S.
International:    Eastern Europe Expert
Languages:       Fluent English, German, French, and Italian; some knowledge of Spanish

## CAREER SKILLS/KNOWLEDGE

o International relations
o Eastern Europe expertise
o European banking relations
o Credit application/approval process
o European financial/cost controls
o European pricing/capital planning
o Manufacturing/factory operations
o European management techniques

o Financial management
o Controller operations/expense control
o Financial planning
o Forecasting/budgeting
o Cost/pricing studies
o Sales/marketing
o Client development
o Closing/customer service

## CAREER ACHIEVEMENTS

o Earned promotion to the much-sought-after position of Director of Finance at a major European operation, the largest such operation in the country, in spite of my negative attitude toward joining the Communist Party: assumed total responsibility for the review and approval of expense outlays for the operation; reduced the multimillion-dollar expense budget 35% while improving overall productivity.

o Upon promotion to Financial Analyst at a European factory, researched and prepared well-conceived financial plans that exceeded cost-reduction targets without sacrificing operational effectiveness; took the lead in negotiating with banks to meet weekly payrolls in the face of critical cash-flow problems.

o Earned rarely achieved first-year promotion within the Cost Department of a European manufacturer based on producing quality multimillion-dollar cost studies: assumed ever-increasing responsibilities with multimillion-dollar signing authority.

o Over a four-year period, planned and executed my escape from the Communist Regime: completed a physical training program; maneuvered access to a waterfront complex; escaped across an inlet and posed as a West German citizen to get to West Germany where the United States granted asylum.

o As a Partner in a San Diego firm, purchase, restore, and successfully market antique furniture; as a Sales Representative for an upscale American business, acted as Assistant Manager and consistently exceeded sales quotas selling $50,000 worth of product in a three-week period: nurtured a loyal client base right up to the unfortunate closing of the business.

## INTERNATIONAL EXPERIENCE

### Eastern European Operation    6/81–3/86

Director of Finance    1/84–3/86
Audited and exercised final approval for all major expense requests for this manufacturer. Achieved substantial cost reductions while improving productivity.

Financial Analyst    5/83–1/84
Formulated financial plans including detailed forecasts and budgets; interacted with managers to reduce expenses and capital expenditures. Worked with financial institutions to address critical cash-flow problems.

Senior Cost Analyst    6/81–5/83
Formulated detailed cost studies as a foundation for better pricing practices. Interacted with departments to accumulate accurate cost data.

## AMERICAN EXPERIENCE

### Insurance Firm, Any City, CA    3/95–Present

Sales Representative: Aggressively cold-call and follow-up to close clients.

### Investment Firm, Any City, CA    3/90–Present

Cofounder: Purchase, restore, and market antique furniture.

### Essex Company, Any City, CA    4/87–3/90

Sales Representative: Sold expensive products and nurtured clients until business closed.

## REFERENCES PROVIDED UPON REQUEST

## PAUL A. CUMMINGS

123 Any Street, Any City, NJ XXXXX (609) 555-1234

Contact Name                                          Date
Title
Company
Street Address
City, State  Zip

Dear Mr./Ms. _____:

**I have applied proficient skills in financial management, planning and analysis, and capital budgeting to generate cost reductions, implement critical systems, expedite budgeting, upgrade controls, and achieve bottom-line results for Fortune 500 companies. Results achieved have been rewarded with multiple promotions.**

I am bringing to your attention my skills, achievements, and talent for developing productive, results-oriented relationships with line managers so that we can discuss my joining _____ as a member of your Financial Management Team.

Results achieved to date:

o Completed ABC International's billion dollar fiscal budget in less than three months versus the six months required to complete the previous year's budget: bottoms-up project covered three major Divisions, 14 Departments, 4 Warehouses, and 52 Outlets.

o Based on in-depth review and analysis, generated significant reductions in ABC's 1991 expense budget: reduced utilities expense $3 million, depreciation $400,000, and benefits $300,000.

o Developed, implemented, and was promoted to centrally manage profitability analysis and capital planning systems for XYZ Corporation.

o Codirected cost-savings from $40,000 up to $1.5 million on capital acquisitions at XYZ; coordinated program reviews of major projects identifying problems and corrective actions.

o Earned rapid promotion from Account Executive to Sales Manager at Acme Finance Company based on my top 10% sales performance: qualified for prestigious Performer's Conference, received the Golden Circle Award, and earned the Charter Professional Award.

I look forward to discussions at which we can determine how I can contribute to your company's future success.

Sincerely,


Enclosure:                                    Paul A. Cummings

## PAUL A. CUMMINGS

123 Any Street, Any City, NJ XXXXX (609) 555-1234

| M.B.A. | Finance | State University of New York | Honors | 1985 |
| B.S. | Finance | University of Colorado | Honors | 1983 |

Licenses: NASD Series 6

Languages: Fluent French

### CAREER SKILLS/KNOWLEDGE

o Financial planning and analysis
o Budget management
o Forecasting
o Capital/expense budgeting
o Variance analysis/reporting
o Auditing operations
o Business planning
o Major program reviews
o Program management
o Program controller

o Line manager interaction
o Staff supervision
o Management reporting
o Capital request approval
o Payback/discount analyses
o Lease versus buy
o Inventory analysis
o Asset turnover
o Aged receivables collection
o Mainframe/micro applications

### CAREER ACHIEVEMENTS

o Completed ABC International's billion dollar fiscal budget in less than three months versus the six months required to complete the previous year's budget: bottoms-up project covered three major Divisions, 14 Departments, 4 Warehouses, and 52 Outlets.

o Based on in-depth review and analysis, generated significant reductions in ABC's 1991 expense budget: reduced utilities expense $3 million, depreciation $400,000, and benefits $300,000.

o Developed, implemented, and was promoted to centrally manage profitability analysis and capital planning systems for XYZ Corporation, its Subsidiaries and Strategic Business Units.

o Codirected cost-savings from $40,000 up to $1.5 million on capital acquisitions at XYZ; coordinated program reviews of major projects identifying problems and corrective actions.

o Earned rapid promotion from Account Executive to Sales Manager at Acme Finance Company based on my top 10% sales performance: qualified for prestigious Performer's Conference, received the Golden Circle Award, and earned the Charter Professional Award.

o During my initial 15 months at Acme, achieved what my boss characterized as an almost unheard record of no policy cancellations: also accelerated my close ratio to over 60%, signing up as many as seven business and individual clients out of every ten appointments.

## CAREER EXPERIENCE

### ACME FINANCE COMPANY, Any Town, NJ   2/93–Present

Sales Manager
Market a full range of financial services including insurance, annuities, pension plans, and mutual funds.

### ABC INTERNATIONAL, INC., Any City, NJ   6/90–2/93

Financial Manager
Responsibilities included:

o Developed and coordinated a new budgeting process.
o Managed $20 million pool of cash.
o Prepared and distributed the flash reports.
o Prepared Proxy Statements for the Annual Report and SEC.
o Prepared Pension and Profit-Sharing Plan statements.
o Created comprehensive Policies and Procedures Manual.

### XYZ CORPORATION, Any City, NJ   7/85–6/90

Financial Supervisor   9/88–6/90
Promoted to this position; expanded responsibilities included:

o Managed profitability analysis and capital planning systems.
o Delivered major presentations on upgrading capital request and financial reporting controls.
o Liaison between XYZ and Profit Centers.

Capital Supervisor   8/86–9/88
Promoted to this position; responsibilities:

o Analyzed and exercised approval authority for all capital appropriations requests.
o Prepared Five-Year Capital Plan.
o Directed preparation of operating reports.

Senior Analyst   1/86–8/86
Promoted to position; controlled major development programs:

o Instituted comprehensive financial controls.
o Performed variance analysis and formulated corrective actions.
o Forecasted sales, planned manpower, implemented controls, and reviewed capital requests.
o Developed and updated five-year plans.

## REFERENCES AVAILABLE UPON REQUEST

# AUDREY A. JONES

**123 Any Street, Any Town, CA  XXXXX  (415) 555-1234**

Contact Name                                               Date
Title
Company
Street Address
City, State  Zip

Dear Mr./Ms. _____:

I have combined two degrees with skills in credit, customer service, client relations, and sales to upgrade service, improve client retention, reduce aged receivables, and achieve the top sales ranking by generating over $1 million in sales for a Utah based company—a revenue growth which doubled total sales. Results achieved have been rewarded with promotions into credit and sales management as well as an offer to take over as General Manager of the Utah company.

I am bringing to your attention my skills, achievements, creative energy, talent for upgrading service operations, and ability to turn around and retain angry customers so that we can discuss my joining _____ as a member of your customer service/credit management team.

Results achieved to date include:

o  As Credit & Collections Manager for an international soda producer, reduced chronically aged receivables and achieved a 94% current status in only a few months by instituting aggressive collection strategies: established constructive dialogue with delinquent customers and made use of stop-shipment leverage; investigated the validity of customer-generated credits recovering 88% of the total.

o  Promoted to Sales Manager at a Utah commercial services company based on number one sales ranking and bottom-line contributions in doubling company revenue: cold-called, closed, and serviced lucrative, difficult-to-sell Fortune 500 and smaller clients including Eagle Supermarkets, Bob Smith Restaurants, Hardee's, Inc., Eckerd Drugstores, and Pizza Hut.

o  Overcame strong resistance to sell, service, and retain major corporate accounts which generated over $1 million in five years for the Utah commercial services company: circumvented strong union resistance to land the lucrative Eagle account; outmaneuvered the competition by offering and delivering better quality service to land the profitable Bob Smith and Hardee's accounts.

o  As liaison to the operations manager and service delivery staff of the Utah services company, significantly upgraded service quality, prevented and resolved customer and employee problems, and enhanced overall morale and productivity: customer complaints dropped 50%; retention of customers with problems increased from 55% to over 93%; employee turnover radically declined.

o  Based on bottom-line sales achievements and demonstrated leadership in turning around the service operations, was offered the General Manager position by the owner of the Utah company: was selected from several candidates to fill this key position created by the relocation of the owner.

I will work hard to achieve bottom-line results and look forward to discussing how I can contribute to your company's future success.

Sincerely,

Enclosure:

Audrey A. Jones

# Credit/Customer Service Management

## AUDREY A. JONES

123 Any Street, Any Town, CA XXXXX (415) 555-1234

| | | | |
|---|---|---|---|
| B.A. | Utah State University | Self-financed | 1986 |
| B.S. | Georgia State University | Self-financed | 1988 |

**Honors/Awards:** Leadership Award (Any Town, CA); Citizenship Award (Any Town, CA)
**Leadership Activities:** Captain/Varsity Player in several sports
**Languages:** Strong German; moderate French and Spanish; studied Asian languages

## CAREER SKILLS/KNOWLEDGE

o Customer service/direct sales
o Client development/retention
o Credit & collection strategies
o Cold-calling/telemarketing
o Competitive maneuvering
o Presentations/demos
o Closing/contract negotiations
o Operations/service/quality control

o Communications/training
o Facilitator/leadership skills
o Platform skills/group presentations
o Team building/training
o Staff development/productivity growth
o IBM/MAC PC applications
o Excel/Lotus 1-2-3/DBase III
o PowerPoint/Harvard Graphics/Wordperfect

## CAREER ACHIEVEMENTS

o As Credit & Collections Manager for an international soda producer, reduced seriously aged receivables and achieved a 94% current status in only a few months by instituting aggressive collection strategies: established constructive dialogue with delinquent customers and made use of stop-shipment leverage; investigated validity of customer-generated credits recovering 88%.

o Promoted to Sales Manager at a Utah commercial services company based on number one sales ranking and bottom-line contributions in doubling company revenue: cold-called, closed, and serviced lucrative, difficult-to-sell Fortune 500 and smaller clients including Eagle Supermarkets, Bob Smith Restaurants, Hardee's Inc., Eckerd Drugstores, and Pizza Hut.

o Overcame strong resistance to sell, service, and retain major corporate accounts which generated over $1 million in five years for the Utah commercial services company: circumvented union resistance to land the lucrative Eagle account; outmaneuvered the competition by offering and delivering better quality service to land the profitable Bob Smith and Hardee's accounts.

o As liaison to the operations manager and service delivery staff of the Utah services company, significantly upgraded service, prevented and resolved customer and employee problems, and enhanced overall morale and productivity: customer complaints dropped 50%; retention of customers with problems increased from 55% to over 93%; employee turnover radically declined.

o Based on bottom-line sales achievements and demonstrated leadership in turning around service operations, was offered the General Manager position by the owner of the Utah company: was selected from several candidates to fill this position created by the relocation of the owner.

o As a member of the Quality Control group at the Acme Corporation, uncovered potentially serious operational problems that had created serious backlogs which threatened the validity of the shelf-life testing process: formulated and gained approval for $100,000 worth of corrective actions which eliminated the backlog and reinstated the validity of the testing process.

## CAREER EXPERIENCE

### AVERY SODA COMPANY, Any Town, CA    1993–Present

Manager of Credit & Collection: Accelerated the collection of high-dollar aged receivables by creating receivables tracking reports for chronically slow-paying customers: over a three-month period, reduced average payment days by as much as 43% for large volume clients.

### ACME CORPORATION, Any Town, CA    1990–1993

Testing Analyst: Implemented Statistical Process Control in testing areas and designed projects for the Quality Control group: gathered and analyzed data for Q.C.; presented data, conclusions, and recommendations to Quality Assurance management; assisted Q.A., Reliability, Advertising, and Development in acquiring test data; tested production and pilot-line samples.

Investigated and uncovered a serious procedural weakness in the sample testing process that allowed leakage to go undetected: corrected the problem by recommending and instituting procedures to supplement the computer testing.

### COMMERCIAL SERVICES COMPANY, Any Town, UT    1988–1990

Sales Manager: Marketed and sold services to Fortune 500 and other businesses: formulated marketing strategies and promotions; developed and presented proposals; negotiated contracts. Also comanaged and upgraded service operations.

Reason for leaving: Relocation to California

### GEORGIA STATE UNIVERSITY, Any Town, GA    1987–1988

Worked and earned a B.S. degree while maintaining a straight A average at this multicampus college: planned special events for and delivered 300 presentations to groups of 400 people; supervised the shipping and receiving department; coordinated advertising and direct mailings.

As part of the leadership training, executed challenging exercises in self-reliance: traveled over a thousand miles without transportation and spent the next several days mountain climbing.

### ESSEX COUNSELING GROUP, Any Town, GA    1986–1987

Program Manager: Promoted this social service agency to the community, school system, and families. Helped clients network with other agencies and followed up on clients to ensure success. Overcame strong attitudinal barriers to convert and sell school officials and the community on the advantages of our programs.

**ADDITIONAL TRAINING:**  Technical Layout Reading; Professional Carpentry
**VOLUNTEER ACTIVITIES:**  Reading Projects and Centers for the Mentally Retarded

**REFERENCES PROVIDED UPON REQUEST**

---

**Stockbroker/Branch Manager**

---

## WILLIAM A. JOHNSON

---

**123 Any Street, Any City, NY  XXXXX  (914) 555-1234**

Contact Name                                                        Date
Title
Company
Street Address
City, State  Zip

Dear Mr./Ms. _____:

Profitably applying brokerage and client relations skills to rank in the top 10% nationwide and earn promotion to Branch Manager at XYZ Securities by age 25, I have demonstrated the ability to produce bottom-line results by generating millions in revenue.

Based on my skills, achievements, and fast-track experience, I would like to initiate discussions about joining _____ as a member of your brokerage management team.

Bottom-line results achieved at XYZ Securities by aggressively applying the skills detailed on the attached resume include:

o  Personally generate up to $2,000,000 annually in "new money."

o  Comanaged the turnaround of the Westchester Operation.

o  Out of over 1,000 brokers nationwide, consistently ranked near the top.

o  Effectively recruit, motivate, and accelerate the productivity of the staff.

I know a face-to-face meeting to determine how I can, likewise, contribute to your firm's future success will be mutually beneficial. I look forward to hearing from you.

Sincerely,

Enclosure:                                                     William A. Johnson

| Stockbroker/Branch Manager |
| :---: |

# WILLIAM A. JOHNSON

123 Any Street, Any City, NY  XXXXX  (914) 555-1234

## BROKERAGE/BUSINESS SKILLS

o Branch management
o New account development
o Client relations
o Underwriting

o Staff recruiting/hiring
o Staff development
o Advertising
o Banking/NASD rules

## BROKERAGE EXPERIENCE/ACHIEVEMENTS

### XYZ SECURITIES, INC., Any Town, NY   6/92–Present

Branch Manager   6/95–Present
Promoted to this position at age 25. Achievements to date:

o Codirected turnaround of Westchester Office.
o Generate up to $2,000,000 annually in "new money."
o Ranked in the top 10% out of over 1,000 brokers nationwide.
o Successfully recruit, motivate, and accelerate productivity of the staff.

## EXPERIENCE TO FINANCE EDUCATION
### Full-time/Part-time

### UNITED DELIVERY SERVICE, Any City, NY   11/88–6/92
Supervisor of Local Operations:  Promoted to this position (part-time).

### ACME ELECTRIC CORPORATION, Any City, NJ   9/88–6/92
Quality Control:  Full-time position during college.

## ACADEMIC/CREDENTIALS

| | | |
| :--- | :--- | :--- |
| B.S. | Business Management | Adelphi University |
| 1992 | Minor: Psychology | |
| | Self-financed 100% of expenses | |

## CERTIFICATIONS

o Registered Full Service Broker Representative  (NASD-Series 7)
o Registered Broker Principal  (NASD-Series 24)
o The Agent  (NASD-Series 63)

## REFERENCES PROVIDED UPON REQUEST

---

# Leasing Industry Professional

---

## BRIAN A. CUMMINGS
---

**123 Any Street, Any City, CA XXXXX (619) 555-1234**

Contact Name                                            Date
Title
Company
Street Address
City, State Zip

Dear Mr./Ms. _____:

I have applied proficient skills in leasing, financial management, accounting, cash management, and systems to upgrade operations, reduce costs, help win multimillion-dollar contracts, turn around cash-flow problems, start up new operations, and help implement mergers and acquisitions. Results achieved have been rewarded with multiple promotions, pay raises, and bonuses.

I am bringing to your attention my skills, achievements, ability to upgrade staff productivity, and talent for improving cash flow and profit margins so that we can discuss my joining _____ as a member of your financial management team.

Major accomplishments to date include:

o As Director of Finance for a division of XYZ Corporation, generated over a million dollars in annual cost reductions by directing the consolidation of major financial functions from 30 decentralized locations to our San Diego offices.

o During a critically important period at XYZ, earned strong feedback for stepping in and effectively directing financial operations: expedited year-end closing, annual report development, and staff training and productivity.

o Created well-received financial package and upgraded the systems at XYZ: project managed installation of an integrated accounting system using a major General Ledger system and Lotus 1-2-3; also implemented cost-saving Sybron accounting package.

o By instituting critically needed financial credibility, helped ABC Company win a $5 million contract increasing the corporation's market value just prior to its scheduled sale; also helped consolidate and merge several companies into one.

o As Controller at Acme Corporation, executed a product leasing study which led to a profitable shift in marketing strategy; also converted a major acquisition to Acme's policies and procedures.

I will work hard to achieve bottom-line results and look forward to discussing how I can contribute to your company's future success.

                                        Sincerely,


Enclosure:                              Brian A. Cummings

# BRIAN A. CUMMINGS

123 Any Street, Any City, CA XXXXX (619) 555-1234

B.S.   Accounting/Business     University of Texas      1980

## CAREER SKILLS/KNOWLEDGE

o Finance/accounting management
o Leasing cycle/financing
o Controller operations
o Operating plan development
o Cash management
o Management reporting
o Budgeting/forecasting
o S.E.C. reporting/compliance
o Software applications/Lotus 1-2-3

o Leasing industry
o Project management
o Business development
o Turnaround strategies
o Margin growth strategies
o Consulting operations
o Franchising operations
o Acquisitions/mergers
o Contract administration

## CAREER ACHIEVEMENTS

o As Director of Finance for a division of XYZ Corporation, generated over a million dollars in annual cost reductions by directing the consolidation of major financial functions from 30 decentralized locations to our San Diego offices.

o During a critically important period at XYZ, earned strong feedback for stepping in and effectively directing financial operations: expedited year-end closing, annual report development, and staff training and productivity.

o Created well-received financial package and upgraded the systems at XYZ: project managed installation of an integrated accounting system using a major General Ledger system and Lotus 1-2-3; also implemented cost-saving Sybron accounting package.

o By instituting critically needed financial credibility, helped ABC Company win a $5 million contract increasing the corporation's market value just prior to its scheduled sale.

o As Corporate Controller at ABC, consolidated and merged several companies: issued new stock, integrated the financials, and earned accolades from the outside accounting firm.

o As Controller at Acme Corporation, executed a product leasing study which led to a profitable shift in marketing strategy; also converted a major acquisition to Acme's policies and procedures.

o As Controller at Essex Leasing Services, turned around cash management by instituting better investment strategies and cash utilization.

## CAREER EXPERIENCE

### XYZ CORPORATION, INC., Any City, CA   7/93–Present

Director of Finance: Supervise staff, systems and reporting, monthly closings, G/L transactions, banking relations, cash flow, investments, payables, and receivables.

### ESSEX LEASING SERVICES, Any City, CA   4/91–7/93

Controller: Upgraded lease financing administration and cash management; initiated leasing software implementation.

Reason for leaving: Company's economic downturn.

### ABC COMPANY, INC., Any City, CA   3/89–4/91

Controller: Performed revenue-generating consulting assignments; merged several separate companies into one; prepared operating plans, financial statements, payroll and related taxes, and management reports; designed and implemented cost accounting system; directed contract administration and compliance to federal regulations.

Reason for leaving: Company was acquired and relocated.

### ACME CORPORATION, Any City, CA   7/87–3/89

Controller: Delivered major presentations to top management. Prepared and analyzed financial statements, operating plans, and cash and sales forecasts.

Reason for leaving: Company relocated to New York.

### SMITH INTERNATIONAL SERVICES, Any Town, CA   6/84–7/87

Manager of Accounting: Chosen for start-up management team by the Franchisor of QRS Services which grew from 20 locations to over 600. Managed growth by establishing financial operations and implementing policies, procedures, and systems.

### RIS COMPANY, Inc., Any City, CA   6/80–6/84

Accounting Department: Promoted to several positions: upgraded cash management, inventory control, and collections.

## REFERENCES PROVIDED UPON REQUEST

# Real Estate Brokerage/Property Management

## ANN Q. JONES

**123 Any Street, Any Town, NJ XXXXX (201) 555-1234**

Contact Name                                                     Date
Title
Company
Street Address
City, State Zip

Dear Mr./Ms. _____:

I have profitably applied skills in real estate brokerage, property management, sales, and marketing to sell $10 million worth of product, earn Million-Dollar-Club status, profitably manage several commercial properties, and generate $5 million in sales in a two-year period.

I am bringing to your attention my skills, achievements, creative energy, work ethic, and ability to sell and achieve bottom-line results even in recessionary markets so that we can discuss my joining _____ as a member of your brokerage team.

Results achieved to date include:

o  As a Residential Real Estate Broker for XYZ Real Estate, Inc., sold $10 million worth of modestly priced housing over a four-year period: qualified for the Million-Dollar Club for several consecutive years generating over $5 million in sales in one two-year period alone.

o  As a Real Estate Broker, achieved bottom-line results by effectively closing the listing sellers and accurately defining the needs of buyers as a basis for selecting and showing only the best alternative products; effectively balanced the needs and demands of the seller versus the buyer.

o  Profitably marketed and managed several apartment buildings over a 12-year period: achieved and maintained a high occupancy rate through aggressive marketing and advertising while attaining a low level of rental income write-offs; directed cost-effective maintenance operations; improved and maintained solid tenant and broker relations.

o  As a veteran Representative on a West Coast Zoning Commission, negotiated directly with architects, developers, and builders exercising right of approval for proposed changes to properties.

o  Earned multiple promotions during three years with a major retailer; based on sales achievements, was promoted within a year to Department Manager in charge of three high-volume departments; was also promoted into Buying and Human Resources at the flagship operation.

I will work hard to achieve bottom-line results and look forward to discussing how I can contribute to your company's future success.

                                                     Sincerely yours,

Enclosure:                                           Ann Q. Jones

# ANN Q. JONES

123 Any Street, Any Town, NJ XXXXX (201) 555-1234

## CAREER SKILLS/KNOWLEDGE

o Real estate professional/broker
o Client development/relations
o Cold-calling/telemarketing
o Sale/rental advertising
o Property appraisals
o Proposals/presentations
o Buyer/seller negotiations
o Overcoming objections
o Closing/customer service

o Property management/ownership
o Occupancy rate strategies
o Rent collection strategies
o Maintenance operations
o Administration management
o Staff supervision/training
o Project management/troubleshooting
o Human resources administration
o Recruiting/hiring/benefits

## CAREER ACHIEVEMENTS

o As a Residential Real Estate Broker for XYZ Real Estate, Inc., sold $10 million worth of modestly priced housing over a four-year period: qualified for the Million-Dollar Club for several consecutive years generating over $5 million in sales in one two-year period alone.

o As a Real Estate Broker, achieved bottom-line results by effectively closing the listing sellers and accurately defining the needs of buyers as a basis for selecting and showing only the best alternative products; effectively balanced the needs and demands of the seller versus the buyer.

o Profitably marketed and managed several apartment buildings over a 12-year period: achieved and maintained a high occupancy rate through aggressive marketing and advertising while attaining a low level of rental income write-offs; directed cost-effective maintenance operations; improved and maintained solid tenant and broker relations.

o As a veteran Representative on a West Coast Zoning Commission, negotiated directly with architects, developers, and builders exercising right of approval for proposed changes to properties.

o As a Program Director for a West Coast Commission on the Homeless, successfully raised tens of thousands of dollars from area corporations in spite of strong resistance from corporate donors.

o Earned multiple promotions during three years with a major retailer: based on sales achievements, was promoted within a year to Department Manager in charge of three high-volume departments; was also promoted into Buying and Human Resources at the flagship operation.

o Upon promotion to Human Resources administration at a major retailer's flagship store, recruited and hired several hundred employees to staff the main floor and part of the lower level retail operations; also dealt firmly and effectively with strong unions; coordinated new hire training and development; effectively handled benefits administration and other personnel administration.

## CAREER EXPERIENCE

### XYZ REAL ESTATE, INC., Any City, NJ   1994–Present

Broker:  Market and sell residential real estate.

### ANOTHER REAL ESTATE INC., Any City, NJ   1989–1994

Broker:  Market and sell residential real estate.

### COMMISSION ON THE HOMELESS, Any Town, WA   1985–1989

Director:  In charge of planning and fund-raising.

### PROPERTY MANAGEMENT, Any Town, WA   1987–1989

Management:  Managed several apartment buildings: in charge of marketing and operations including rental advertising, tenant relations, maintenance operations, and rent collection.

### ZONING COMMISSION, Any Town, WA   1986–1987

Representative:  Negotiated with architects, developers, and builders on proposed projects.

### REALTY MANAGEMENT COMPANY, Any Town, WA   1983–1986

Human Resources:  Recruited staff for the properties managed by the company.

### MAJOR RETAILER, Any Town, WA   1980–1983

Department Manager:  Managed major departments. Completed well-respected Training Program.

## CREDENTIALS

College:  Attended University of Seattle   1979–1982

Certifications:  Real Estate License (NJ); Graduate Real Estate Institute; Licensed Appraiser

## REFERENCES PROVIDED UPON REQUEST

# DANIEL A. CUMMINGS

**123 Any Street, Any City, CA XXXXX (619) 555-1234**

Contact Name                                                    Date
Title
Company
Street Address
City, State  Zip

Dear Mr./Ms. _____:

I have applied proficient skills in advertising, marketing, and sales promotion within the travel, cruise line, and transportation industries to achieve bottom-line results. As Director of Advertising and Sales Promotion at a major international cruise line, converted Corporate Advertising into a first-rate $20 million operation which facilitated the company's expansion from 58 to 120 ships.

I am bringing to your attention my skills, achievements, creative energy, and guarantee to generate revenue several times my compensation so that we can discuss my joining _____ as a member of your advertising management team.

Additional results achieved to date include:

o Helped achieve worldwide occupancy rate of over 75% by upgrading the quality, creativity, and payback of Acme Cruise Lines' advertising and sales promotions: instituted local management accountability and significantly improved readership response and marketing analysis.

o Recipient of numerous major advertising and sales promotion awards: we were the only cruise line to ever win a Gold Award from the Art Director's Club, which selected Acme Cruise Lines, Inc., from thousands of entries.

o As Vice President and Account Director at the XYZ Advertising Agency, successfully executed politically sensitive multimillion-dollar campaigns for the San Diego Transportation Authority.

o As a Sales Vice President at a Fortune 500 Corporation, increased annual billing $20 million by signing and managing major accounts including the much sought after Essex Cruise Line.

I look forward to a meeting at which we can focus on how I can contribute to your company's future success.

Sincerely,

Enclosure:                                                    Daniel A. Cummings

## DANIEL A. CUMMINGS

123 Any Street, Any City, CA XXXXX (619) 555-1234

### MARKETING SKILLS/KNOWLEDGE

o Advertising/sales promotion
o Agency operations/relations
o Domestic/international campaigns
o Multimedia planning/buying
o Direct marketing
o Brochure/catalog development

o Travel industry
o International cruise line industry
o Transportation industry
o Off-peak sales strategies
o New market development
o Public relations

### CAREER ACHIEVEMENTS

o As Corporate Director of Advertising and Sales Promotion at Acme Cruise Lines, converted Corporate Advertising into a first-rate $20 million operation which helped facilitate expansion from 58 to 120 ships worldwide.

o Helped achieve worldwide occupancy rate of over 75% by upgrading the quality, creativity, and payback of Acme Cruise Lines' advertising and sales promotions: instituted local management accountability and significantly improved readership response and marketing analysis.

o Introduced several major changes and innovations to Acme's advertising and promotional material including the use of world-class photographers and illustrators.

o As Vice President and Account Director at the XYZ Advertising Agency, successfully executed politically sensitive multimillion-dollar campaigns for the San Diego Transportation Authority.

o As a Sales Vice President at a Fortune 500 Corporation, increased annual billing $20 million by signing and managing major accounts including the much sought after Essex Cruise Line.

o Significantly improved sales and profit growth at Smith Transportation Company; stimulated off-peak sales achieving a load factor in excess of 87%.

### MAJOR ADVERTISING AND PROMOTION AWARDS

o Art Directors' Club Award: Print Advertising
o Magazine Editors Association: Joseph M. Reilly Award
o American Advertising Awards: Consumer Advertising
o Atlantic Travel Association Award: Trade Advertising
o Cruise Line Sales Association Awards: Direct Marketing
o Travel Agents and Travellers Awards: Competitive Surveys

<h1 style="text-align:center">CAREER EXPERIENCE</h1>

## FREELANCE CONSULTANT, Any Town, CA   1995–Present

Promotional Consultant
Develop and present comprehensive proposals for major cruise lines.

## XYZ ADVERTISING AGENCY, Any Town, CA   1989–1995

Vice President and Account Director
Responsible for direct mail programs for the San Diego Transportation Authority; supervised vacation package program for the San Diego Chamber of Commerce. Developed proposals to generate new business from tourism sector. Consultant on Acme Cruise Lines and SRO Cruise Lines.

## ACME CRUISE LINES, INC., Any Town, CA   1986–1989

Director of Advertising
Supervised creative staff and administered $20 million budget:

o Worked with outside advertising firms to develop strategies and execute global media plans.
o Monitored activities of European and South American offices.
o Upgraded promotional materials to generate better response.
o Upgraded staff training and development; created and distributed operating manuals.

## FORTUNE 500 CORPORATION (ESSEX DIVISION), Any Town, CA   1982–1986

Vice President of Sales & Marketing
Accelerated product acceptance and signed major cruise lines. Managed and accelerated the billings from our largest cruise line account.

## SMITH TRANSPORTATION COMPANY, INC., Any City, CA   1978–1982

Manager of Advertising and Public Relations
Directed sales, advertising, communications, and public relations.

<h1 style="text-align:center">EDUCATION</h1>

B.S.        Brown University
M.B.A.    UCLA Graduate School of Business Administration

<h1 style="text-align:center">REFERENCES PROVIDED UPON REQUEST</h1>

# JOANNE A. SMITH

**Any Street, Any City, NJ XXXXX (201) 555-1234**

Contact Name                                              Date
Title
Company
Street Address
City, State Zip

Dear Mr./Ms. _____:

I have combined a Stanford M.B.A. with skills in systems consulting, software, client relations, and programming to develop custom software applications, audit and upgrade systems, streamline programs, reduce processing time, produce multilingual software products, and generate lucrative consulting fees from major private and public sector clients.

I am bringing to your attention my skills, achievements, technical prowess, and talent for satisfying the most demanding clients so that we can discuss my joining _____ as a member of your systems consulting team.

Results achieved to date include:

o  As a Senior Consultant at XYZ Corporation, project managed the design and development of a German language version of the company's Modified Client Survey: traveled to Frankfurt to document the client's specifications and streamlined the complex conversion procedures.

o  Upon graduation from Stanford, was chosen for the selective management development program at Acme Corporation: among other assignments, completed a major systems audit at a Consumer Products Division generating recommendations which upgraded surveillance, improved backup procedures, and helped correct out-of-control financial reporting.

o  Received written commendations for streamlining the data input and calculation process for Acme's Executive Benefits Plan—reduced the processing time from several days to only a few minutes; also corrected previously undetected errors in the division financial reports resulting in tens of thousands of dollars in favorable adjustments.

o  Earned promotion to Project Head at ABC Corporation based on the on-time development of processing systems for financial institutions: effectively handled tough clients in developing custom back and front office software; generated additional consulting fees by convincing clients to expand the scope of the original projects.

I look forward to discussions at which we can determine how I can contribute to your company's future success.

                                        Sincerely,


Enclosure:                              Joanne A. Smith

## JOANNE A. SMITH

**123 Any Street, Any City, NJ XXXXX (201) 555-1234**

| | | | | |
|---|---|---|---|---|
| M.B.A. | Marketing/Finance | Stanford University | Self-financed | 1990 |
| B.S. | Quantitative Analysis | University of Chicago | Self-financed | 1986 |

Graduate Studies: Completed several accelerated computer science courses
Publications: Article on Computerization: Systems Management Magazine (1983)
International: Traveled throughout South America and Europe

### CAREER SKILLS/KNOWLEDGE

- o MIS/systems consulting
- o Proprietary databases
- o Real-time analysis/graphics display
- o SPSS/DBase III Plus
- o Spreadsheets/Lotus 1-2-3/Excel
- o Design/testing/debugging
- o Fortran/Basic/Pascal/Algol/C

- o Marketing/account management
- o Client relations/development
- o Government relations
- o Corporate relations
- o European relations
- o Market research studies
- o Strategic planning/forecasting

### CAREER ACHIEVEMENTS

o As a Senior Consultant at XYZ Corporation, project managed the design and development of a German language version of the company's Modified Client Survey: traveled to Frankfurt to document the client's specifications and streamlined the complex conversion procedures.

o Upon graduation from Stanford, was chosen for the selective management development program at Acme Corporation: among other assignments, completed a major systems audit at a Consumer Products Division generating recommendations which upgraded surveillance, improved backup procedures, and helped correct out-of-control financial reporting.

o Received written commendations for streamlining the data input and calculation process for Acme's Executive Benefits Plan—reduced the processing time from several days to only a few minutes; also corrected previously undetected errors in the division financial reports resulting in tens of thousands of dollars in favorable adjustments.

o Saved Acme expensive outside systems consulting fees by initiating and leading an in-house effort to upgrade and purge the database systems; applied in-depth knowledge of Lotus and complex financial databases to execute this assignment.

o Earned promotion to Project Head at ABC Corporation based on the on-time development of processing systems for financial institutions: effectively handled tough clients in developing custom back and front office software; generated additional consulting fees by convincing clients to expand the scope of the original projects.

o As a programmer on a consulting assignment to Boeing, earned promotion to Senior Associate at Essex, Inc., based on my contribution to the programming on major assignments: helped develop real-time data and graphics display of test information; created software to generate key reports from a confidential database.

## CAREER EXPERIENCE

## AVERY FINANCIAL GROUP, Any City, NJ   1996–2001

Director
Performed industry research, executed sophisticated supply/demand analyses, and developed economic and financial models.

Reason for leaving: Massive restructuring due to corporation's bankruptcy.

## XYZ CORPORATION, Any City, NJ   1991–1996

Senior Consultant
Developed models, statistical data, management reports, and safeguards for proprietary software: designed databases for planning and scheduling corporate consulting assignments; designed and developed multilingual versions of software; conducted industry analyses.

## ACME CORPORATION, Any City, NJ   1990–1991

Senior Planner
Upgraded the massive database systems; executed comprehensive systems reviews; generated a research study which documented critically needed marketing, competitive, and demographic information.

## ABC CORPORATION, Any City, NJ   1987–1988

Project Head
Promotion. Developed processing systems for financial institutions. Managed a team of analysts.

Reason for leaving: To attend graduate school.

## ESSEX, INC., Any City, WA   1986–1987

Senior Associate
Promotion. Programmer on a consulting assignment to Boeing for: development of real-time data and graphics display of test information; creation of software for management reporting from a confidential database.

Reason for leaving: Relocation to New Jersey.

## REFERENCES PROVIDED UPON REQUEST

## JOHN A. JONES

**123 Any Street, Any City, WA XXXXX (206) 555-1235**

Contact Name                                                    Date
Title
Company
Street Address
City, State  Zip

Dear Mr./Ms. _____:

I have applied executive skills in production, materials management, engineering, and sales to turn around out-of-control operations and build a multimillion-dollar company known for its state-of-the-art products, cost-effective manufacturing, and substantial market shares. Achievements have been rewarded with profit-sharing and awards for the on-time delivery of major systems.

I am bringing to your attention my leadership skills, achievements, ability to turn around problem operations, and proven talent for accelerating profits to produce financial security for others and myself so that we can discuss my joining _____ as a member of your materials management/operations team.

Major accomplishments to date include:

o  Turned around out-of-control quality and distribution problems at XYZ Technology increasing on-time shipments from 38% to 95%; also turned around purchasing operations generating $3 million a year in cost reductions while reducing inventory $3 million.

o  As Director of Procurement at Acme Company, generated $4 million in annual cost savings and reduced inventory $2 million by resolving serious cost control and material control problems.

o  As founder of ABC, Inc., started and built this profitable high-tech electronics company known over 20 years for its innovative products and low-cost volume production: negotiated and executed the lucrative sale of the company to a major corporation.

o  More than doubled ABC's revenue by marketing breakthrough products to over 40 countries and major Fortune 500 corporations: developed damage-proof and modular products; introduced concept of placing electronics into clothing; developed communications systems for space projects, carriers, train systems, executive aircraft, and bank machines.

o  Became one of the world's largest producers of specialized communication devices by focusing on the high volume global market; instituted "people-based" engineering to extend the life of electronic equipment and produce safety-conscious communications for major clients.

Should we reach mutually agreeable terms, I will work hard to help accelerate or turn around operating performance contributing to your future success.

Sincerely,


Enclosure:                                                     John A. Jones

# Production/Materials Management

## JOHN A. JONES

123 Any Street, Any City, WA XXXXX (206) 555-1235

| | | | |
|---|---|---|---|
| M.B.A. | Management | Wharton | 1974 |
| B.S. | Electrical Engineering | Stanford University | 1972 |
| B.A. | Economics | Stanford University | 1972 |

### CAREER SKILLS/KNOWLEDGE

- o Operations/materials management
- o Manufacturing/Q.C.
- o Procurement operations
- o Production & inventory control
- o Cost reductions/productivity
- o Cost-effective production
- o R&D/systems engineering
- o Distribution/transportation
- o Electronics industry

- o International marketing/sales
- o General management/finance
- o Start-up operations/organization
- o Major client development
- o Product management
- o Competitive maneuvering
- o Expansion/turnaround strategies
- o Profit/market share growth
- o New product marketing/pricing

### CAREER ACHIEVEMENTS

o Turned around out-of-control quality and distribution problems at XYZ Technology increasing on-time shipments from 38% to 95%; also turned around purchasing operations generating $3 million a year in cost reductions while reducing inventory $3 million.

o As Director of Procurement at Acme Company, generated $4 million in annual cost savings and reduced inventory $2 million by resolving serious cost control and material control problems.

o As founder of ABC, Inc., started and built this profitable high-tech electronics company known over 20 years for its innovative products and low-cost volume production: negotiated and executed the lucrative sale of the company to a major corporation.

o Awarded a coveted medal by a foreign government for producing and delivering, in less than 60 days, critically needed communications systems vital to their national defense: crash program cut four months off the schedule.

o More than doubled ABC's revenue by marketing breakthrough products to over 40 countries and major Fortune 500 corporations: developed damage-proof and modular products; introduced concept of placing electronics into clothing; developed communications systems for space projects, carriers, train systems, executive aircraft, and bank machines.

o Became one of the world's largest producers of specialized communication devices by focusing on the high volume global market; instituted "people-based" engineering to extend the life of electronic equipment and produce safety-conscious communications for major clients.

## CAREER EXPERIENCE

### ACME COMPANY, Any City, WA   1996–Present

Director of Procurement
Instituted much needed budget systems; upgraded material control, developed off-shore vendors, reduced materials shortages, and stopped downtime; generated cost savings and reduced inventory.

### XYZ TECHNOLOGY CORPORATION, Any Town, WA   1995–1996

Project Director
In a series of manufacturing, technical, and procurement assignments, instituted modern management techniques: improved production quality, cut costs, reduced inventory, and established on-time delivery:

o Upgraded Q.C. operations, policies, and procedures.
o Tightened vendor product quality standards.
o Instituted competitive bidding and second sourcing.
o Introduced Japanese methods of inventory stocking.

### ABC, INCORPORATED, Any Town, WA   1974–1995

Founder
Founded and managed a high-tech company which grew to over 150 employees:

o Expanded through innovation, systems engineering, and cost-effective manufacturing.
o Oversaw new product development from inception through design, engineering, and production.
o Established and monitored marketing and pricing objectives.
o Developed client relations with major corporations and numerous countries.
o Continuously expanded into new markets.
o Redesigned and improved products to reduce costs.
o Established rigid quality control standards.
o Designed a plant layout which dramatically improved assembly productivity.
o Consistently met tight delivery schedules.

## REFERENCES PROVIDED UPON REQUEST

# ELIZABETH A. JOHNSON

123 Any Street, Any City, VA  XXXXX  (703) 555-1234

Contact Name                                                              Date
Title
Company
Street Address
City, State  Zip

Dear Mr./Mrs. _____:

Combining skills in operations, project management, systems, and technical service with an Engineering degree from M.I.T., I identified and resolved serious systems problems that were costing ABC Company $500 million annually. My ability to achieve bottom-line results has been rewarded with multiple promotions, classification as a high-potential manager, and a salary package in the 90s at age 28.

I am presenting for your review my skills, achievements, and ability to execute high-impact projects so that we can initiate discussions about my joining _____ as a member of your Operations/Project Management Team.

Results achieved at ABC Company by applying the skills detailed on the attached resume include:

o  Researched, identified, and developed corrective actions for major problems in the service system which were costing ABC $500 million annually; created and implemented nationwide a comprehensive training package that will prevent these losses and accelerate profits.

o  Due, in part, to the above training package which I designed to prevent massive revenue losses, the Southern Region won ABC's Excellence Award.

o  Created and implemented a marketing campaign to motivate technicians to sell: achieved 250% of sales objective; was successfully introduced in other districts.

o  Codeveloped and implemented nationwide a major service program which saved $30 million.

o  In preparing for a major corporate-wide restructuring, established a separate service center which became the company's prototype: implemented manual operations, achieving balanced workloads, cost controls, and stable productivity in a crisis environment.

A face-to-face meeting to determine how I can contribute to your company's future success might well be to our mutual benefit.

                                        Sincerely,


Enclosure:                              Elizabeth A. Johnson

## ELIZABETH A. JOHNSON

123 Any Street, Any City, VA XXXXX (703) 555-1234

B.S.   Massachusetts Institute of Technology   Electrical Engineering   Honors   1992

### CAREER SKILLS/KNOWLEDGE

- o Operations/technical service
- o Project management
- o Major program implementation
- o Marketing campaign development
- o Productivity improvements
- o Staff management/training
- o Training package design
- o Negotiating skills
- o Expense control/reductions
- o Corrective action plans

- o Telecommunications
- o Installation/maintenance
- o Field Service Center set-up
- o Field Service Center management
- o Crew supervision
- o Workload management
- o Labor relations
- o Systems implementation
- o User training
- o UNIX Operating System

### CAREER ACHIEVEMENTS

o Researched, identified, and developed corrective actions for major problems in the service system which were costing ABC $500 million annually; created and implemented nation-wide a comprehensive training package that will prevent these losses and accelerate profits.

o Due, in part, to the above training package which I designed to prevent massive revenue losses, the Southern Region won ABC's Excellence Award.

o Codeveloped and implemented nationwide a major service program which saved $30 million.

o Implemented a major program to equip technicians with portable computers, eliminating the clerical interface between the field and the billing, inventory, and reporting systems; trained personnel in 23 districts including 4,500 technicians.

o Created and implemented a marketing campaign to motivate technicians to sell: achieved 250% of sales objective; was successfully introduced in other districts.

o As manager of one of the largest service centers, negotiated a ground-breaking agreement with the local Union permitting ABC to substitute work locations.

o In preparing for a major corporate-wide restructuring, established a separate service center which became the company's prototype: implemented manual operations, achieving balanced workloads, cost controls, and stable productivity in a crisis environment.

## CAREER EXPERIENCE

## ABC COMPANY, Any Town, VA   5/92–Present

### L.S.R. HEADQUARTERS, Any Town, VA   8/95–Present

Manager of Operations   3/96–Present
Direct staff responsible for:

o Major field productivity programs designed to generate millions in revenue and cost reductions; also provide support to service organizations.
o While on assignment to the Group Director, implemented a major service program as well as a program to equip technicians with portable computers.

Manager of Systems   8/95–3/96
Responsibilities executed:

o Identified and resolved service system weaknesses costing ABC hundreds of millions.
o Provided applications support for 1,400 field personnel who relied on in-house systems to handle 150,000 maintenance and installation requests weekly.

### MANAGEMENT TRAINING, Any Town, VA   5/92–8/95

Marketing Manager   10/94–8/95
Exceeded goals in over 90% of the objectives established: created marketing campaign to accelerate Technician sales; reduced backlog of orders not invoiced from 16,000 to 500.

Service Manager   10/93–10/94
Promotion to manage one of the largest centers:

o Installed and maintained communication systems.
o Elevated the responsibility and reliability of technicians in order to improve productivity.
o Negotiated with the XYZ Union.

Operations   5/92–10/93
Major assignments included:

Center Manager: established the prototype operation.
Supervisor: produced on-time installations and repairs.
Installations Supervisor: Promotion; managed major cutovers.
Foreman: turned around lowest-rated crew; accelerated productivity 48%.
Testing Supervisor: Promotion; ensured on-time service.

## REFERENCES AVAILABLE UPON REQUEST

## JAMES A. SMITH

**123 Any Street, Any City, NY XXXXX (914) 555-1234**

Contact Name                                                    Date
Title
Company
Street Address
City, State  Zip

Dear Mr./Ms. _____:

I have combined an E.E. degree with management skills in product development, electronics, system engineering, and marketing to create state-of-the-art products, develop high-tech market research devices for the Executive Branch, accelerate revenue and profits, and play a central role in producing one of the most profitable ventures in the history of ABC Company.

I am bringing to your attention my skills, achievements, creativity, technical prowess, and talent for accelerating revenue and profits so that we can discuss my joining _____ as a member of your product development/engineering management team.

Results achieved to date include:

o As director of a key development group at XYZ, a subsidiary of ABC Company, developed several state-of-the-art communication products in five years creating one of the company's most profitable ventures: ground-breaking systems overcame restrictive limitations permitting peripherals to be located 70 miles away from a computer mainframe.

o As cofounder of a start-up venture, led development of Single Board Computer, a processor board for industrial applications requiring less coding than other processor boards: protected product through legal means and marketed it to major Fortune 500 clients.

o As founder of an E.E. consulting firm, developed a proprietary computer-based device called the "XYZ Product" for the chairman of a market research firm under contract to the executive branch: earned fees based on the development, usage, and subsequent sale of the product to the executive branch.

o Started and marketed two business ventures during the past year generating six-figure sales: expanded an E.E. consulting firm; started a hazardous material consulting service.

o Directed a software-intensive group in executing state-of-the-art changes to a major machine at Acme Company: led development of coding printer executing all of the complex software and hardware tasks in harnessing the speed-printing technology.

I will work hard to achieve bottom-line results and look forward to discussing how I can contribute to your company's future success.

Sincerely,

Enclosure:                                                    James A. Smith

## JAMES A. SMITH

123 Any Street, Any City, NY XXXXX (914) 555-1234

B.S.E.E.   University of Rochester   Self-financed   1985

Honors:
- Earned top grade for Senior project: designed hand-held scanner
- Who's Who Among Students in American Colleges
- Graduated with Honors; Dean's List

### CAREER SKILLS/KNOWLEDGE

- Product development
- Project management
- System engineering
- Electronics/mechanical
- Digital/analog technology
- PCB design/development
- Computer science/programming
- Biomedical engineering

- Sales/marketing
- Product creation/introduction
- Revenue/profit growth
- Client development
- Cold-calling/telemarketing
- Proposals/presentations
- Closing/customer service
- Business start-up

### CAREER ACHIEVEMENTS

- As director of a key development group at XYZ, a subsidiary of ABC Company, developed several state-of-the-art communication products in five years creating one of the company's most profitable ventures: ground-breaking systems overcame restrictive limitations permitting peripherals to be located 70 miles away from a computer mainframe.

- As cofounder of a start-up venture, led development of Single Board Computer, a processor board for industrial applications requiring less coding than other processor boards: protected product through legal means and marketed it to major Fortune 500 clients.

- As founder of an E.E. consulting firm, developed a proprietary computer-based device called the "XYZ Product" for the chairman of a market research firm under contract to the executive branch: earned fees based on the development, usage, and subsequent sale of the product.

- Started and marketed two business ventures during the past year generating six-figure sales: expanded an E.E. consulting firm; started a hazardous material consulting service.

- Directed a software-intensive group in executing state-of-the-art changes to a major machine at Acme Company: led development of coding printer executing all of the complex software and hardware tasks in harnessing the speed-printing technology.

- Successfully developed, for a major automotive company, the 4066 product which provided tape drive channels for customers without dedicated communications facilities: required complete restructuring of XYZ's 6088 product line.

## CAREER EXPERIENCE

### JAMES SMITH ASSOCIATES, Any Town, NY  1990–Present
E.E. Consulting: Developed feeder mechanism critical to development of a mail machine to be marketed by an electronics firm. Created "XYZ Product" proprietary computer-based data-entry device used to measure responses to words, phrases, and ideas. Worked on a computer-based automated routing system for Essex Corporation.

### HAZARDOUS WASTE CONSULTING CORPORATION, Any Town, NY   1994–Present
Started and manage consulting business.

### ACME COMPANY, Any City, NY  1992–1994
Directed a product development effort aimed at instituting critical changes to a major machine: introduced speed-printing technology to new code printer.

### XYZ SUBSIDIARY, ABC COMPANY, Any Town, NY  1987–1992
Director: Developed high-speed data communications equipment for mainframes; designed PC compatible interface card for serial and parallel transfer to proprietary product. Codeveloped high-speed logic board using FAST series logic and programmable devices; implemented 64K deep high-speed FIFO capable of a 5 Mega word throughput; employed error detection and correction with the RAM array.

### COMPUTER START-UP VENTURE, Any Town, NY  1987–1988
Cofounder/Partner: Designed and marketed a single board computer using the Intel 8051 microcomputer: incorporated ROM memory mapping, 8155 I/O ports/RAM/Timers, Electronically Erasable PROM, and RS-232 serial communication using the on-board UART of the 8051.

### A FORTUNE 500 ELECTRONICS COMPANY, Any Town, NY  1986–1987
Electronic Engineer: Earned positive feedback for systems testing and authoring critical test sections of major proposal.

### A SMALLER ELECTRONICS COMPANY, Any City, NY  1985–1986
Electronic Engineer: Developed control system software for custom molding machines; generated assembly language and PLM programs for the Intel 8085 processor.

## REFERENCES PROVIDED UPON REQUEST

# DEBORAH A. SMITH

**123 Any Street, Any City, CA XXXXX (619) 555-1234**

Contact Name                                               Date
Title
Company
Street Address
City, State  Zip

Dear Mr./Ms. _____:

I have applied executive skills in program administration, operations, and marketing to direct the administration of a $300 million project and generate over $1 million in documented cost savings for a major electronics firm. I also started up a multimillion-dollar electronics company, generated half of its total sales, and expanded the client base of another high-tech company.

I am bringing to your attention my skills, achievements, nationwide network of electronics industry contacts, and ability to produce results under crisis management conditions so that we can discuss my joining _____ as a member of your administration management team.

Results achieved to date include:

o As Director of Program Administration for a major $300 million program at ABC Corporation, direct all planning, budgeting, scheduling, and reporting: am recognized for executing crisis projects with little advance notice including critical design reviews for the board.

o As administrative manager for a $60 million project at ABC, generated over $1 million in documented cost savings by recommending alternative vendors who offered better prices, quality, and service.

o As Manager of Administration for a $500 million ABC system, acted as liaison to a foreign government interacting up to the Cabinet level: enforced security, coordinated state visits and relocations, and expedited shipment of top priority hardware.

o Recipient, for the third consecutive year, of the ABC Service Award which is awarded based on outstanding service and contributions by individuals to ABC and important team projects.

o As cofounder and Sales Vice President for Acme Electronics, Inc., accelerated revenue growth and directly generated 60% of the gross sales for this high-tech multimillion-dollar company.

I look forward to discussing how I can contribute to your company's future success.

Sincerely,

Enclosure:                                               Deborah A. Smith

## DEBORAH A. SMITH

123 Any Street, Any City, CA XXXXX  (619) 555-1234

| | | |
|---|---|---|
| B.S. | University of Colorado | 1980 |
| M.S. Candidate | University of San Diego | 1997 |

### CAREER SKILLS/KNOWLEDGE

| | |
|---|---|
| o R&D program administration | o Sales/marketing |
| o Project management | o Market expansion strategies |
| o Liaison to officials | o Cold-calling/telemarketing |
| o Planning/budgeting | o Client development/relations |
| o Scheduling/reporting | o Overcoming objections/closing |
| o Senior program reviews | o Entrepreneurial start-ups |
| o Cost reduction strategies | o Operations/manufacturing |
| o Corrective action plans | o Staff development/productivity |
| o Internal consulting | o Materials/procurement |

### CAREER ACHIEVEMENTS

o As Director of Program Administration for a major $300 million program at ABC Corporation, direct all planning, budgeting, scheduling, and reporting: am recognized for executing crisis projects with little advance notice including critical design reviews for the board.

o Recipient, for the third consecutive year, of the ABC Service Award which is awarded based on outstanding service and contributions by individuals to ABC and important team projects.

o As administrative manager for a $60 million project at ABC, generated over $1 million in documented cost savings by recommending alternative vendors who offered better prices, quality, and service.

o As Manager of Administration for a $500 million ABC system, acted as liaison to a foreign government interacting up to the Cabinet level: enforced security, coordinated state visits and relocations, and expedited shipment of top priority hardware.

o Overcame strong resistance to persuade ABC's Layout Manager to designate our project location a test site; resulted in a total renovation of our facility greatly improving productivity.

o As cofounder and Sales Vice President for Acme Electronics, Inc., accelerated revenue growth and directly generated 60% of the gross sales for this high-tech multimillion-dollar company.

o Directed Acme Electronics' operations, instituting better training which accelerated productivity and upgrading procurement which improved quality and reduced cost of materials 30%.

o As Sales Account Specialist for XYZ Distributors, Inc., generated major multimillion-dollar accounts expanding the client base 40%.

## PROJECT MANAGEMENT/ADMINISTRATION EXPERIENCE

### ABC CORPORATION, Any City, CA    5/88–Present

Director of Program Administration ($300 million project)   3/94–Present
Coordinate inter-departmental planning, budgeting and reporting:

o  Assure cooperation; avoid duplication of effort; foster communication.
o  Identify prime and supporting objectives; prepare schedules; participate in progress reviews.
o  Prepare status reports; recommend and implement corrective actions.

Manager of Administration ($500 million project)   5/88–3/94
Liaison to clients and upper management; established procedures to insure performance compliance; developed and administered plan to monitor objectives and manpower utilization.

## SALES/OPERATIONS EXPERIENCE

### ACME ELECTRONICS, INC., Any Town, CA    4/86–5/88

Cofounder/Vice President of Sales and Operations
Directed Sales and Operations for this electro-mechanical company: Developed client network, cold-called and closed deals; directed production; instituted second sourcing; negotiated contracts.

### HIGH-TECH MANUFACTURER, Any City, CA    10/84–4/86

Regional Sales Manager
Sold panel meters to test equipment companies, military electronics companies, and medical instrumentation companies.

### A.B. ENTERPRISES, INC., Any Town, CA    9/82–10/84

Sales Representative:  Sold electro-mechanical products.

### XYZ DISTRIBUTORS, INC., Any City, CA    8/81–9/82

Sales Representative:  Sold electronic components and test equipment.

### A SMALL ELECTRONICS FIRM, INC., Any Town, CA    6/80–8/81

Sales Representative
Managed almost 100 accounts, specializing in OEMS, military electronics companies, and medical equipment companies; worked with engineers to spec out components/meters/test equipment.

## CERTIFICATE PROGRAMS

| Accounting for the Non-Accounting Manager | San Diego State | 1989 |
| Managing for Growth | San Diego State | 1990 |
| Three-month Management Course | ABC Corporation, Inc. | 1992 |
| Negotiating Skills | San Diego State | 1994 |

# VINCENT A. JONES

**123 Any Street, Any City, WA XXXXX (206) 555-1234**

Contact Name
Title
Company
Street Address
City, State  Zip

Date

Dear Mr./Ms. _____:

Written quote from a Group President of Acme Corporation:

"It's not easy for a marketing guy, like myself, to run a company like Acme, Inc. Because of Vincent (Jones), we have a better understanding of the work that is required in staffing a growing organization. I learn every day, that is every day I find someone whom I respect for their talents and would like to emulate. Vincent Jones is one of those people."

I have applied diverse skills in human resources management to achieve bottom-line results in corporate staffing, sales force staffing and development, productivity growth, turnover reduction, accident prevention, and cost control. I am presenting for your review my skills, achievements, and proven track record so that we can discuss my joining _____ as a Human Resources Manager.

Results achieved by persistently applying the skills detailed on the attached resume include:

o Successfully staffed the sales force for selected Acme dealerships which generate a substantial portion of total company revenue.

o Developed and implemented accelerated training programs at a regional XYZ Company: significantly improved manager/employee relations and measurably upgraded individual performance.

o Through aggressive yet selective staffing techniques, reduced average unfilled requisitions at Acme from 20 per month to 8 per month.

o Established a new regional record for Accident Free Days at a regional XYZ Company through the aggressive efforts of the accident prevention committee which I instituted.

I look forward to a face-to-face meeting which will give us the opportunity to discuss how I can contribute to your company's future success.

Sincerely,

Enclosure:

Vincent A. Jones

## VINCENT A. JONES

123 Any Street, Any City, WA  XXXXX  (206) 555-1234

"Recruiting good people is always difficult at best. Through Vince Jones' staffing effort, we were able to hire excellent prospective sales people. All of us here at Acme look forward to the next opportunity of working with Vince."
—Corporate Vice President

### CAREER SKILLS/KNOWLEDGE

| | |
|---|---|
| o Human resources management | o Sales force staffing |
| o Employee relations | o Sales force development |
| o Staffing strategies | o Dealer relations |
| o Wage/salary administration | o Training programs |
| o Benefits administration | o Recruiting: exempt/non-exempt |
| o Affirmative action plans | o Monthly reporting |
| o Accident prevention programs | o Extensive travel |
| o Outplacement counseling | o Newsletter publication |
| o Unemployment cost control | o Community affairs |
| o Suspensions/terminations | o Counseling-outreach program |
| o Worker compensation | o Correctional counseling |

### SELECTED ACHIEVEMENTS

o Successfully staffed the sales force for selected Acme dealerships which generate a substantial portion of total company revenue.

o Through aggressive yet selective staffing techniques, reduced average unfilled requisitions at Acme from 20 per month to 8 per month.

o Developed and implemented accelerated training programs at a regional XYZ Company: significantly improved manager/employee relations and measurably upgraded individual performance.

o Researched and implemented major wage scale revisions at a regional XYZ Division: substantially reduced company turnover.

o Established a new regional record for Accident Free Days at a regional XYZ Company through the aggressive efforts of the accident prevention committee which I instituted.

o Organized and executed Acme's participation in career days at various employment fairs: screened an average of 40 candidates in four days, hiring an average of 5.

o Researched and wrote Acme's well-received 1986 Equal Employment Opportunity Program.

## CAREER EXPERIENCE

### ACME CORPORATION, Any Town, WA   9/93–Present

HR Manager
Responsibilities executed include:

o  Employee staffing—exempt and non-exempt
o  Sales force recruiting/branch relations
o  Wage and salary administration
o  Benefits administration
o  Unemployment cost control
o  Worker compensation
o  Affirmative action plans
o  Outplacement counseling

### XYZ COMPANY, INC., Any Town, CA   6/86–9/93

HR Manager—XYZ Division, Any Town, KY   6/90–9/93
Managed Human Resources for over 500 employees. Generalist functions executed included staffing, employee relations, training and development, salary administration, orientations, accident prevention, benefits administration, and unemployment cost control.

HR Supervisor—XYZ Division, Any Town, CA   5/88–6/90
Managed personnel functions for over 1,500 employees at one of XYZ's largest operations. Responsibilities included: staffing, terminations, unemployment cost control, and accident prevention.

## EDUCATION/CREDENTIALS

| | | |
|---|---|---|
| B.A. Philosophy/English | San Diego State University | 1986 |
| Certified HR Training | University of California | 1986 |

Additional Training: Completed several comprehensive Human Resource Management courses and workshops.

## REFERENCES PROVIDED UPON REQUEST

# Training and Development Professional

## JENNIFER A. SMITH

123 Any Street, Any City, WA XXXXX (206) 555-1234

Contact Name                                                        Date
Title
Company
Address
City, State Zip

Dear Mr./Ms. _____:

I have applied proven skills in training and development, HR management, recruiting, redeployment, and systems to turn around training and development operations, institute critically needed training programs, and achieve challenging HR recruiting objectives for Fortune 500 corporations. Bottom-line achievements have been rewarded with bonuses and several promotions.

I am bringing to your attention my skills, achievements, high energy, and talent for upgrading the training process and accelerating worker productivity so that we can discuss my joining _____ as a member of your training and development management team.

Results achieved to date include:

o As HR Director at the Essex Company, upgraded Human Resources for over 3,000 employees: filled over 500 openings annually improving candidate quality while cutting the recruiting cycle in half; instituted critically needed training programs as well as comprehensive cross-training; reduced benefits operating costs; upgraded systems, policies, and procedures.

o As HR Manager at ABC Corporation, project managed the start-up of a new headquarters: coordinated the logistics and successfully recruited, hired, and directed the training and development of over 400 employees in only seven months; also directed and accelerated the productivity of the administrative support staff.

o Directed Acme Development Center's Human Resources start-up and operation: achieved first-year staffing and training objectives in less than nine months and instituted comprehensive employee relations programs.

o Turned around Acme's Personnel Cross-Training and Redeployment Program achieving over a 90% placement rate through well-received seminars and workshops.

o Directed the highly successful implementation of Acme's critically needed $12 million Human Resource, Benefits, and Payroll system.

I look forward to discussing how I can, likewise, contribute to your company's future success.

Sincerely,


Enclosure:                                              Jennifer A. Smith

# JENNIFER A. SMITH

123 Any Street, Any City, WA XXXXX (206) 555-1234

B.A.  Honors Communications  Smith College  GPA 3.7/4.0  1980

## CAREER SKILLS/KNOWLEDGE

| | |
|---|---|
| o Human resources professional | o Systems implementation |
| o Training and development | o Systems consulting/design |
| o Recruiting techniques | o Installation troubleshooter |
| o Seminar/workshop development | o User training/support |
| o Video role playing/feedback | o Computer-based training |
| o Payroll/benefits administration | o Micro/mainframe applications |
| o Performance appraisal/merit guidelines | o Excel/LOTUS 1-2-3 |
| o Communications/public relations | o Administration |
| o Outplacement counseling | o Staff supervision |

## CAREER ACHIEVEMENTS

o As HR Director at the Essex Company, upgraded Human Resources for over 3,000 employees: filled over 500 openings annually improving candidate quality while cutting the recruiting cycle in half; instituted critically needed training programs as well as comprehensive cross-training; reduced benefits operating costs; upgraded systems, policies, and procedures.

o As HR Manager at ABC Corporation, project managed the start-up of a new headquarters: coordinated the logistics and successfully recruited, hired, and directed the training and development of over 400 employees in only seven months; also directed and accelerated the productivity of the administrative support staff.

o Directed Acme Development Center's Human Resources start-up and operation: achieved first-year staffing and training objectives in less than nine months and instituted comprehensive employee relations programs.

o Turned around Acme's Personnel Cross-Training and Redeployment Program achieving over a 90% placement rate through well-received seminars and workshops.

o Directed the highly successful implementation of Acme's critically needed $12 million Human Resource, Benefits, and Payroll system.

o Created and executed job search and redeployment workshops for the homeless in Seattle.

## CAREER EXPERIENCE

### ESSEX COMPANY, Any Town, WA  7/94–Present

HR Director
Directed recruiting, managed multimillion-dollar benefits plan, computerized operations, instituted aggressive cost-reduction programs, and upgraded policies and procedures.

## ABC CORPORATION, Any Town, WA    2/89–7/94

HR Manager
Project managed the logistics and staffing of a new headquarters.

## ACME, INC., Any Town, WA    3/84–2/89

Corporate Benefits Administration    1/88–2/89
Performed benefits evaluations and upgraded several outdated HR manuals.

Corporate HR Systems Analyst    12/86–1/88
Project managed the implementation of a major HR system designed to support in excess of 200,000 employees.

Personnel Redeployment    3/85–12/86
Executed well-received Redeployment Programs.

HR Administrator    3/84–3/85
Recruited and hired all staff for the Development Center; established Communications and Benefits Groups; also developed EEO Plans and authored several policies and procedures.

## AVERY SERVICE CORPORATION, Any Town, WA    6/80–3/84

HR Administrator
Accelerated cost reduction programs; upgraded and assisted in the administration of relocations, recruiting, terminations, payroll, benefits, and employee orientations.

## VOLUNTEER ACTIVITIES

o  Created job search seminars for the homeless
o  Provided support of the learning disabled
o  Taught reading skills to adults

## REFERENCES PROVIDED UPON REQUEST

## WILLIAM Q. SAMPLE        International Marketing Executive

**123 Any Street Address, Any Town, NJ XXXXX (201) 555-1234**

Contact Name                                 Date
Title
Company
Street Address
City, State Zip

Dear Mr./Ms. _____:

As a follow-up to our recent discussion, I am forwarding the information about which we spoke. As Executive Vice President for the U.S. Division of a European corporation, I have applied skills in international sales, marketing, client development, and operations to outmaneuver the competition, deal with volatile exchange rates, accelerate growth of the corporate client base, and achieve a fivefold increase in sales—a revenue level which accounts for 40% of global sales.

I am presenting for your review my skills, achievements, technical degree, global contacts, and talent for creating productive marketing organizations and achieving aggressive revenue goals so that we can discuss my joining _____ as a member of your senior management team.

Results achieved during the past decade with Acme International include:

o Earned multiple promotions up to Executive Vice President of Sales at a U.S. Division of Acme International, one of Europe's largest industrial corporations: created a highly productive sales organization and achieved a fivefold increase in revenue turning the U.S. Division into a $20 million business which now accounts for almost 40% of the subsidiary's global sales.

o In spite of high turnover and chronically unfavorable exchange rates, which adversely impacted the U.S. Division's pricing structure, generated a 500% increase in Acme's customer base through an accelerated client development program which emphasized quality and service to offset the unfavorable pricing.

o In spite of global competition, closed multimillion-dollar clients including Western Electric, AT&T, Boeing, and John Deere: accelerated the AT&T account from zero to $9 million representing half of total sales; generated a ninefold sales increase from the Harvester Division of John Deere; produced an eightfold increase in the Western Electric and Boeing accounts.

o Significantly reduced overhead and logistics expenses and all but eliminated aged receivables and write-offs by creating and enforcing conservative credit policies at Acme; in order to meet scheduled delivery dates through on-time shipments from Europe, also established a first-rate logistics function.

I look forward to discussing how I can help accelerate or turn around the performance of your international operations.

                                         Sincerely,

Enclosure:                                William Q. Sample

## Over-50 Manager Marketed to Career Position

## WILLIAM Q. SAMPLE        International Marketing Executive

123 Any Street Address, Any Town, NJ XXXXX (201) 555-1234

| | | |
|---|---|---|
| B.S. Electrical Engineering | International University | Comprehensive Six-Year Program |
| B.A. Business Administration | Lehman College | Managerial Studies |

| | |
|---|---|
| International: | Traveled throughout Europe, Asia, South America, and North America |
| Languages: | Fluent French, and Spanish |

### CAREER SKILLS/KNOWLEDGE

- o Sales/marketing executive
- o International sales/markets
- o European relations
- o Strategic/marketing plans
- o Market share strategies
- o Major client development
- o Competitive maneuvering
- o Exchange rate strategies
- o Organizational development
- o Staff supervision/development

- o Operations/materials/engineering
- o Purchasing operations
- o Cost controls/reductions
- o Global distribution/logistics
- o Heavy industry clients
- o Aircraft engine market
- o Engineering operations
- o Electrical/systems engineering
- o New product design
- o Plant operating systems design

### CAREER ACHIEVEMENTS

o Earned multiple promotions up to Executive Vice President of Sales at a U.S. Division of Acme International, one of Europe's largest industrial corporations: created a highly productive sales organization and achieved a fivefold increase in revenue turning the U.S. Division into a $20 million business which now accounts for almost 40% of the subsidiary's global sales.

o In spite of high turnover and chronically unfavorable exchange rates, which adversely impacted the U.S. Division's pricing structure, generated a 500% increase in Acme's customer base through an accelerated client development program which emphasized quality and service to offset the unfavorable pricing.

o In spite of global competition, closed multimillion-dollar clients including Western Electric, AT&T, Boeing, and John Deere: accelerated the AT&T account from zero to $9 million representing half of total sales; generated a ninefold sales increase from the Harvester Division of John Deere; produced an eightfold increase in the Western Electric and Boeing accounts.

o Significantly reduced overhead and logistics expenses and all but eliminated aged receivables and write-offs by creating and enforcing conservative credit policies at Acme; in order to meet scheduled delivery dates through on-time shipments from Europe, also established a first-rate logistics function.

o Earned several promotions up to director within the Engineering Department of a Florida-based division of Essex Corporation: directed high-quality product designs, upgraded operating systems critical to the production process, and effectively troubleshooted the complex power supply systems.

## CAREER EXPERIENCE

### ACME INTERNATIONAL CORPORATION, Any Town, NJ   1984–Present

Executive Vice President of Sales   1987–Present
Direct the Sales Organization with responsibility for direct sales, marketing, strategic planning, client development, import operations, logistics, distribution, and credit.

Vice President of Sales   1984–1987
Directed sales, marketing, strategic planning, and related functions.

### ESSEX CORPORATION, Any Town, FL   1975–1984

Director of Engineering   1980–1984
Earned several promotions based on engineering achievements in directing low-tolerance design and systems engineering projects. Also successfully planned and executed high-visibility manufacturing projects.

## MILITARY EXPERIENCE

European Military:   Honorably Discharged


**Affiliations:**      Society of U.S. Engineers; Production Engineers of the Northeast
**Citizenship:**      U.S. Citizen


## REFERENCES AVAILABLE UPON REQUEST

## DANIEL A. JOHNSON                    Brokerage Candidate

**123 Any Street, Any City, CA  XXXXX  (619) 555-1234**

Contact Name                                        Date
Title
Company
Street Address
City, State  Zip

Dear Mr./Ms. _____:

Having profitably applied skills in sales, marketing, client development, and dealer relations, I have consistently demonstrated the ability to start up and grow high-risk ventures which have generated substantial revenue and profits over the past decade.

I am very interested in exploring the possibility of joining _____ as a member of your brokerage team.

Specific results achieved by applying the skills detailed in the attached resume:

o Founded a highly profitable publishing firm, producing and marketing sophisticated how-to books which are highly marketable supplements to a popular how-to series marketed by Time-Life; consistently achieved aggressive, six-figure revenue goals.

o Authored the initial how-to book and through creative and persistent sales techniques, overcame intense resistance to form an international distribution network for my book series: retail distributors sold included such major chains as Barnes & Noble, Lauriats, and Doubleday.

o Cofounded and assumed the marketing and sales leadership role in a successful renovation business; substantial revenue growth well into six figures was achieved by aggressively marketing our contract services to Fortune 500 and smaller clients.

o Consistently exceeded targeted sales and profit goals throughout all stages of my business and entrepreneurial career.

A face-to-face meeting will afford us the opportunity to determine how I might be of service. You may contact me at your earliest convenience to set up an appointment. I look forward to our discussion.

Sincerely,

Enclosure:                                          Daniel A. Johnson

## Entrepreneur Marketed to Top Brokerage Firm

**DANIEL A. JOHNSON**                                        **Brokerage Candidate**

123 Any Street, Any City, CA XXXXX (619) 555-1234

## CREDENTIALS

B.A.   Drew University   GPA 3.5/4.0    1986

Honors/Activities:   Graduated with Honors; College Varsity Sports; Class President; Editor-in-Chief; Authored and scored plays; Studied with well-known artists

## MARKETING SKILLS/KNOWLEDGE

o Sales/marketing
o Direct sales/client development
o Product distribution/dealer relations
o Brochure development
o Corporate client interaction
o Cold-calling/telemarketing
o Proposal development/presentations
o Closing the sale
o Entrepreneurial/business owner

o Marketing strategies
o Creating markets
o Product piggybacking
o Product development
o Staff supervision/development
o Budgeting/finance/accounting
o Cost control
o Author/editor
o PC applications

## CAREER ACHIEVEMENTS

o Founded a highly profitable publishing firm, producing and marketing sophisticated how-to books which are highly marketable supplements to a popular how-to series marketed by Time-Life; consistently achieved aggressive, six-figure revenue goals.

o Authored the initial how-to book and through creative and persistent sales techniques, overcame intense resistance to form an international distribution network for my book series: retail distributors sold included such major chains as Barnes & Noble, Lauriats, and Doubleday.

o Cofounded and assumed the marketing and sales leadership role in a successful renovation business; substantial revenue growth well into six figures was achieved by aggressively marketing our contract services to Fortune 500 and smaller clients.

o Created and implemented effective marketing strategies to promote the concept of floor renovation as a cost-effective substitute for replacement—successfully sold services to large corporate clients as well as smaller companies.

o Codeveloped a new floor renovation product composed of a special mixture of penetrating oils; resulted in improved customer servicing.

o Consistently exceeded targeted sales and profit goals throughout all stages of my business and entrepreneurial career.

## CAREER EXPERIENCE

### ACME PUBLISHING CORPORATION, Any Town, CA    8/93–Present

Founder/President
Started firm; directed global marketing of how-to books:

o Formulated and implemented overall marketing and operational strategies.
o Authored and coauthored books.
o Established international distribution network including Barnes & Noble and Doubleday.
o Used PC applications for word processing, graphics, and transmission.
o Instituted tight financial and accounting controls.

### ABC RENOVATION CORPORATION, INC., Any Town, CA    6/86–8/93

Vice President of Sales and Marketing/Cofounder
Responsible for the start-up and marketing of this floor renovation company:

o Developed marketing and sales strategies.
o Scoped out and tapped new markets.
o Directed sales to Fortune 1000 and smaller clients.
o Coordinated staffing and supervision.
o Executed new product development.
o Instituted effective cost controls.

## REFERENCES AVAILABLE UPON REQUEST

## JOHN A. JOHNSON                              Sales/Marketing

**123 Any Street, Any City, NY XXXXX (212) 555-1234**

Contact Name                                        Date
Title
Company
Street Address
City, State  Zip

Dear Mr./Ms. _____:

I have combined proven leadership with skills in communication, strategic planning, organization, training, and logistics to restructure multimillion-dollar operations, turn around out-of-control situations, upgrade performance standards, direct record-setting campaigns, and accomplish what had been described as "the toughest challenges." Results achieved have been rewarded with top performance reviews and rapid promotion.

I am bringing to your attention my skills, achievements, talent for overcoming obstacles, ability to achieve bottom-line results, and desire to contribute to your revenue growth so that we can discuss my joining _____ as a member of your professional sales team.

Results achieved to date include:

o As Company Commander with responsibility for a rapid deployment force and $500 million in equipment, significantly improved unit's combat readiness by restructuring the training, maintenance, fitness, and property accountability: achieved operational readiness rating of 96%.

o As Brigade Logistics Officer for an Air Assault Division, was cited for making lasting contributions to Brigade's combat readiness: upgraded unit movement plans, directed motorpool reorganization, fielded several hundred High Mobility Vehicles, and directed the logistics for successful no-notice Emergency Deployment Exercises.

o Directed one of the most successful fund-raising drives ever conducted at Fort XYZ; exceeded established goals by orchestrating television and print media campaigns, mailing over 20,000 marketing letters, and developing automated control systems.

o Upon promotion to Operations and Training Officer, a position normally held by a higher ranking officer, authored the first documented Post Defense Plan, upgraded Special Forces training, streamlined Alert Notification Procedures, and radically revised NCO training programs achieving 30% better test scores.

I will work hard to achieve bottom-line results and look forward to discussing how I can contribute to your company's future success.

Sincerely,


Enclosure:                                          John A. Johnson

## JOHN A. JOHNSON                                    Sales/Marketing

123 Any Street, Any City, NY XXXXX (212) 555-1234

### ACADEMIC/MILITARY CREDENTIALS

B.S.        Distinguished Graduate        Ohio State University        1984

Additional Studies

o Completed graduate marketing courses toward Masters Degree
o Graduate of Combined Arms and Services Staff School
o Completed 20 comprehensive military courses including Advanced Officer Courses

### CAREER ACHIEVEMENTS

o As Company Commander with responsibility for a rapid deployment force and $500 million in equipment, significantly improved unit's combat readiness by restructuring the training, maintenance, fitness, and property accountability: achieved operational readiness rating of 96%.

o As Brigade Logistics Officer for an Air Assault Division, was cited for making lasting contributions to Brigade's combat readiness: upgraded unit movement plans, directed motorpool reorganization, fielded several hundred High Mobility Vehicles, and directed the logistics for successful no-notice Emergency Deployment Exercises.

o Directed one of the most successful fund-raising drives ever conducted at Fort XYZ; exceeded established goals by orchestrating television and print media campaigns, mailing over 20,000 marketing letters, and developing automated control systems.

o Upon promotion to Operations and Training Officer, a position normally held by a higher ranking officer, authored the first documented Post Defense Plan, upgraded Special Forces training, streamlined Alert Notification Procedures, and radically revised NCO training programs achieving 30% better test scores.

o Upon promotion to Executive Officer, upgraded operations directly contributing to Company B's much improved readiness position: reorganized supply system increasing accountability; upgraded maintenance program achieving higher availability; developed equipment loading plans which considered all possible contingency missions.

o Introduced zero-based budgeting in developing the Division's current and long-range training budgets: authored budgeting book which became the model and developed a program which created much greater understanding of the Training Management System.

o Turned around a tactically and logistically poor performing mortar platoon instituting combat readiness: proved that what had been considered impossible was possible by creating and executing a concept for mortar employment in rough terrain.

## CAREER EXPERIENCE

## UNITED STATES ARMY    10/84–Present

Officer in Charge, Fort XYZ, GA   4/95–Present
Doubled the number of training courses and instructional hours at no additional cost.

Brigade Logistics Officer, Fort XYZ, GA   6/92–4/95
Coordinated logistical support for the training exercises and contingency plans.

Company Commander, Fort XYZ, GA   3/90–6/92
Maintained a combat ready force capable of rapid deployment.

Operations and Training Officer, Fort ABC, FL   9/88–3/90
Created and developed effective mobilization and Post Defense.

Executive Officer/Captain, Fort GHI, OR   2/88–9/88
Responsible for logistical, administrative, and maintenance operations of an infantry company.

Platoon Leader, Fort GHI, OR   7/87–2/88
Planned and coordinated rough terrain survival training.

Platoon Leader, Fort DEF, OR   6/85–7/87
Formulated well-received fighting positions; significantly upgraded poor performing platoon.

Project Officer/1st Lieutenant, Fort ABC, FL   10/84–6/85
Managed production of visual aids; coordinated logistics for production in rough terrain.

## REFERENCES PROVIDED UPON REQUEST

## SAMUEL A. JONES (Version 2)                    International Sales/Finance

123 Any Street, Any Town, CA  XXXXX  (619) 555-1234

Contact Name                                                         Date
Title
Company
Address
City, State  Zip

Dear Mr./Ms. _____:

I have combined in-depth knowledge of Eastern Europe with skills in sales, finance, manufacturing, banking, credit, and management to generate revenue, resolve serious cash shortages, achieve critical cost savings, and accelerate productivity for American and Eastern European operations. Achievements at a major European company were rewarded with multiple management promotions in spite of my unwillingness to join the Communist Party.

I am bringing to your attention my skills, achievements, ability to achieve results under negative conditions, and talent for executing tough projects including my escape from Eastern Europe so that we can discuss my joining _____ as a member of your International Sales or Finance Team.

Major achievements to date include:

o  Earned promotion to the much-sought-after position of Director of Finance at a major European operation, the largest such operation in the country, in spite of my negative attitude toward joining the Communist Party: assumed total responsibility for the review and approval of expense outlays for the operation; reduced the multimillion-dollar expense budget 35% while improving overall productivity.

o  Upon promotion to Financial Analyst at a European factory, researched and prepared well-conceived financial plans that exceeded cost-reduction targets without sacrificing operational effectiveness; took the lead in negotiating with banks to meet weekly payrolls in the face of critical cash-flow problems.

o  Earned rarely achieved first-year promotion within the Cost Department of a European manufacturer based on producing quality multimillion-dollar cost studies: assumed ever-increasing responsibilities with multimillion-dollar signing authority.

o  Over a four-year period, planned and executed my escape from the Communist Regime: completed a physical training program; maneuvered access to a waterfront complex; escaped across an inlet and posed as a West German citizen to get to West Germany where the United States granted asylum.

o  As a Partner in a San Diego firm, purchase, restore, and successfully market antique furniture; as a Sales Representative for an upscale American business, acted as Assistant Manager and consistently exceeded sales quotas selling $50,000 worth of product in a three-week period: nurtured a loyal client base right up to the unfortunate closing of the business.

I look forward to discussing how I can contribute to your international revenue and profit growth.

                                                         Sincerely,


Enclosure:                                               Samuel A. Jones

## SAMUEL A. JONES                    International Sales/Finance

123 Any Street, Any City, CA XXXXX  (619) 555-1234

|        | B.S.   Finance/Economics   Finance Institute   1981 |

Honors:         Chosen to attend selective Institute
                Recipient of major scholarship; Graduated with honors

Citizenship:    U.S.
International:   Eastern Europe Expert
Languages:      Fluent English, German, French, and Italian; some knowledge of Spanish

### CAREER SKILLS/KNOWLEDGE

o International relations
o Eastern Europe expertise
o European banking relations
o Credit application/approval process
o Manufacturing/factory operations
o European management techniques
o European financial/cost controls
o European pricing/capital planning

o Sales/marketing
o Client development
o Closing/customer service
o Financial management
o Controller operations/expense control
o Financial planning
o Forecasting/budgeting
o Cost/pricing studies

### CAREER ACHIEVEMENTS

o Earned promotion to the much-sought-after position of Director of Finance at a major European operation, the largest such operation in the country, in spite of my negative attitude toward joining the Communist Party: assumed total responsibility for the review and approval of expense outlays for the operation; reduced the multimillion-dollar expense budget 35% while improving overall productivity.

o Upon promotion to Financial Analyst at a European factory, researched and prepared well-conceived financial plans that exceeded cost-reduction targets without sacrificing operational effectiveness; took the lead in negotiating with banks to meet weekly payrolls in the face of critical cash-flow problems.

o Earned rarely achieved first-year promotion within the Cost Department of a European manufacturer based on producing quality multimillion-dollar cost studies: assumed ever-increasing responsibilities with multimillion-dollar signing authority.

o Over a four-year period, planned and executed my escape from the Communist Regime: completed a physical training program; maneuvered access to a waterfront complex; escaped across an inlet and posed as a West German citizen to get to West Germany where the United States granted asylum.

o As a Partner in a San Diego firm, purchase, restore, and successfully market antique furniture; as a Sales Representative for an upscale American business, acted as Assistant Manager and consistently exceeded sales quotas selling $50,000 worth of product in a three-week period: nurtured a loyal client base right up to the unfortunate closing of the business.

## INTERNATIONAL EXPERIENCE

### Eastern European Operation   6/81–3/86

Director of Finance   1/84–3/86
Audited and exercised final approval for all major expense requests for this manufacturer. Achieved substantial cost reductions while improving productivity.

Financial Analyst   5/83–1/84
Formulated financial plans including detailed forecasts and budgets; interacted with managers to reduce expenses and capital expenditures. Worked with financial institutions to address critical cash-flow problems.

Senior Cost Analyst   6/81–5/83
Formulated detailed cost studies as a foundation for better pricing practices. Interacted with departments to accumulate accurate cost data.

## AMERICAN EXPERIENCE

### Insurance Firm, Any City, CA   3/95–Present

Sales Representative:  Aggressively cold-call and follow-up to close clients.

### Investment Firm, Any City, CA   3/90–Present

Cofounder:  Purchase, restore, and market antique furniture.

### Essex Company, Any City, CA   4/87–3/90

Sales Representative:  Sold expensive products and nurtured clients until business closed.

## REFERENCES PROVIDED UPON REQUEST

## LAURA A. JONES                    Professional Sales

**123 Any Street, Any City, PA XXXXX (215) 555-1234**

Contact Name                                        Date
Title
Company
Street Address
City, State  Zip

Dear Mr./Ms. _____:

Having recently been promoted to Assistant Sales Manager in a computer industry corporation, a role in which I have responsibility for both a direct sales quota and sales management,
I have proven my ability to achieve bottom-line results. Sales skills which I have developed
and applied to achieve quota include: aggressive cold-calling; telemarketing; effective presentations; overcoming objections; closing; customer training; effective follow-through to
promote future sales.

I am very interested in discussing the possibility of joining _____ as a
professional salesperson.

Specific results achieved to date include:

o Rank among the top revenue-producers with Telco Corporation, a computer industry company; earned promotion to Assistant Sales Manager while retaining an aggressive sales
  quota.

o Quote from the President of Telco: "Ms. Jones has generated more prospects and sales appointments and produced more custom proposals for prospects than anyone in the company with equivalent time and experience. After only seven months, she is performing at
  the level of a two-year veteran."

o Selected as the first salesperson at Telco to break into the tough, highly competitive
  Philadelphia market; made significant inroads and accelerated unit sales through persistent
  cold-calling and telemarketing combined with disciplined follow-up and persuasive closes.

o Received strong feedback and lucrative deals from Telco customers who characterized my
  overall approach from initial contact to proposal presentation as thorough and professional.

I feel that it will be mutually advantageous to meet and talk face-to-face. You may contact me
at the above number so that we can make the necessary arrangements. Thank you in advance
for your consideration.

                                        Sincerely,


Enclosure:                              Laura A. Jones

# LAURA A. JONES                                Professional Sales

123 Any Street, Any City, PA  XXXXX  (215) 555-1234

## CREDENTIALS

| M.S. | University of Pennsylvania | 1985 | GPA 3.8/4.0 |
|------|----------------------------|------|-------------|
| B.S. | State University of New York | 1983 | Self-financed |

Courses at Studies for Professional Women (Philadelphia, PA 1989):

> o The Successful Marketing of High-Tech Products
> o Proven Strategies in Achieving Corporate Objectives

Attended Workshops on "Prospecting and Cold-calling Tactics"

| Honors: | Earned Commendation for Master's Thesis; Graduated with Honors |
|---------|----------------------------------------------------------------|
| Member: | National Association of Computer Professionals |
|  | Pennsylvania Women and Men in Computer Sales |

## SALES/MARKETING ACHIEVEMENTS

o Rank among the top revenue-producers with Telco Corporation, a computer industry company; earned promotion to Assistant Sales Manager while retaining an aggressive sales quota.

o Quote from the President of Telco: "Ms. Jones has generated more prospects and sales appointments and produced more custom proposals for prospects than anyone in the company with equivalent time and experience. After only seven months, she is performing at the level of a two-year veteran."

o Selected as the first salesperson at Telco to break into the tough, highly competitive Philadelphia market; made significant inroads and accelerated unit sales through persistent cold-calling and telemarketing combined with disciplined follow-up and persuasive closes.

o Received strong feedback and lucrative deals from Telco customers who characterized my overall approach from initial contact to proposal presentation as thorough and professional.

o As an Account Executive for a Philadelphia-based Personnel Firm, achieved and exceeded placement quotas.

## SALES SKILLS/KNOWLEDGE

o Cold-calling/telemarketing
o Decision-maker contact/client development
o Effective proposals/presentations
o Cost-benefit studies development
o Overcoming objections
o Negotiations/closing
o Follow-up/training/support

## SALES EXPERIENCE

### TELCO, INC. (COMPUTER INDUSTRY), Any Town, PA    2/96–Present

Assistant Sales Manager    4/96–Present
Promotion. Responsibility for both direct sales and sales management:

o  Recruiting, hiring, and training and development including: prospecting, overcoming objections, proposals, presentations, and closing.
o  Continue to generate sales through aggressive client development.

Sales Representative    2/96–4/96
Chosen as the first salesperson assigned to the tough South Philadelphia territory. With the goal of establishing an initial client base, cold-called, prospected, and followed-up leads. Worked with clients as a computer consultant to close sales. Received on-going product and sales training.

### ABC PERSONNEL, INC., Any Town, PA    7/95–2/96

Account Executive
Responsibilities executed:

o  Developed and maintained new business in downtown Philadelphia; designed sales strategies; cold called; formulated sales tactics.
o  Scoped out and assessed prospect needs; prepared tailored sales presentations; interacted with decision makers; negotiated agreements; monitored service quality.
o  Maintained sales reports and records; analyzed sales results; assisted in the design and development of sales literature.
o  Demonstrated strength in overcoming obstacles; received excellent feedback based on results.

## OTHER EXPERIENCE

Metropolitan Health Care, Inc., Any Town, PA    8/88–7/95

Director of Activities
Directed the support staff in the creation and execution of the Activities Programs.

The Essex Center, Any Town, PA    6/85–8/88

Activities Director
Created and instituted Activities Programs for the mentally challenged.

## REFERENCES AVAILABLE UPON REQUEST

## WALTER A. CUMMINGS                    IT/Systems Professional

123 Any Street, Any City, NJ XXXXX (201) 555-1234

Contact Name                                                Date
Title
Company
Street Address
City, State  Zip

Dear Mr./Ms. _____:

Having developed a full command of the EDP Operations of both large and small data centers during the last nine years, I have demonstrated the ability to apply technical and managerial skills to consistently meet tight deadlines and achieve bottom-line results. I would like to bring my skills, accomplishments, and take-charge attitude to the attention of your company.

I am very interested in exploring the possibility of joining _____ as a member of your systems management team.

Specific MIS skills applied to meet even the most aggressive production schedules and achieve other targeted goals (related to my multiple DP supervisory and technical roles) include: operations management; production planning; production scheduling; tape library management; IBM System 3033 management; negotiation of management priorities; and additional EDP technical and supervisory skills.

I feel it will be to our mutual benefit to meet and talk face-to-face. You may contact me at the above number to set up an appointment. I look forward to our meeting.

                                        Sincerely,


Enclosure:                              Walter A. Cummings

## WALTER A. CUMMINGS                    IT/Systems Professional

123 Any Street, Any City, NJ XXXXX (201) 555-1234

## CAREER SKILLS/KNOWLEDGE

- o Operations management—System 32
- o Tape library supervision
- o Scheduling supervision/negotiation
- o IBM System 3033
- o IBM Systems 360/370
- o Job Control Language (JCL)
- o Peripheral equipment usage

- o UCCI Tape Management System (TMS)
- o ROSCOE application
- o Abend analysis
- o JCL maintenance
- o Knowledge of utilities
- o Table development
- o Retention management

## CAREER EXPERIENCE/ACHIEVEMENTS

### A FORTUNE 100 CORPORATION, Any City, NJ    4/92–Present

Production Planning Supervisor
Promoted to this position; responsibilities include:

- o Develop and implement realistic systems output schedules based on user requirements, optimum systems usage, and lead-times.
- o Negotiate compromises to accommodate conflicting user objectives.
- o Screen all new program packages to verify programmer meets standards relative to JCL—will accept or reject packages.
- o Access two IBM 3033s via ROSCOE terminal.
- o Monitor schedule for projects to be processed for next-day completion; retrieve scheduled jobs from Partitioned Data Set to set up for running based on notes and commentary in the JCL.
- o Perform maintenance/changes to JCL; run utilities—copy tapes, scratch files, catalog files, etc.

Results achieved to date include:

- o Consistently meet scheduled completion dates relative to major project output.
- o Implemented UCC1 on-line system for tape library management—a major productivity improvement.
- o Designed and implemented corporate wide a critically needed disaster recovery program.
- o Successfully developed and applied computer, human-interaction, and negotiating skills to achieve targeted goals.

### ANOTHER FORTUNE 100 CORPORATION, Any City, NJ    6/88–4/92

Scheduling Supervisor
Promoted to this position. Responsibilities included: supervised tape library and scheduled computer time; analyzed and corrected JCL and system abends.

Improved on-time performance by over 30%; significantly improved departmental efficiency.

## ABC COMPANY, Any Town, NJ    7/86-6/88

Operations Supervisor
Responsibilities included:

o  Supervised and trained operations staff.
o  Operated IBM System 32 minicomputer.
o  Performed system maintenance.
o  Implemented department standards and procedures.

Significant improvements were achieved in processing turnaround time and overall productivity.

Reason for leaving: Company discontinued operations.

## OTHER EXPERIENCE

## XYZ SALES COMPANY, Any City, NJ    6/85-7/86

Credit Analyst
Promotion. Researched financial background of prospective accounts and compiled detailed
financial profiles for management review. Collected past due interest totaling $150,000.

## ESSEX CORPORATION, Any City, NJ    3/84-6/85

Tape Librarian
Developed training manual for new tape librarians and implemented department standards
and procedures. Supported and maintained on-line tape library management system.

## QRS SYSTEMS, Any City, NY    1/82-3/84

Service Support
Maintained portfolios for individuals and banks; updated transaction reports.

## EDUCATION

**College:**    57 hours of college credits: data processing, programming, and general business

**Training:**    o  JCL/Utilities Course by IBM
o  Credit Financial Analysis by Dun & Bradstreet
o  Speed Reading Course

## REFERENCES PROVIDED UPON REQUEST

# Part II

# Launching a Job Search Campaign in the Twenty-First Century

━━━━━━━━━━━━━━ **REALITY CHECK** ━━━━━━━━━━━━━━

In the career and job search game, the only thing that really matters is results. As demonstrated through real-life case histories, clients who combined our market-tested resume and cover letter packages with our Expansionist Theory have enjoyed a placement success rate that far surpassed the outplacement industry norm.

# 8

# Top Ten Rules of the Job Market: What Worked for Satisfied Clients

_____ **REALITY CHECK** _____

In the career and job search game, the only thing that matters is results. As demonstrated through the real-life case histories featured throughout this text, clients who combined our choice marketing packages with Montag Associates' Expansionist Theory achieved their targeted career and job search goals.

As a preface to the discussion of our Expansionist Theory in Chapter 9, here are 10 market-tested rules that helped clients and readers produce job offers even in the worst job markets of the past two decades. While the competition dawdled, clients of Montag Associates were busy outmarketing them by applying the following principles:

*Rule 1. Failure to Take Control of Your Career and Job Search Planning Forfeits Control to Others.* In the final analysis, each one of us is, and should have always been, responsible for our own job satisfaction and security. Yet, as we enter the twenty-first century, this take-charge philosophy—and the tools to implement it—

continue to elude a workforce whose servitude to corporate America has left it short of the professional job search skills required to take control. This skills deficit spurred hundreds of blue-chip managers to pay thousands of dollars each to the author of this text—which is dedicated to rectifying this deficiency.

*Rule 2. Taking Control of Your Career and Job Life Is Anything but a Straightforward Task.* How naive is our workforce regarding the effort required to conduct a competent search? This is best answered by saying that I will scream bloody murder if I hear one more job seeker tell a network news reporter, "I've done everything possible to get a job. I mailed out 100 resumes in the past six months." Admitting in front of several million viewers that it took six months to do three days' work makes the American workforce look absurd. Here and now, let it be understood that a search is equal to a full-time job, period.

*Rule No. 3. To Take Advantage of Luck and Timing, Your Paperwork Must Be in the Right Hands at Exactly the Right Moment.* The search process is, and will always be, a numbers game. Universal failure to play the numbers game—buoyed by logic that says 100 contacts are somehow just as good as 2,000—is so baffling that it makes the workforce look asinine. Speaking selfishly on behalf of clients and readers, this widespread folly is good news since it gives a huge competitive edge to those who do play the game. Clients of Montag Associates have repeatedly outdistanced the competition with a winning formula that says power packaging plus *high-volume marketing* equals multiple interviews and job offers.

*Rule No. 4. You Can't Get an Invitation to Interview with Your Resume and Cover Letter in Your Briefcase.* This rule was born one night long ago when I shouted these words across the room to a client who had just arrived after a 12-hour day at a job she hated. She was so angry at her obnoxious advisor that she immediately accelerated her stalled campaign. Within six weeks, we were celebrating a great job offer from 3M Corporation.

*Rule No. 5. There Are Smart Ways to Work, But No Shortcuts to the Right Interviews.* This rule has given clients a major competitive edge that resulted in multiple job offers.

*Rule No. 6. The Real Power in a Job Search Is the Power to Say No.* Anyone can say yes to the first job offer. Producing multiple job offers affords the freedom to turn down bad ones. This is power. This is taking control of your career and job life. (Exception:

Accepting the first offer in order to pay the bills and finance your ongoing job search is, of course, an exception to the rule. Buying time to achieve career goals is certainly taking control.)

*Rule No. 7. In an Era of Fleeting Job Security, the Twenty-First-Century Workforce Must Cast Off Traditional Definitions of Employment and Security.* Old ideas about job security have been rendered null and void. Most of the workforce has yet to accept this reality. This mass denial—and corresponding inaction—is good news for those who can exploit the possibilities accompanying change.

*Rule No. 8. The Circa 2002 Global Economy Mandates That Contract Job Openings Be Treated as a Near-Equivalent of Permanent Employment.* The growth in outsourcing and executive temp services—offering high-paying, long-term assignments—reflects a historic growth in demand for contingent workers who now make up more than one-third of the total workforce. According to the prestigious Washington, DC-based *Conference Board*, managerial and professional contract workers will assume an ever-increasing role in the twenty-first century. It's readily apparent that contract jobs are now only marginally less secure than permanent jobs in a corporate world addicted to downsizing.

*Rule No. 9. Never Underestimate the Mega-Power of the Internet/World Wide Web (WWW).* Those of you who have yet to harness this power should realize you are aiding and abetting the competition—who are already employing this 24/7 job search tool to supplement the research library, post office, word processing service, copy shop, and hard-copy classifieds. Want ads from around the globe can now be accessed, researched, and answered within minutes at such respected Internet Web sites as www.CareerJournal.com, www.Futurestep.com, www.BrilliantPeople.com, www.ChiefMonster.com, www.CareerBuilder.com, www.SpencerStuart.com, www.ExecuNet.com, www.PamDixon.com, www.RileyGuide.com, www.Weddles.com, www.CareerDoctor.org, www.JobStar.org, and hundreds of other great Web sites identified in *The 24/7 Online Job Search Directory* (Chapter 11). Internet service providers like America Online (AOL), CompuServe (CS), and Microsoft Network (MSN) make accessing the Internet easy—log on now.

*Rule No. 10. Recognize the Exceptional Power of the Telephone to Produce Results.* This rule is designed to encourage those fearless enough to tap the singular power of the telephone. A case in point is a client who literally phoned his way into a major corporation that had all but frozen new hiring. Determined to join this recovering blue-chip, George exercised his skills as a top-ranked sales manager to telephone his way up the chain of command at IBM. Refusing to accept no for an answer, he cold-called, circumvented, and neutralized a dozen bureaucrats before unearthing the right connection. After the initial interview, George followed with more calls that produced more interviews that, in turn, produced a lucrative job offer. For those with fortitude, the telephone can work miracles.

These proven principles combined with our power packaging, Expansionist Theory (Chapter 9), and 24/7 Online Job Search Directory (Chapter 11) will give you the same competitive edge that has produced thousands of satisfied clients and readers—who took control of their work lives.

# 9

## Launching the Search: The Expansionist Theory

_____ **REALITY CHECK** _____

In comparing restrictive search theories to our Expansionist Theory, remember this simple truth: You can never be guilty of making too many contacts, but you can certainly be guilty of making too few. Widespread failure to heed this fact has ceded a big competitive edge to our clients who surpass the competition with high-volume marketing that gets job offers.

### INTRODUCTION: A WINNING FORMULA

Armed with the market-tested resume and cover letter packages drafted in Part I, you already hold a competitive edge that will facilitate and expedite your job search. While it's true that the resume alone will not get you a job, it's equally certain that quality marketing packages can produce the right interviews, including many that our clients would have otherwise failed to land. Power packaging coupled with our Expansionist Theory and use of the World Wide Web (see Chapters 10 and 11) has been a winning formula for clients of Montag Associates—who repeatedly outmarket, outsmart, and outdistance the competition.

## THE EXPANSIONIST THEORY:
## NO RESTRICTIONS, NO DUPLICITY

First, let's separate the wheat from the chaff. The literary chaff of the career genre is the harmfully restrictive guidance that imposes arbitrary limits on the job search process. Although exclusionary advice comes from many sources, the disciples of networking have effected the most damage on a workforce already stifled by its servitude to corporate America. Sometimes employing scare tactics regarding breaches of confidentiality that could endanger your present job, the networking gurus have persuaded millions to reject direct company contact and other equally viable search methods—that are relegated to secondary status. Speaking selfishly on behalf of readers and clients—85% of whom got results through means other than networking—this widespread inertia is good. It gives an enormous competitive edge to those who understand that networking is just one step of a multistep, high-volume, patented process that we call the *Expansionist Theory.* While their peers bow to the gurus, clients of Montag Associates are busy outmarketing them by at least 1,000%—achieving a placement success rate that buries the competition.

### REALITY CHECK

To capitalize on luck and timing, your marketing package must be in the hands of the decision maker at exactly the right moment. A job search is, and will always be, a numbers game. Widespread failure to play the game has benefited those who do, including clients of Montag Associates who simply outclass the competition.

## EXPANSIONIST THEORY, STEP ONE:
## DIRECT COMPANY CONTACT

The unqualified success of direct company contact stands as the sharpest rebuke to the irresponsible disciples of networking. Ignoring unsubstantiated drivel about breaches of confidentiality and overexposure, over half of the executives and professionals served by our firm in the past decade achieved career moves through this method. Armed with power packaging, CD-ROM listings, the *Directory of Corporate Affiliations*, and the Web, clients have researched, selected, and queried thousands of executive decision makers, who have responded very well to our skills and achievement-oriented

---

**FIGURE 9.1a. The Power of Direct Company Contact: A Case History**

---

**Client:** Robert A. Gordon

**Volume of direct company contacts:** over 1,300 packages mailed/e-mailed/faxed (continuous process)

**Results achieved within three months:**

| | |
|---|---|
| Favorable responses (phone): | 73 (plus 1 to 2 calls/day going into the fourth month) |
| Formal telephone interviews: | 38 (calls still coming in going into the fourth month) |
| Formal in-person interviews: | 19 (calls still coming in going into the fourth month) |
| Formal job offers received: | 8 (formal offer letters) |

Companies extending job offers:   Agra Financial Services Corporation (pseudonym)
      Accepted
  Mont Blanc Capital Corporation (pseudonym)
  Electronic Industries, Inc. (pseudonym)
  Babcock Industries, Inc.
  Bowater, Inc.
  Irving Trust Company
  Perkin-Elmer Corporation
  U.S. Concord Corporation

**The bottom line:** Within three months this client had generated eight good offers through direct contact.

---

packages. Clients have been told repeatedly that the first paragraph of the letter *hooked* the reader, enticing him/her to review the entire package, so never underestimate the power of the words that you drafted in Part I. At the end of the day, the sheer magnitude and quality of our marketing campaigns have produced extraordinary results for clients, period.

## A Definitive Case History

The power of direct contact is exemplified in the fast-track career of Bob Gordon, who became the youngest executive in a financial services division of a European giant. As a long-time client who has conducted multiple searches in the past decade, Bob has progressed from a recent graduate of a state university to a financial manager with a six-figure salary (one of several offers that emerged from a job search detailed in Figure 9.1a). As shown in Figure 9.1a, his job search campaign included mass mailing customized packages (Figures 9.1b to 9.1d) to more than 1,300 companies. Armed with CD-ROM listings obtained from Web sites like www.reedref.com and www.nwbuildnet.com, Bob completed the mailing in under three weeks. The responses were immediate and positive. In order to eliminate nonstarters, Bob screened callers more rigorously than they screened him. Within three months, our direct campaign had generated countless phone calls, 73 positive responses, 38 phone interviews, 19 on-site interviews, and 8 good job offers (Figure 9.1a). As always, this client, whose talent and charisma yield an imposing interview-to-offer ratio, was firmly in control of his career and work life. Power packaging combined with high-volume marketing had once again produced results.

## EXPANSIONIST THEORY, STEP TWO: RECRUITER CONTACTS

Clients of Montag Associates deal with the maligned recruiting industry for one reason—they have job orders. But our clients deal from strength. Since recruiters are only one step of a process, clients never have to depend on an industry whose loyalty naturally lies with their client companies. The bottom line is that recruiters are vital to any search as long as you don't rely on them. Although the retainer firms—represented by such icons as Korn/Ferry International and Heidrick & Struggles—are often considered more reputable, the contingency firms should not be overlooked. Recruiters in both categories have helped our clients. Armed with CD-ROM or floppy-disk versions of the *Directory of Executive Recruiters* (available at (800) 531-0007 or www.kennedyinfo.com), our clients outmarket the competition by contacting at least 500 search firms. Volume counts, period.

### A Definitive Case History

The power of recruiter contacts is illustrated in the career of Leslie Barnes, a training and development executive whose talent has been rewarded with endless company awards and a vice presidency. Another long-time client of ours, she encountered the indiscriminate wrath of a new executive who was equally vile to all. Realizing it was time to take action, Leslie called to update her marketing package and initiate a search that would include recruiters, direct contact, the classifieds, and networking. As shown in Figure 9.2a, she sent custom resume and cover letter packages (Figures 9.2b to 9.2d) to more than 700 search firms. Armed with the *Directory of Executive Recruiters* on CD-ROM, she completed the mailing in just a few weeks. Within four months, our recruiter campaign produced countless phone calls, 26 formal telephone interviews, 29 on-site interviews and

**ROBERT A. GORDON**          Auditing/Finance/Management/Consulting

One Sutton Place, New York, NY 10022  Telephone: (212) 555-1234  e-mail: rgmanager@aol.com

Contact Name                                                Date
Title
Company
Street Address
City, State  Zip

Dear Mr./Ms. _____:

As the division's youngest department director—reporting to an executive vice president—I assumed full responsibility for restructuring, automating, and expanding the corporate audit department at Global Resource Corporation. Results achieved over the past five years were rewarded with rapid promotions and a 220% growth in salary.

I am presenting for your review my skills, P&L accomplishments, and talent for turning around weak operations so that we can discuss my joining _____ as a member of your corporate finance/audit management team.

Results achieved at Global Resource Corporation (GRC) include:

o Promoted from Manager to Director of Corporate Audit after profitably redefining and expanding our corporate charter: shifted focus from routine compliance audits to unstructured operational reviews designed to identify and resolve high-impact problems within GRC; the immediate payback of these in-depth audits led to further expansion of our charter as corporate audit was elevated to chief investigatory arm of GRC's top management.

o Reinforced our growing credibility by investigating and stopping potential crises including legal and financial exposures related to our non-compliance with state and local tax laws (applicable to customer lease payments): corrective actions included automating out-of-control manual processes; also recommended critically needed systems integration, as well as organizational changes that ultimately produced a major staff realignment.

o Worked directly with GRC and C&L top management to effect major cost savings in year-end audit fees: saved tens of thousands of dollars in charges by developing new CAAT applications for use by C&L; created an automated account confirmation process for GRC/GR of Quebec; provided strong technical support generating special reports and complex analyses; expanded year-end audits to include other financial service subsidiaries.

o Exposed and corrected control problems related to multimillion-dollar streams of cash flowing back and forth between GRC and its vendors: stopped big dollar overpayments to vendors caused by poorly trained staffers who had failed to net current/overdue amounts owed to GRC by vendors against amounts owed to vendors by GRC.

It should be to our benefit to meet and discuss the possibilities. I look forward to discussing how I can contribute to your company's future success.

                                                Best Regards,


Enclosure:                                      Robert A. Gordon

## ROBERT A. GORDON      Auditing/Finance/Management/Consulting

One Sutton Place, New York, NY 10022   Telephone: (212) 555-1234   e-mail: rgmanager@aol.com

### CAREER SKILLS/KNOWLEDGE

o Auditing operations/internal consulting
o Department management/turnaround
o Annual audit plan development/budgeting
o Computerized audit department start-up
o Manpower planning/staff development
o Major cost reductions/productivity growth
o Major operational/financial audits
o Process improvement/compliance audits
o Services/manufacturing/government/defense
o Year-end audits/outside auditor fee savings
o Major report writing/communications
o Easytrieve/Panaudit Plus/ACL

o Financial/administration/leasing
o Financial controls/collections turnaround
o Leasing and financing revenue audits
o Asset remarketing/maturity programs
o Dealer activity and control audits
o Upgraded wholesale flooring controls
o Upgraded dealer rate participation controls
o Upgraded sales/property tax administration
o MIS/EDP operational reviews/security
o Hardware/software policy development
o Lotus macros/databases/utilities
o MVS (TSO, ISPF, JCL)

### CAREER ACHIEVEMENTS AT GLOBAL RESOURCE CORPORATION (GRC)

o Earned rapid promotions by significantly improving the image, credibility, and productivity of corporate audit: introduced state-of-the-art auditing techniques and upgraded our obsolete systems in spite of strong resistance from senior systems management; ultimately enlightened the MIS Director who implemented required software upgrades; project managed the implementation and instituted training seminars to accelerate the conversion.

o In our new role as the president's chief investigatory arm, identified and reported high-dollar/legal exposures that led to major corrective actions in several areas including commodity validation/ dealer guarantee programs.

o Exposed high-dollar problems in the lease/remarketing program that led to the formation of a corporate office, as well as upgraded staffing and systems at GR of Quebec: found virtually no controls over repossessed inventory, asset disposal, and loss recovery; over a 10-month period, the inventory of repossessed items aged over 120 days increased from 17% to 56% of total assets; poor loss recovery led to a doubling of write-offs.

o Expanded our region audit coverage—and reviewed $450 million in credit transactions—by creating a library of standard CAAT applications for sample selections, data integrity tests, analytical reports, and IRR calculations; further improved coverage by auditing big dollar exposures including dealer interest and charge delinquencies; this audit led to immediate corrective actions and collection of nearly a million dollars in overdue payments.

o Based on an interest rate verification program designed and programmed in Easytrieve/Panaudit Plus, exposed numerous deviations from customer finance program guidelines: because unexplained variances were detected in 44% of the contracts issued during a one-month period, IA issued company-wide bulletins, prepared monthly reports for top management, and worked with the regions to institute critically needed manual/systems controls.

o Sanctioned immediate corrective actions to address the absence of centralized strategic planning and controls within MIS: forced its management to define GRC's systems requirements, justify multimillion-dollar budgets, and correct poor budget controls—that had caused at least a million dollars in unwarranted expenditures.

ROBERT A. GORDON

## CAREER EXPERIENCE

### GLOBAL RESOURCE CORPORATION, New York, NY    4/91–Present

Director of Corporate Audit    2/95–Present
As the company's youngest department director, assumed full P&L responsibility for corporate audit.

Manager of Corporate Audit    3/93–2/95
As the company's youngest department manager, assumed coresponsibility for the corporate audit staff.

Audit Leader    8/92–3/93
Major promotion. In charge of planning, staff development, and auditing operations.

Senior Audit Specialist    4/91–8/92
Promotion with significant salary increase.

### SUNBEAM CORPORATION, Miami, FL    4/89–4/91

Senior Operational Auditor    11/89–4/91
Double promotion. In auditing a major division, found millions in committed-yet-unapproved appropriations, out-of-control inventory, and unjustified project delays; uncovered millions of dollars in purchases without valid PO numbers as well as weak competitive bidding. During a major manufacturing audit, ordered a product disassembly that disclosed serious and costly discrepancies between the actual parts, BOM, and engineering drawings.

Associate Auditor/Corporate Management Training Program    4/89–11/89
Chosen for one of six training slots. After just a few months, acted as in-charge auditor for an unstructured review of a problem division: created the audit plan and uncovered millions of dollars in cannibalized company property.

## EDUCATION

BS Accounting    University of Illinois    Dean's List    Self-financed    1989

## CREDENTIALS/MANAGEMENT TRAINING

o  Active Member: Institute of Internal Auditors (IIA)
o  Zenger-Miller: Front-line Leadership Development Program
o  French and Spanish Languages: semi-fluent

## COMMUNITY/VOLUNTEER ACTIVITIES

o  Active Advisor/Consultant: Junior Achievement (Teach Economics/Entrepreneurialism)
o  Active Volunteer: Harbor/River Watch Program (water testing project)

---

**FIGURE 9.2a. The Power of Recruiter Contacts: A Case History**

---

**Client:** Leslie A. Barnes

**Volume of recruiter contacts:** over 700 packages mailed/e-mailed/faxed (continuous process)

**Results achieved within four months:**

| | |
|---|---|
| Recruiters responding (by phone): | 129 (plus activity going into the fifth month) |
| Client company interviews—phone: | 26 (calls still coming in going into the fifth month) |
| Client company interviews—on-site: | 29 (calls still coming in going into the fifth month) |
| Formal job offers received: | 4 (bona fide offer letters) |

| | | |
|---|---|---|
| Companies extending job offers: | Grumman Corporation (pseudonym) | Accepted |
| | General Reinsurance Corporation | |
| | Philips Medical | |
| | General Electric Corporation | |

**The bottom line:** Within four months this client had generated four good offers through recruiter contacts.

---

4 good job offers (Figure 9.2a). She accepted a job as Vice President of Training and Development for a high-tech division of a Fortune 500 company. A quality, high-volume campaign got the job done once again.

## EXPANSIONIST THEORY, STEP THREE: THE CLASSIFIED ADS

As detailed in Chapters 10 and 11, the World Wide Web has virtually nullified all the old excuses for failing to answer classified ads promptly. It has ended the agony of reading, analyzing, and sorting hard-copy classifieds—whose tiny print has all but blinded readers. Using online classifieds is so easy that it's hard to make a mistake. Clients simply sign on to an Internet service provider and type in "www.CareerBuilder.com" to get instant access to the help-wanted sections of several leading newspapers. They next enter key words, job classifications, and geographic preferences to pinpoint relevant job openings that are then conveniently listed. They have finished a task that once took days or even weeks, and they can transmit their responses to the ads in record time. The 24/7 Internet job search is fully explored in the next two chapters (10 and 11).

## LESLIE A. BARNES          Human Resources/Training Executive

199 Washington, Briarcliff Manor, NY  10510   Telephone: (914) 555-1234  e-mail: dmanager@aol.com

Contact Name                                                     Date
Title
Company
Address
City, State  Zip

Dear Mr./Ms. _____:

As Director of Training and Development, I earned awards for achieving strategic goals within
tight budgets. Tough vendor negotiations and judicious use of internal resources allowed T&D
to achieve bottom-line results including Daytron's first-ever: middle-management TQM; self-
managed production teams; technical skills inventory; and off-site strategic planning.

As an achiever who has survived a 75% reduction in staff, I am presenting for your review
my skills and talent for getting the job done so that we can discuss my joining one of your
client companies as Vice President of T&D.

Results achieved during the past several years at Daytron Systems include:

o As director of our cross-functional Training Council, ensured that T&D did everything possible to
   meet business plan requirements within limited budgets: met all functional requirements and employee development needs by identifying and resolving any and all shortfalls in training and basic
   education; stretched our budget dollars by initiating and directing after-hours and state-funded
   courses at nominal cost to the corporation.

o At the request of Daytron's Chairman, restructured and directed the strategic business review process: drafted members of the Chairman's senior staff to lead teams accountable for resolving issues
   critical to the survival of the business; led to corrective actions that increased productivity and generated high dollar cost savings.

o As part of Daytron's desperate search for additional operating capital, initiated and directed over 11
   months of intense and hard fought negotiations that produced a $2 million commitment from the
   State of New York.

o Chosen by the Vice President of Human Resources to head a steering committee chartered to create
   TQM teams composed of cross-functional middle managers addressing management-level business
   issues: facilitated the definition of specific business issues around which some 20 teams were
   formed; among other major process improvements, these teams significantly reduced the cycle for
   producing multimillion-dollar proposals from 75 to 19 days.

o Recruited to build Daytron's first training department: overcame initial barrage of opposition and
   cynicism to start and direct a cost-effective department that has offered hundreds of programs to
   thousands of employees.

I look forward to discussing how I can contribute to one of your clients' future success.

                                                    Sincerely,


Enclosure:                                          Leslie A. Barnes

## LESLIE A. BARNES — Human Resources/Training Executive

199 Washington, Briarcliff Manor, NY 10510  Telephone: (914) 555-1234  e-mail: dmanager@aol.com

### CAREER SKILLS/KNOWLEDGE

o T&D management/HR senior staff
o Budgeting/cost controls/corrective actions
o Training department start-up
o Management/staff development
o Strategic planning process
o Succession planning/manpower planning
o Marketing/sales professional
o Business start-up/independent consulting

o Self-managed production teams
o Process improvement teams/ISO-9000
o Needs analysis/skills inventory system
o Diversity/sexual harassment
o Surveys and culture change
o Technical training
o Basic skills training
o Multiple computer applications

### CAREER ACHIEVEMENTS AT DAYTRON SYSTEMS

o As T&D Director, earned sundry management awards for creating and managing a state-of-the-art department that achieved and exceeded major business goals: in spite of downsizing and budget cuts, achieved results through good people, tough vendor negotiations, and optimum use of internal and government resources.

o Exceeded the hours of training per employee target by 50%; earned corporate commendation for implementing first-ever technical skills inventory; scored highest among all divisions in diversity training; also implemented automated tracking systems adopted by other business units; doubled participation in basic education classes.

o Won the Chairman's Citation for facilitating adoption and implementation of self-managed production teams: fully trained and prepared the facilitators and team members for this important transition.

o Initiated and facilitated Daytron's first-ever senior staff off-site strategic planning and team-building meetings: produced the first group-developed and group-supported strategic plans and MBOs.

o Initiated and implemented state-of-the-art missile systems training, as well as proposal development training that materially improved the accuracy of our proposals while streamlining the cumbersome development cycle.

o Initiated corrective actions to address deteriorating communication between senior and middle management: introduced and facilitated a series of Chairman-interchange meetings that encouraged open dialogue between the Chairman's staff and our normally reticent middle managers.

o As Daytron's representative on a headquarters employee relations council, codirected several events including an annual gathering that honored the corporation's top performing employees and vendors.

## CAREER EXPERIENCE

### DAYTRON SYSTEMS, INC., White Plains, NY    11/91–Present

Director of Training and Development: Human Resources
Implement management, technical, and basic skills training in support of our strategic plan; secure commitment and financial support from management; direct company-wide needs assessment and skills inventory; facilitate implementation of self-managed work teams and strategic business review process; identify and implement cost reductions; direct vendor negotiations; facilitate and expedite employee development dictated by annual reviews; review and update instructor training; and communicate Daytron's business plan and leadership philosophy.

### HOLLINGER ENGINEERING, New York, NY    9/88–11/91

Director of Training
Created, organized, and directed T&D for this electronics firm. Trained over 3,000 employees; introduced 81 programs, 80% of which were designed and implemented in-house. These broad-based training programs covered such critical areas as management development, succession planning, sales, technical, and basic skills.

### BARNES CONSULTING, White Plains, NY    2/87–9/88

Founder and Trainer
Created, marketed, and provided customized training programs to such clients as Texaco, Citgo, General Motors, Peat Marwick, SCM Corporation, IBM, and GTE. Designed and conducted numerous Women in Management programs for IBM. Initiated, designed, and produced sophisticated training packages for PM's interactive videotex subsidiary. Designed an advertising training program marketed nationwide by IBM.

### TRAINING TECHNOLOGY, INC., Webster, NY    6/84–2/87

Manager Training and Development
Comanaged start-up and operation of this company which designed and published both customized and off-the-shelf training products. Created, marketed, and executed innovative management and basic skills training. Also recruited, directed, and trained a talented staff of 30 professionals.

## CAREER AWARDS AT DAYTRON SYSTEMS

**Chairman's Award:** for initiating adoption and implementation of self-directed work teams
**Leadership Awards:** based on outstanding achievements throughout the 1990s
**Excellence in Performance Program (EIP) Awards:** exceeded major goals established by senior management
**Corrective Action Awards:** for leadership in improving Daytron's work environment

EDUCATION: BA   Hunter College   1984

## A Definitive Case History

The one-two punch of classified ads and custom packaging is illustrated in the career of Ken Allen, a veteran entrepreneur who achieved his goal of transitioning to the Fortune 500. In the midst of direct mailings, recruiter contacts, and networking, Ken saw some online ads that persuaded him to try the big corporations, where he wanted to be a division sales director. Operating under the premise of "no-guts, no-glory," we tailored his package (Figures 9.3a to 9.3c) to accomplish three things: meet the ad specifications, stress bottom-line results, and boldly assert Ken's unabashed pride in being an entrepreneur although he is thoroughly qualified to be a corporate department head. (Employed judiciously, this in-your-face, never-apologize strategy does work.) The 10 special packages initially sent produced two good interviews. We had gotten him in the door. As a powerful communicator with a gift for neutralizing opposition, Ken survived the standard callbacks and gauntlet of bureaucratic interviews, where his entrepreneurial background was viewed with skepticism. He received and accepted an offer and is doing very well. A combination of astute packaging and a talented client had beaten the system.

## EXPANSIONIST THEORY, STEP FOUR: NETWORKING

———— **REALITY CHECK** ————

Exploit networking for all it's worth, but assume that you must achieve a career move on your own. At the end of the day, we must rely primarily on ourselves.

As one step of a process, networking is obviously vital. Although many networking books offer excellent guidance and strategies regarding the relationship-building process, others have detoured into duplicitous tactics. They endorse bogus schemes to gain access to decision makers so that the topic of jobs can be broached at a later more opportune time. Those amenable to these roundabout tactics can certainly employ them. In the past decade, I have had few clients who would comfortably abide this subterfuge. Our clients have instead adopted forthright tactics including third-party introductions which can be extremely effective as shown in our case history that follows. While nurturing and sustaining work and social relationships is a top priority, the fact remains that 85% of our clients achieved career

## KENNETH A. ALLEN                Sales Executive/General Management

11 Tunic Road, Larchmont, NY  10538   Telephone: (914) 555-1234 e-mail: kamanager@aol.com

John Smith                                                        Date
Senior Vice President of Sales
Division of a Fortune 500 company
118 Wilmot Avenue
Paramus, NJ  05432

Dear Mr. Smith:

I have exercised skills in sales, marketing, operations, and general management to start, expand, and manage two million-dollar businesses that were later sold at a sizable profit. I have
repeatedly outmaneuvered the competition, penetrated new markets, and expanded operations to achieve financial security both for others and myself. I can and will accomplish these
same bottom-line results as a division sales director in your Fortune 500 company.

I am bringing to your attention my skills, achievements, and talent for thwarting competitors
to achieve sales goals so that we can discuss my joining your Fortune 500 division as Director
of Sales.

Results achieved to date include:

o Rapidly promoted to Vice President of Sales and Operations at United Spring Water Company after
   achieving a nine-fold increase in revenue within a highly competitive market: increased our sales
   from less than $100,000 to almost $1,000,000—setting the stage for the company's acquisition by the
   largest Eastern distributor of Pepsi-Coca.

o Profitably competed within the ruthless soft-drink industry by outmaneuvering the competition
   and penetrating new markets: introduced 24-hour service; expanded narrow product lines; formed
   and nurtured new territories; created and administered combative marketing campaigns; and
   helped reduce unfair industry practices.

o Surmounted potentially disastrous competitive threats from the majors: drafted a marketing plan
   that secured critically needed capital funding from two New York City banks; purchased and installed state-of-the-art equipment that allowed United Spring Water to enter the lucrative concentrated syrup market.

o As the founder and CEO of a building and remodeling business, increased revenue from $78,000 to
   almost $2.1 million: ultimately sold the company at a premium to a $50 million corporation.

o More than tripled company sales over a two-year period through strategic changes to our organization and marketing: formed a partnership; expanded our facilities; developed a client base of large
   builders; emphasized lucrative commercial work; participated in major home shows; and computerized our operation.

As an entrepreneur and rainmaker who never acquired the less desirable habits of corporate
America, I am fully qualified to join your company. I would like an appointment to discuss
how I can accelerate your sales growth.

                                                        Sincerely,


Enclosure:                                              Kenneth A. Allen

## KENNETH A. ALLEN         Sales Executive/General Management

11 Tunic Road, Larchmont, NY 10538  Telephone: (914) 555-1234  e-mail: kamanager@aol.com

Bachelors Degree  Cum Laude  Illinois Institute of Technology  1988

### CAREER SKILLS/KNOWLEDGE

o Marketing/Sales
o Revenue/profit growth
o Competitive maneuvering
o Product/market development
o Turnaround strategies
o Pricing/market penetration
o Advertising/direct mail
o Networking/promotions
o Service strategies
o Territory planning/management

o General management
o Start-up venture
o Operations/cost control
o Business planning/budgeting
o Funding/capitalization
o Negotiating/acquisitions
o Productivity improvements
o Staff development/supervision
o Computerization/PC applications
o Inventory management/control

### CAREER ACHIEVEMENTS

o As Vice President of Sales and Operations at United Spring Water Company, achieved a several-fold increase in revenue within a highly competitive market: increased sales from $100,000 to almost $1,000,000—setting the stage for our acquisition by the largest East Coast distributor of Pepsi-Cola.

o Competed within the cut-throat soft-drink industry by outsmarting the competition and penetrating untapped markets: introduced 24-hour service, expanded product lines, developed new territories, executed effective marketing campaigns, and helped mitigate unfair industry practices.

o Surmounted potentially disastrous competitive threats from the major soft-drink companies: drafted a business and marketing plan that secured needed funding from New York City banks to finance the installation of state-of-the-art electronic equipment needed for expansion into concentrated syrups.

o As the founder and CEO of a $2 million building and remodeling business, negotiated the lucrative sale of the company to a $50 million corporation.

o Initiated actions that nearly quadrupled company sales over a two-year period: formed partnership, expanded facilities, developed a client base of large builders, focused on commercial work, participated in home shows, and computerized operations.

o Accelerated revenue growth through aggressive marketing and expansion: emphasized lucrative kitchen renovations, targeted high-end markets, developed network of architects, created productive ad campaigns, and expanded our facilities and staff.

KENNETH A. ALLEN                                                                              Page 2

## CAREER EXPERIENCE

### WHITE PLAINS BUILDERS, INC., New York, NY    1998–Present

Vice President of Sales and Marketing
Initiated, researched, and negotiated a deal to sell Technical Builders, Inc. to this $50 million
company. Currently honoring a multi-year agreement to manage the company.

### TECHNICAL BUILDERS, INC., Larchmont, NY    1996–98

Cofounder/President/Marketing VP
Organized and directed this building and remodeling partnership:

o Created and staffed organization; tripled size of facility.
o Developed network of high-end builders; focused on commercial work.
o Planned and executed participation in lucrative home shows.
o Directed operations; computerized all planning and administration.

### ALLEN'S BUILDING & REMODELING, INC., Larchmont, NY    1992–96

Founder/President/Marketing VP
Founded and directed growth of this building and remodeling company:

o Created and executed marketing/advertising campaigns.
o Developed network of architects; focused on kitchen renovations.
o Instituted professional cold-calling, proposal writing, and closing.
o Directed operations; upgraded and expanded staff and facilities.

### UNITED SPRING WATER COMPANY, Port Chester, NY    1988–92

Vice President of Sales and Operations
Directed all sales, marketing, operations, and administration:

o Supervised department heads composed of production manager, route manager, and service director.
o Established and monitored sales and profit objectives.
o Expanded product line introducing new cocktail mixers.
o Restructured product line to include full-line syrups.
o Designed marketing campaigns including direct mail.
o Evaluated and expanded territories; established/monitored routes.
o Negotiated and purchased all materials and equipment.
o Established inventory and quality control systems.
o Established credit and collection procedures; supervised financials.
o Reduced transportation costs through truck fleet conversion.

## REFERENCES PROVIDED UPON REQUEST

KATHERINE POWERS                                    Presenting Lawrence V. Chambers

Telephone: (212) 555-1234 ext. 567 e-mail: kpmanager@gcc.com

**Confidential Eyes Only: Presenting Mr. Lawrence V. Chambers**


Ross Murdoch                                                        Date
President and CEO
Global Communications Corporation
One Park Avenue
New York, NY 10016

Based on discussions with a long-time business associate, I am introducing Mr. Lawrence V. Chambers.

As per the attached curriculum vitae, Mr. Chambers might well be able to expedite our circa 2003 to 2010 goals.

As Executive Vice President reporting to the Board of a global financial services firm, Mr. Chambers planned and directed the turnaround of its ailing international division—that is once again a significant earnings contributor. He added some $275 million in revenue by leveraging his extensive global network and accelerating cross-regional business development. He contributed over $56 million to profits by restructuring product development strategies.

At the Chairman's request, Mr. Chambers orchestrated the same organizational changes at the Geneva headquarters that marked his profitable tenure at the North American operation. He transformed the corporation into an investment-banking and deal-oriented business committed to management by objectives and bottom-line accountability. His rise to one of the firm's top executives reflects of his singular abilities and brainpower.

As an investment banker and global deal-maker with the drive and spirit of a chief executive, Mr. Chambers is interested in shifting to a corporate setting within global communications. He covets international assignments—and would gladly perform such for our company.

Mr. Chambers is working stateside for the next month. He would be glad to meet at a time convenient to both your calendars. He is confident that he can make important contributions to our international growth plans.

I will call you on Friday to follow up.

                                                        Best Regards,



Enclosure:                                              Katherine Powers
                                                        Corporate Vice President

## LAWRENCE V. CHAMBERS

## Global Marketing/Management/ Business Development

West Swedeland Road, Geneva, Switzerland  Telephone: (0114122) 555-1234  e-mail: lvcmanager@aol.com

### Confidential Curriculum Vitae: Mr. Lawrence V. Chambers

### CAREER EXPERIENCE

### GLOBAL FINANCIAL SERVICES OF GENEVA, Geneva, Switzerland  9/90–Present

Executive Vice President and General Manager/International Division  3/95–Present
Reporting to the Board, helped return the international division to profitability. Added $275 million in revenue by leveraging global contacts and expanding business development. Added $56 million to profits by restructuring marketing and product development. Enhanced global marketing by ensuring that players like Microsoft received equal attention in Europe and Asia. Ensured that reciprocal tax treaties were integrated into financing solutions.

Strengthened our balance sheet by exploiting profitable market developments. Cognizant that investment bankers can no longer compete by excelling on the advisory, structuring, underwriting, and financing side, shifted focus to the distribution side by expanding product development to encompass the entire product chain. Also eliminated all underperforming assets by packaging and selling them off to third-party investors.

Appointed by the Chairman to orchestrate the same organizational transformation that reshaped North American operations. Achieved P&L goals by cultivating inter-divisional teams that required employees to act as CEOs in order to better define customers' needs. Changed attitudes from that of a traditional lender to that of an investment-banking and deal-oriented operation committed to maximizing revenue opportunities.

Representing all of the Swiss financial institutions, negotiated with the IMF and former Iron Curtain governments. Reduced a potential $2.75 billion loss to $550 million by minimizing debt forgiveness and optimizing the mix of exchanged debt instruments for maximum trading appreciation. Established a LDC bond portfolio that produced an average ROC of 195%—representing one of our most successful desks.

Assumed regional responsibility for Africa and the Middle East.

Managing Director—Corporate Finance: North American Operations  1/93–3/95
Directed staff of 94. As chief architect of a total turnaround in the North American operations, accelerated income and orchestrated radical shifts in our tarnished image. Recast the operation as a global player by generating a 265% growth in return while tripling its asset base to $8.6 billion. Gained market penetration by opening offices in the Midwest and South. Converted weak South American unit to capital market/M&A advisors.

Senior Vice President—Corporate Finance: North American Operations  6/91–1/93
Rebuilt organization. Recruited ten VPs and formed five marketing teams. Expanded client base via strategy that required new VPs to act as CFOs through adoption of a value-added, activist, and proactive marketing philosophy.

LAWRENCE V. CHAMBERS                                                                    Page 2

Confidential Curriculum Vitae: Mr. Lawrence V. Chambers

## CAREER EXPERIENCE

### GLOBAL FINANCIAL SERVICES OF GENEVA, Geneva, Switzerland    9/90–Present

Vice President—Corporate Finance: North American Operations   9/90–6/91
Recruited by the Board to plan and direct crucial changes to the motivation and focus of the entire North American operation. Achieved a record 260% growth in return (on risk-adjusted capital employed) by totally restructuring the organization, staffing, marketing, and product mix. With carte blanche support from the Board, planned and executed a ground-breaking reorganization that transformed the North American group to an investment-banking and deal-oriented operation committed to management by objectives and bottom-line accountability.

### CHASE MANHATTAN BANK, New York, NY    1/87–9/90

Vice President Global Merchant Banking, 2/89–9/90: Generated $11 million in revenue by saving 80% of the at-risk accounts. Increased fees/ROA by focusing on corporate finance and asset sales.

Vice President Corporate Banking, 8/88–2/89: Leveraged contacts to market corporate and capital market products. Generated $5 million in added NI and achieved a 330% growth in fees.

Manager Business Development—European Energy Group, London, England, 1/87–8/88: Recruited to start and direct new BD group. Established productive project finance and lending operation that generated $400 million in new business within two years with a ROE of 17%. Closed lucrative deals including a much sought after $400 million project with a global energy company.

### GLOBAL FINANCIAL SERVICES OF CANADA, Calgary    9/85–1/87

Division Head, 2/86–1/87: Started office and exceeded goals by generating new business of $180 million.

Principal Lending, 9/85–2/86: Expanded multinational accounts tripling pretax NI to $2.95 million.

### EDUCATION AND OTHER CREDENTIALS

Education:          BS Finance with honors; University of Virginia   1985
Languages:          Fluent in German, French, Spanish, and Swedish

moves through means other than networking. Even the best networking is no substitute for our multistep, high-volume search process that outclasses the competition by applying a truth that the workforce invariably sidesteps, namely, that you can never be guilty of making too many contacts, but you can certainly be guilty of making too few.

### A Definitive Case History

The power of networking and third-party introductions is shown in the career of Lawrence V. Chambers, a long-time client who has tripled his annual compensation during our long association. The challenge of his most recent search was to balance a need for aggressiveness with a need for caution due to his high profile within global finance. We resolved this quandary by employing a discreet version of the Expansionist Theory. To secure pledges of confidentiality, we called company contacts and recruiters before sending packages. Unblinded classifieds were also contacted; blind ads were jettisoned. Our networking included discreet phone calls by Larry and third-party introductions by past clients who were well-connected in their companies. The latter produced results. Another long-time client, Katherine Powers, submitted Larry's package (Figures 9.4a to 9.4c) to the CEO of her company. It produced an important first interview that led to follow-up interviews and a lucrative offer that Larry ultimately accepted.

## EXPANSIONIST THEORY, STEP FIVE:
## RADICAL TELEPHONY (optional)

This optional step is based on the success of a minority of clients who are fearless enough to tap the advanced power of the telephone. Such a client was George Henderson, whose mastery allowed him to talk his way into a corporation that had all but stopped hiring. Determined to join this recovering blue-chip, George exercised his skills as a top-ranked sales manager to telephone his way up the chain of command at IBM. Refusing to accept no for an answer, he cold-called, circumvented, and nullified a dozen bureaucrats before finding the right connection. After an initial interview, he followed with more calls that produced more interviews that, in turn, produced a job offer. George recently celebrated another anniversary with IBM. For those with fortitude, the telephone can work miracles.

The bottom line is that the Expansionist Theory works, period.

# 10

# The 24/7 Internet Job Search: Registering with CareerJournal.com from the Wall Street Journal

---

**REALITY CHECK**

Never underestimate the mega-power of the Internet/World Wide Web. Those of you who have yet to harness this power should realize that you are aiding and abetting the competition who are already employing this easy-to-use, 24/7 job search tool to supplement the research library, post office, word processing service, copy shop, and hard-copy classifieds. Want ads from around the globe can now be accessed, researched, and answered within minutes at such respected Internet Web sites as www .CareerJournal.com, www.Futurestep.com, www.BrilliantPeople .com, www.ChiefMonster.com, www.CareerBuilder.com, www .SpencerStuart.com, www.ExecuNet.com, www.PamDixon.com, www.RileyGuide.com, www.Weddles.com, www.CareerDoctor .org, www.JobStar.org, and hundreds of other great Web sites identified in *The 24/7 Online Job Search Directory* (Chapter 11). Internet service providers like America Online (AOL), Compu-Serve (CS), Microsoft Network (MSN), and other ISPs make accessing the Internet easy—so log on right now.

---

## EXPANSIONIST THEORY REDUX: THE WORLD WIDE WEB IS NOT ENOUGH

While the Internet is the core of the information revolution dominating the twenty-first century, the spirit of the Expansionist Theory™ detailed in Chapter 9 mandates that the career planning and job search process include both the Internet and conventional job search tools. Even though most companies and recruiters accept cold-call inquiries and classified ad responses through electronic mail (e-mail), this does not preclude the use of conventional job search methods in tandem with electronic communication. Mailing hard-copy letter/resume packages through the U.S. Postal Service still makes good sense. Employing the telephone as a powerful device for making initial and follow-up contacts makes equally good sense. In fact, the overwhelming volume of e-mail flooding into hiring companies often necessitates multistep strategies for replying to job openings—you can stand out from the crowd by responding to much-sought-after positions through both electronic and conventional mail, supplemented by follow-up phone calls to decision makers. As detailed in Chapter 9, clients who generated the most interviews and offers were those who did more not less—they embraced the Internet as a miracle tool, but not to the exclusion of conventional job search methods that continue to generate interviews and offers.

The bottom line is that you should capitalize on the power of the Internet as a research, communications, and job search tool—then do more.

## TWO QUICK TECHNICAL POINTS BEFORE REGISTERING WITH CAREERJOURNAL.COM

While this chapter is obviously not intended to be a technical primer on the Internet (there are already countless books on the subject), this chapter addresses two quasitechnical issues that can seriously impact the quality and speed at which you execute your online job search. The first issue focuses on the selection of Internet service providers (ISPs) through which to gain access to the Internet. The second issue centers on choosing the most productive Internet connectivity option from alternate sources.

### Internet Service Providers (ISP): Selection Process

There are literally thousands of Internet service providers through which to gain access to the Web. The latest ISP count stands at 3,454, according to ISP Finder™ (ISP Finder, Inc., www.ispfinder.com, 9 May 2002). These numbers aside, it's safe to assume that most readers follow the same or similar pattern as my managerial and professional clients—most of whom connect to the Internet through such major ISPs as America Online (AOL), CompuServe (CS), or Microsoft Network (MSN). These leading ISPs are user-friendly and offer generally reliable customer service and exclusive proprietary features (e.g., instant messaging, Web site bookmarking, career chat rooms, exclusive Web sites, and countless research tools) that clearly expedite the job-search process. The monthly fee charged by these major ISPs is still less than a dollar a day—a bargain for a user-friendly service that affords 24/7 access to global job listings, research tools, and international communication links connecting users to tens of millions of people. As a long-time customer of AOL—with no stock or other vested interest in AOL Time Warner—I can state objectively that it is the leading ISP for a good reason: They have done a good job of satisfying their tens of millions of customers. In any case, any of the major ISPs can do the job.

### Connectivity Options: The Selection Process

The second and last technical issue centers on three popular communications options for connecting your computer to the ISP/Internet—telephone dial-up service, high-speed Internet cable modem, and high-speed digital subscriber line (DSL), which transforms ordinary telephone lines into high-speed digital lines for Internet access. Based on firsthand experience with painfully slow and arduous telephone dial-up services, I urge readers to upgrade to either Internet cable modem service—offered by many local cable television companies, or high-speed DSL—offered by many local telephone companies. While these high-speed services were once prohibitively expensive for personal use, prices have fallen, as cable operators and telephone companies seek to expand their Internet customer base to the home market. Even in high cost of living areas like my home state Connecticut, the prices for Internet cable modem services have fallen to the point where the total monthly cost for ISP services accessed through Internet cable modem—which downloads data at speeds up to 100 times faster than traditional phone connections—is, in some instances, actually the same or less than the total cost of ISP services accessed by telephone dial-up. This is due, in part, to the fact that major ISPs like AOL offer a substantial discount on their monthly fee when customers switch from telephone dial-up access to DSL or Internet cable modem.

The bottom line is that your job search will be optimized and expedited by securing the services of a major ISP accessed through high-speed cable modem or DSL.

## GETTING STARTED: REGISTERING WITH CAREERJOURNAL.COM

Describing a career and job search Web site as "the premier career site for executives, managers, and professionals" might well sound like Madison Avenue hype—unless that Web site is owned and operated by CareerJournal.com from the *Wall Street Journal*. Career-Journal and other premium Web sites described in *The 24/7 Online Job Search Directory* (Chapter 11) will remain an integral part of your career planning for many years to come.

Since there are no fees for registering with their confidential resume database, there's no time like the present to sign up with CareerJournal.

### A Case History: Real-Life Client Registers with CareerJournal.com

Using the same steps followed by one of my clients, Bob Gordon (Figures 10.1a to 10.1c), will have you registered with CareerJournal.com in less than an hour. Your completed letter/resume package developed in earlier chapters, combined with word-processing tools that let you copy and paste text from your word-processing files to CareerJournal's input forms, will expedite the process.

Follow the next several steps as Bob Gordon completes the registration process:

*Step 1:* Bob enters his password and signs on to his ISP. He starts the registration process by deleting the text in the web address window on the toolbar at the top of the ISP screen. He types www.CareerJournal.com into the address window and clicks the "go" button or hits "return." Within seconds, he views the home page of CareerJournal.com (Figures 10.2a and 10.2b). In order to expedite future access to this site, Bob bookmarks this page by saving it to his "Favorites" or "Bookmarks" folder. *Note:* AOL or CompuServe users can simply click on the red heart in the upper right hand corner of the web page and select "Add to Favorites" from the menu. MSN users should click "Favorites" on the MSN toolbar and select "Add to Favorites" from the menu.

**FIGURE 10.1a. Power of the Internet: Real-Life Client Registers with Career-Journal.com: Accomplishments Copied and Pasted to CareerJournal Directly from Cover Letter Below**

---

ROBERT A. GORDON                    Risk Management/Audit Management

---

One Sutton Place, New York, NY 10022 (212) 555-1234 e-mail: rgmanager@aol.com

Date

Contact Name
Title
Company
Street Address
City, State Zip

Dear Mr./Ms. _____ :

In a key risk management role chartered to integrate finance and operations at Agra Financial Services, identified and mitigated the downside risk of major fiscal exposures that ultimately required hundreds of millions of dollars in charges to the P&L. Slashed a massive billion-dollar exposure in half by initiating corrective actions to address out-of-control inventory, weak remarketing, and depleted reserves at AFS.

I am presenting for your review my risk management skills, tangible achievements, and talent for making bottom-line contributions so that we can discuss my joining _____ as a member of your senior risk management team or senior audit management team.

As resident expert regarding reserves, losses, residuals, and audit process, achieved the following at AFS:

o Exposed and assuaged serious downside risks: based on huge inventory of used agricultural equipment, poor remarketing, and scant reserves, persuaded management to take drastic measures including major organizational changes and a $92 million lump sum write-off followed by monthly charges to P&L of $12 million to build reserves; failure to act would have doubled the losses recorded between 1997 and 2001.

o In spite of losses generated by AFS, forestalled downgrading of credit rating by preparing and delivering strong reports to Moody's and S&P detailing corrective action plans; added $125 million to the bottom line by producing a study that allowed AFS to reduce residual reserves for key products from 7% to 6%.

o Shifted $78.9 million from deferred income to P&L by completing—and negotiating approval for—complex analysis of residual supports paid to AFS by N.A. subsidiaries: negotiated early end to payment supports allowing AFS to shift over $60 million from deferred income to the P&L over a three-year period.

o In response to massive volume of lease maturities engulfing the Seattle CSC, initiated and managed a temporary remarketing phone bank at our New York City HQ: aggressive remarketing eliminated backlog and quickly produced over 400 lease extensions, 190 customer purchases, and 212 continued billings.

o After AFS merger with Deere & Company, was offered promotion to Manager of Portfolio Risk Management with responsibility for JD Financial lease portfolios for U.S. and Europe: accountabilities included profit maximization, policies, reporting, and strategic projects related to business development, residual financing and remarketing; based on factors that precluded relocation to the Midwest, declined the offer.

It may well be to our mutual benefit to discuss how I can likewise contribute to your future success.

Best regards,

Robert Gordon

Enclosure:

## ROBERT A. GORDON        Risk Management/Audit Management

One Sutton Place, New York, NY 10022 (212) 555-1234 e-mail: rgmanager@aol.com

### FINANCIAL/RISK MANAGEMENT SKILLS

o Risk management skills

o Leasing/retail financing

o Quality/reengineering

o P&L management/systems

o Balance sheet management/systems

o Portfolio risk management

o Leveraged leasing

o Residual value analysis/reserves

o Loss reserves

o Provision for reserves

o Delinquency analysis/monitoring

o Inventory monitoring/remarketing

o Inventory write-downs

o Write-offs and loss recovery

o Auditing/financial management skills

o General portfolio accounting

o Marketing support/subvention

o Portfolio systems accounting security

o Business planning/aviation/ABL

o Annual audit plan development/budgeting

o Computerized audit department startup

o Manpower planning/staff development

o Year-end audits/outside auditor controls

o Major operational and financial audits

o Financial controls/collections turnaround

o Process improvement/compliance audits

o IT operational reviews/security

o Cost reductions/productivity growth

### CAREER EXPERIENCE

### Agra Financial Services Corporation (AFS), New York, NY 4/97–Present

#### Manager of Risk and Portfolio Accounting 4/97–Present

In a risk management position designated to integrate finance and operations, played strategic role in identifying and alleviating the downside risk of serious fiscal exposures. Major accomplishments:

o Obtained top management approval for actions that alleviated billion-dollar inventory problems: initiated lump sum write-offs and monthly multi-million-dollar charges to P&L; initiated early warning reports that brought corporate oversight and visibility to delinquencies; spurred organizational changes and systems upgrades to correct weak inventory reporting; reduced billion-dollar exposure to $350 million.

o Countered costly gouging by equipment dealers who exploited problems at AFS: poor inventory controls and remarketing allowed dealers to purchase used equipment from AFS for twenty cents on the dollar; dealers then charged AFS $20,000 per unit to repair same equipment bought at deep discounts; dealers then resold equipment at premium prices; limits on repairs and better remarketing alleviated the problem.

o Produced and presented high-profile report that persuaded headquarters' management to rescind their high-level mandate to write off delinquent accounts aged over 180 days: mandate would have severely impacted the P&L to the tune of tens of millions of dollars; the mandate was also in violation of GAAP.

o Managed quality project that spurred total reengineering of month-end closing cycle— which was reduced from twelve working days to four; automated manual entries and reconciliation process; purged useless and redundant reports, entries, and GL accounts; realigned work processes to gain maximum efficiencies.

o Managed project team that corrected costly errors in our Portfolio Accounting System (PAS): sent shock waves through headquarters based on a security review that revealed serious breaches—that allowed injudicious access to confidential information; restructured policies and systems to close security gap.

ROBERT A. GORDON                                                                         Page 2

## CAREER EXPERIENCE

### Global Resource Corporation (GRC), New York, NY 4/91–3/97

Director of Corporate Internal Audit 2/95–3/97
Major bottom-line accomplishments included:

o Expanded IA's charter and radically restructured annual audit plans: shifted focus from compliance to unstructured operational audits as chief investigative arm of senior management; introduced state-of-the-art auditing techniques and computerized manual operations in spite of strong resistance from IT.

o Exposed and resolved potentially disastrous legal and financial exposures related to non-compliance with state and local taxes applied to customer lease payments: automated out-of-control processes; initiated much needed systems integration; and effected major organizational and policy changes.

o Worked with GRC and C&L senior management in scheduling and executing year-end audits: saved tens of thousands of dollars in fees by developing new CAAT applications for use by C&L; created automated account confirmation process; expanded the year-end audits to include GRC subsidiaries.

o Exposed and fixed weak controls over multi-million-dollar streams of cash flowing between GRC and its equipment dealers: stopped big dollar overpayments to dealers caused by untrained staffers who failed to net current and overdue amounts owed to GRC by dealers against amounts owed to dealers.

o Saved failed remarketing program by forcing GRC Quebec to establish a corporate office with new staff: fixed weak controls over Repo Inventory that had caused inventory aged over 90 days to rise from 17% to 56% of total assets; rectified weak controls over Loss Recovery that had caused doubling of write-offs.

o Corrected legal/high-dollar exposures related to GRC's dealer network: mandatory recommendations resolved deficiencies in many areas including commodity verification and dealer guarantee programs.

o Expanded region audit coverage—and reviewed $450 million in credit transactions—by creating library of standard CAAT applications for sample selection, data testing, and IRR calculation; further improved our coverage—and expedited the collection of several hundred thousand dollars in overdue payments—by auditing high-dollar exposures including wholesale dealer interest and flat charge delinquencies.

o Armed with retail interest rate verification tool programmed in Easytrieve, found unexplained variances in 44% of the contracts issued during a one-month period: IA issued urgent bulletins, prepared monthly reports for senior management, and worked with regions to institute critically needed systems controls.

o Sanctioned immediate corrective actions that helped address a crisis in IT: lacking centralized strategic planning and controls, IT had no operating plans to justify its multi-million-dollar budgets; poor budget controls had resulted in bad lease/buy decisions and unjustified expenditures in the million-dollar range.

### Sunbeam Corporation, Miami, FL 4/89–4/91

Senior Operational Auditor 11/89–4/91
Government division audits exposed: millions of dollars in committed-yet-unapproved appropriations; out-of-control inventory; unjustified project delays; high-dollar purchases without valid POs. Manufacturing audits exposed major discrepancies between the actual parts, BOM, and engineering drawings.

**Education:** BS Accounting University of Illinois Dean's List Self-financed 1989

**Community Activities:** Initiated GRC's sponsorship of River Watch Program and Junior Achievement

**FIGURE 10.2a.   Power of the Internet: Real-Life Client Registers with www.CareerJournal.com: Home Page: CareerJournal.com from *The Wall Street Journal***

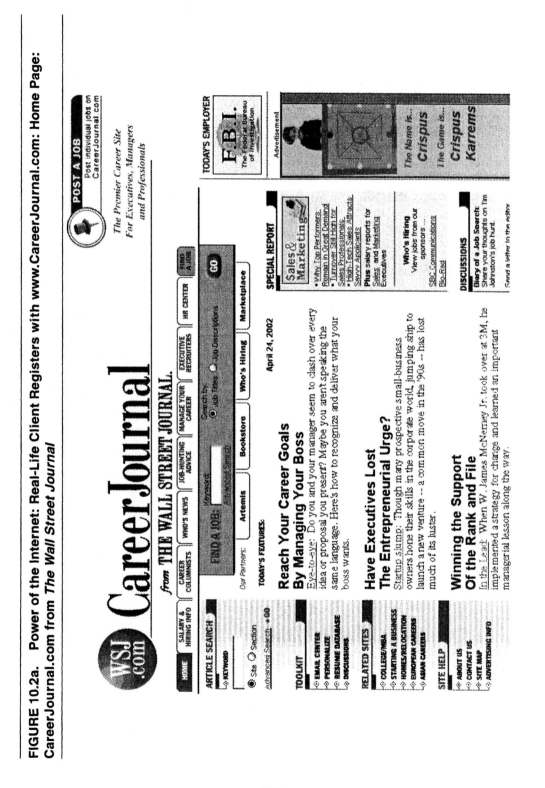

**FIGURE 10.2b.   Power of the Internet: Real-Life Client Registers with www.CareerJournal.com: Home Page: CareerJournal.com from *The Wall Street Journal***

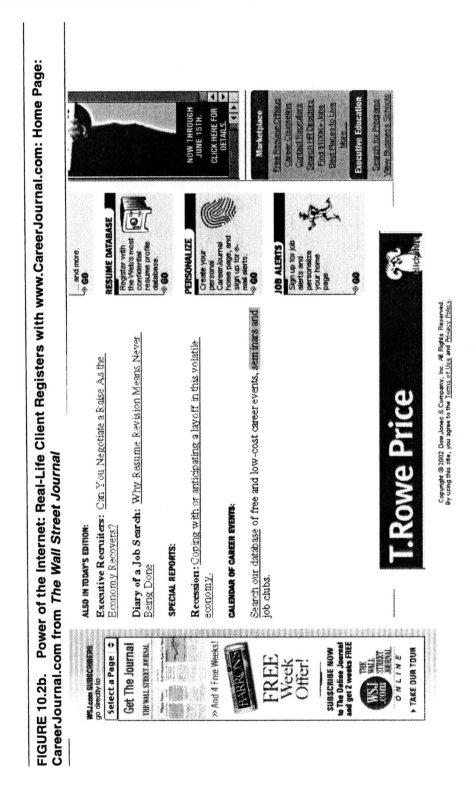

*Step 2:* After reviewing the home page (Figures 10.2a and 10.2b) to familiarize himself with the CareerJournal's features and contents, Bob guides his mouse arrow to the "navigational table of contents" located on the left-hand column of the page. Under the "Site Help" menu, he clicks the "About Us" link. This page (Figures 10.3a and 10.3b) gives Bob a brief overview.

*Step 3:* After reviewing the "About Us" page, Bob returns to the "Site Help" menu on the left-hand column of the page and clicks the "Site Map" link. He studies the "Site Map" (Figures 10.4a and 10.4b), which provides an overview of CareerJournal's products and services.

*Step 4:* On the site map, Bob clicks the "Resume Database" link under the "Find a Job" column. He briefly reviews the "Confidential Resume Database" overview page (Figure 10.5), which offers two options for inputting data. Quoting directly from this web page, "Under *option one* the job seeker can create a brief, confidential profile that can be searched by corporate and executive recruiters. If your qualifications match available jobs, recruiters will send CareerJournal.com an e-mail, which they will forward to you. Then, only you can decide whether to respond. CareerJournal.com will not share your contact information with a recruiter. Under *option two*, you can create multiple full resume/CVs to apply to job openings." CareerJournal employs the ResumeBuilder tool—with its step-by-step instructions—to help create your resume, which will be securely stored on CareerJournal's site. You can revise your resume package anytime, as required. Note that both options afford total confidentiality.

*Step 5:* After considering these options, Bob Gordon chooses option two. He clicks the "Create a Resume" link (Figure 10.5) which takes him to the "Post a Resume" web page (Figures 10.6a and 10.6b). He scans down the "Post a Resume" page and clicks on the "Build a Resume Step-by-Step" link (Figure 10.6b). This takes him to the "ResumeBuilder" input forms (Figures 10.7a to 10.7d). Armed with word processing tools that will let him copy and paste text directly from his MS Word letter and resume package (Figures 10.1a to 10.1c), he starts the input form.

*Step 6:* At the top of the ResumeBuilder input page (Figure 10.7a), Bob quickly types in the "Account Information/Contact Information," as well as the "Miscellaneous Information" regarding relocation preferences, languages, and salary desired.

**FIGURE 10.3a. Power of the Internet: Real-Life Client Registers with www.CareerJournal.com: "About Us" Web Page: CareerJournal.com from *The Wall Street Journal***

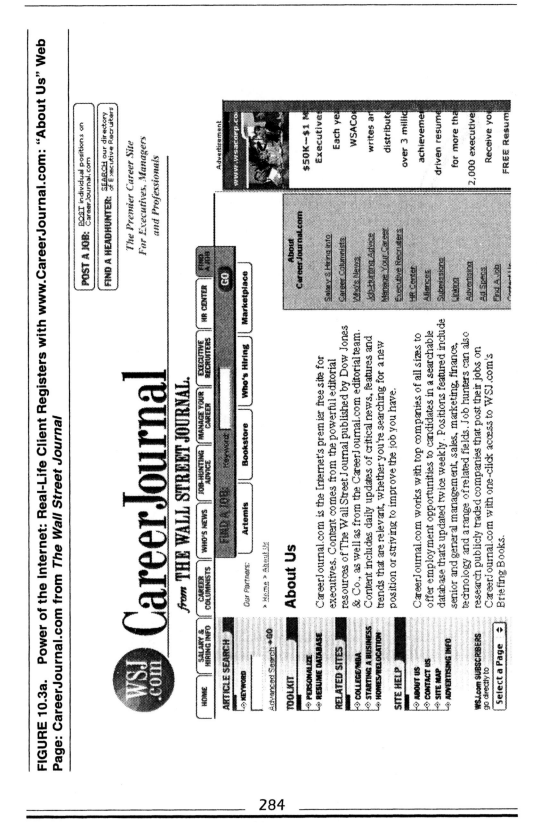

**FIGURE 10.3b. Power of the Internet: Real-Life Client Registers with www.CareerJournal.com: "About Us" Web Page: CareerJournal.com from *The Wall Street Journal***

Site Map

Help/FAQs

When you access CareerJournal.com, you'll see our Main Page, which highlights the day's top stories and our Find A Job and JobAlert features. By using the navigational table of contents down the left-hand side of the screen, you can link to our extensive collection of editorial content, databases and other services throughout the site.

## CareerJournal.com

Published by Dow Jones & Co.
P.O. Box 300, Princeton, N.J. 08543-0300

Tony Lee
Editor in Chief, General Manager

Laura Lorber
Managing Editor

Pat Rodeawald
Assistant Director

Perri Capell
Senior Correspondent

Loretta Tracy
Account Coordinator

Sarah Needleman
Associate Editor

Elaine Richardson
Staff Assistant

Christian Knoebl
Executive Producer

Valerie Patterson
Senior Producer

Anthony Catalano
Associate Producer

WSJ.com
Go to WSJ.com

THE WALL STREET JOURNAL
Subscribe to
The Wall Street Journal

BARRON'S
Subscribe to Barron's

Critiqu

Marke
Evaluatio

with our fr
information pac

Helping Executive
Since 1976
www.wsacorp.co

**FIGURE 10.4a.** Power of the Internet: Real-Life Client Registers with www.CareerJournal.com: "Site Map" Web Page: CareerJournal.com from *The Wall Street Journal*

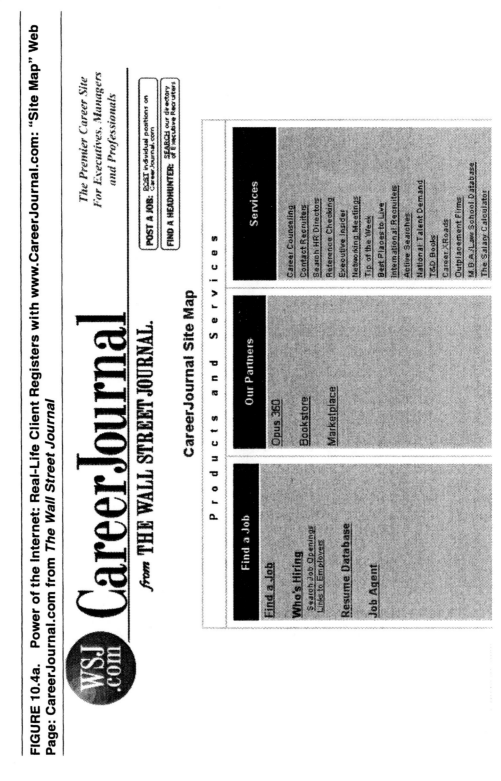

**FIGURE 10.4b.** Power of the Internet: Real-Life Client Registers with www.CareerJournal.com: "Site Map" Web Page: CareerJournal.com from *The Wall Street Journal*

## Articles

### Salary & Hiring Info
Negotiation Tips
Career Indicators
Hot Issues
Options
Regional News
Salary Calculator
Powered by ExecuNet:
Active Searches
National Talent Demand

### Career Columnists
Career Corner
In the Lead
Work & Family
A Balanced Life
Careers Q & A
From My Perspective
Working Wounded
Work Week
A Little Humor
Editor's Choice

### Who's News
Getting Ahead
Pivot Point

### Job-Hunting Advice
Resumes & Cover Letters
Interviewing
Changing Careers
Networking
Search Strategies
Using the Net
After a Job Loss
Working Abroad
Negotiation Tips
Help Wanted
Relocation Info
Options & Benefits
    Retirement
    Stock Options
    Health Benefits

### Manage Your Career
Climbing the Ladder
Management Style
Success Stories
Career Killers
Survive a Crisis
Plan for Retirement
Negotiation Tips
Diversity Issues
50 + Professionals
Working Abroad
Return to School
    Powered by Peterson's:
    Search M.B.A. Programs
    Search Law School Programs
Office Life
Legal Concerns
Workspaces
Work & Family
Business-School Guide

### Executive Recruiters
Working with Executive Recruiters
Recruiter Profiles
The Jungle

### HR Center
News Briefs
Feature Articles
Weddle's Internet Recruiting Guide
SHRM® Center
    White Papers
    Articles from HR Magazine
ASTD Center
    @Work
    Selected Features
    Training & Development
Benefit News Center
CareerJournal.com HR Alliances

### CareerJournal Discussions
Discussion FAQ

### Business-School Guide

### Calendar of Career Events

### Personalized Home Page

### Resource Centers
AESC
SHRM
ASTD
Benefit News
IPMA

## Site Information

### About Us/FAQs
Contact Us

### Advertise
Alliances

### Terms of Use
Privacy Policy

**FIGURE 10.5. Power of the Internet: Real-Life Client Registers with www.CareerJournal.com: "Confidential Resume Database" Overview: CareerJournal.com from *The Wall Street Journal***

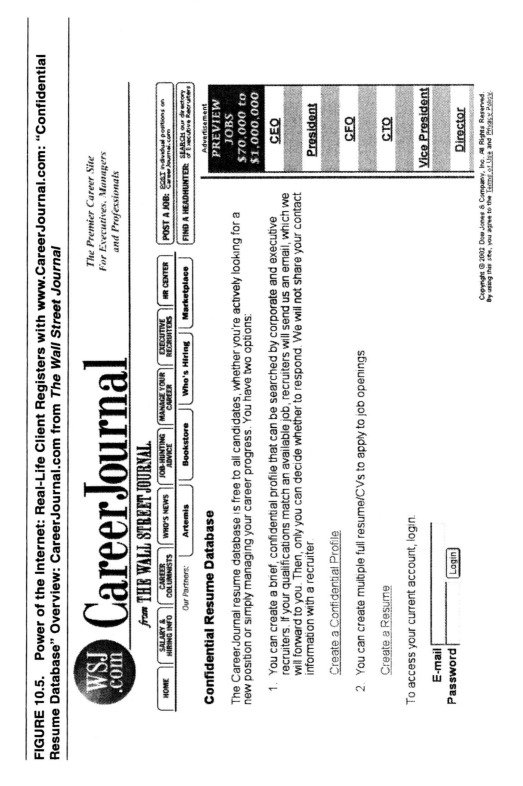

**FIGURE 10.6a. Power of the Internet: Real-Life Client Registers with www.CareerJournal.com: Post a Resume: CareerJournal.com from *The Wall Street Journal***

WSJ.com

## CareerJournal

*from* THE WALL STREET JOURNAL

*The Premier Career Site For Executives, Managers and Professionals*

| HOME | SALARY & HIRING INFO | CAREER COLUMNISTS | WHO'S NEWS | JOB-HUNTING ADVICE | MANAGE YOUR CAREER | EXECUTIVE RECRUITERS | HR CENTER |

Our Partners:   Ariemis   Bookstore   Who's Hiring   Marketplace

POST A JOB:  POST individual positions on CareerJournal.com

FIND A HEADHUNTER:  SEARCH our directory of Executive Recruiters

### Post a resume

Create one or more resumes to apply to jobs in our JobSeek data. No recruiters will see this resume unless you send it to them. An asterisk (*) indicates a required field.

**Contact Information**

*First Name: [Title ▼]

*Last Name:

*Home Phone:

*Work Phone:

*Email:

Address:

*City:

State: [State ▼]

Zip:

Password:*

*Confirm Password:

**Employment Information**

Current Employer:

*Job Title:

Language(s): [English / Arabic / Cantonese]

☑ Authorized to work in the U.S.

☐ Security clearance

Education [▼]

*Salary Desired [▼]

☐ I am willing to relocate to:

**FIGURE 10.6b.  Power of the Internet: Real-Life Client Registers with www.CareerJournal.com: Post a Resume: CareerJournal.com from** *The Wall Street Journal*

Copy and Paste a text version of your resume or <u>build a resume step-by-step</u>

**Resume:**

**Resume Name:**

**Primary Skills:**

Save

Note: Click the "build a resume step-by-step" link.

FIGURE 10.7a. Power of the Internet: Real-Life Client Registers with www.CareerJournal.com: Completed "ResumeBuilder" Input Form: CareerJournal.com from *The Wall Street Journal*

**FIGURE 10.7b. Power of the Internet: Real-Life Client Registers with www.CareerJournal.com: Completed "ResumeBuilder" Input Form: CareerJournal.com from *The Wall Street Journal***

**Skills:** (Simple HTML allowed)

Career Skills/Key Words Include:

Risk management skills: Leasing/retail financing; Quality/reengineering; P&L management/systems; Balance sheet management/systems; Portfolio risk management; Leveraged leasing; Residual value analysis/reserves; Loss reserves; Provision for reserves; Delinquency analysis/monitoring; Inventory monitoring/remarketing; Inventory write-downs; Write-offs and loss recovery.

Additional Skills/Key Words:

Auditing/financial management skills: General portfolio accounting; Marketing support/subvention; Portfolio systems accounting security; Business planning/aviation/ABL; Annual audit plan development/budgeting; Computerized audit department startup; Manpower planning/staff development; Year-end audits/outside auditor controls; Major operational and financial audits; Financial controls/collections turnaround; Process improvement/compliance audits; IT operational reviews/security; Cost reductions and productivity growth.

**Employment History:**

| Current Employer: | From: | To: |
|---|---|---|
| Agra Financial Services | 4/97 | Presen |

| Job Title: | Industry: |
|---|---|
| Manager of Risk and Portfo | Financial |

**Accomplishments/Responsibilities:** (Simple HTML allowed)

- Exposed and assuaged serious downside risks; based on huge inventory of used agricultural equipment, poor remarketing, and scant reserves, persuaded management to take drastic measures including major organizational changes and a $92 million lump sum write-off followed by monthly charges to P&L of $12 million to build reserves; failure to act would have doubled the losses recorded between 1997 and 2001.

- In spite of losses generated by AFS, forestalled downgrading of credit rating by preparing and delivering strong reports to Moody's and S&P detailing corrective action plans; added $125 million to the bottom-line by producing a study that allowed AFS to reduce residual reserves for key products from 7% to 6%.

- Shifted $78.9 million from deferred income to P&L by completing—and negotiating approval for—complex analysis of residual supports paid to AFS by N.A. subsidiaries: negotiated early end to payment supports allowing AFS to shift over $60 million from deferred income to the P&L over a three-year period.

- In response to massive volume of lease maturities engulfing the Seattle CSC, initiated and managed a temporary remarketing phone bank at our New York City HQ: aggressive remarketing eliminated backlog and quickly produced over 400 lease extensions, 190 customer purchases, and 212 continued billings.

- After AFS merger with Deere & Company, was offered promotion to Manager of Portfolio Risk Management with responsibility for JD Financial lease portfolios for U.S. and Europe: accountabilities included profit maximization, policies, reporting, and strategic projects related to business development, residual financing and remarketing; based on factors that precluded relocation to the Midwest, declined the offer.

**FIGURE 10.7c.    Power of the Internet: Real-Life Client Registers with www.CareerJournal.com: Completed "ResumeBuilder" Input Form: CareerJournal.com from *The Wall Street Journal***

| Previous Employer: | From: | To: |
|---|---|---|
| Global Resource Corporat | 4/91 | 3/97 |

| Job Title: | Industry: |
|---|---|
| Director of Corporate Inter | Financial |

**Accomplishments/Responsibilities:** (Simple HTML allowed)

- Expanded IA's charter and radically restructured annual audit plans: shifted focus from compliance to unstructured operational audits as chief investigative arm of senior management; introduced state-of-the-art auditing techniques and computerized manual operations in spite of strong resistance from IT.
- Exposed and resolved potentially disastrous legal and financial exposures related to noncompliance with state and local taxes applied to customer lease payments; automated out-of-control processes; initiated much needed systems integration; and effected major organizational and policy changes.
- Worked with GRC and C&L senior management in scheduling and executing year-end audits: saved tens of thousands of dollars in fees by developing new CAAT applications for use by C&L; created automated account confirmation process; expanded the year-end audits to include GRC subsidiaries.
- Exposed and fixed weak controls over multimillion dollar streams of cash flowing between GRC and its equipment dealers; stopped big dollar overpayments to dealers cause by untrained staffers who failed to net current and overdue amounts owed to GRC by dealers against amounts owed to dealers.
- Saved failed remarketing program by forcing GRC Quebec to establish a corporate office with new staff; fixed weak controls over Repo Inventory that had caused inventory aged over 90 days to rise from 17% to 56% of total assets; rectified weak controls over Loss Recovery that had caused doubling of write-offs.

| Previous Employer #2: | From: | To: |
|---|---|---|
| Sunbeam Corporation | 4/89 | 4/91 |

| Job Title: | Industry: |
|---|---|
| Senior Operational Auditor | Manufacturing |

**Accomplishments/Responsibilities:** (Simple HTML allowed)

Government division audits exposed: millions of dollars in committed-yet-unapproved appropriations; out-of-control inventory; unjustified project delays; high-dollar purchases without valid POs. Manufacturing audits exposed major discrepancies between the actual parts, BOM, and engineering drawings.

**FIGURE 10.7d. Power of the Internet: Real-Life Client Registers with www.CareerJournal.com: Completed "ResumeBuilder" Input Form: CareerJournal.com from *The Wall Street Journal***

*Step 7:* Bob next focuses on the "Skills" and "Accomplishments" sections. Note that the skills and accomplishment sections of ResumeBuilder (Figures 10.7b and 10.7c) correspond exactly to the skills and accomplishment sections of Bob's letter/resume package (Figures 10.1a to 10.1c) developed in earlier chapters—this will significantly expedite the registration process.

*Step 8:* After opening the MS Word files containing his letter and resume, Bob highlights (with the mouse) and copies the two-column skills section of his resume (Figure 10.1b). He then pastes these skills into the "Skills" section of ResumeBuilder. Because ResumeBuilder does not allow for columns, it left justifies the two columns (see page 295). Because this vertical formatting does not make the most effective use of space, Bob makes some quick manual adjustments in Step 9.

**Skills Copied from MS Word to ResumeBuilder: Columns Are Left-Justified (Adjust in Step 9)**

Career Skills/Key Words Include:

o Risk management

o Leasing/retail financing

o Quality/reengineering

o P&L management/systems

o Balance sheet management/systems

o Portfolio risk management

o Leveraged leasing

o Residual value analysis/reserves

o Loss reserves

o Provision for reserves

o Delinquency analysis/monitoring

o Inventory monitoring/remarketing

o Inventory write-downs

o Write-offs and loss recovery

Additional Skills/Key Words:

o Auditing/financial management

o General portfolio accounting

o Marketing support/subvention

o Portfolio systems accounting security

o Business planning/aviation/ABL

o Annual audit plan development/budgeting

o Computerized audit department startup

o Manpower planning/staff development

o Year-end audits/outside auditor controls

o Major operational and financial audits

o Financial controls/collections turnaround

o Process improvement/compliance audits

o IT operational reviews/security

o Cost reductions/productivity growth

*Step 9:* To make better use of space, Bob reformats the left-justified, vertical listing of skills/key words. He creates a horizontal listing of skills/key words separated by colons and semi-colons (see page 296 and Figure 10.7b). This completes the skills section of ResumeBuilder.

**Adjusted/Reformatted Skills List to Replace Above Vertical List
(see ResumeBuilder Figure 10.7b)**

Career Skills/Key Words Include:
Risk management: Leasing/retail financing; Quality/reengineering; P&L management/systems; Balance sheet management/systems; Portfolio risk management; Leveraged leasing; Residual value analysis/reserves; Loss reserves; Provision for reserves; Delinquency analysis/monitoring; Inventory monitoring/remarketing; Inventory write-downs; Write-offs and loss recovery.

Additional Skills/Key Words:
Auditing/financial management: General portfolio accounting; Marketing support/subvention; Portfolio systems accounting security; Business planning/aviation/ABL; Annual audit plan development/budgeting; Computerized audit department startup; Manpower planning/staff development; Year-end audits/outside auditor controls; Major operational and financial audits; Financial controls/collections turnaround; Process improvement/compliance audits; IT operational reviews/security; Cost reductions and productivity growth.

*Note:* Because employers use key words to search resume databases, these skills listings/key words are pivotal to the job search.

*Step 10:* Bob proceeds to the "Employment History" section of ResumeBuilder, where he will once again extract information directly from his letter/resume package. For "Current Employer," "Previous Employer," and "Previous Employer 2" (Figures 10.7b and 10.7c), Bob quickly types in company names, dates, and job titles—and selects the "Industries" of his three past employers from the listing provided by ResumeBuilder.

*Step 11:* Bob next addresses the "Accomplishments/Responsibilities" to be entered for each employer. Accessing his MS Word letter and resume files, Bob reviews and selects bulleted accomplishments for inclusion in ResumeBuilder. The reader should follow the steps Bob used to extract information from his letter/resume package.

*Step 11A:* For his current employer, Agra Financial Services, Bob selects, copies, and pastes into ResumeBuilder (Figure 10.7b) five bulleted achievements from his cover letter (Figure 10.1a). Even though his resume (Figure 10.1b) contains additional achievements at Agra Financial, he chose not to include them in ResumeBuilder since the five accomplishments in the letter (Figure 10.1a) adequately reflect his success at AFS. When selecting achievements for inclusion in ResumeBuilder, a good rule of thumb is to choose the top five or six accomplishments for each employer. This should be sufficient to make your case.

*Step 11B:* For his previous employer (Global Resource Corporation), Bob selects, copies, and pastes into ResumeBuilder (Figure 10.7c) the first five achievements under GRC from page 2 of his resume (Figure 10.1c). Bob once again chose not to include all of his achievements. The first five adequately reflect his success at GRC.

*Step 11C:* For previous employer 2 (Sunbeam Corporation), Bob copies and pastes into ResumeBuilder (Figure 10.7c) the brief paragraph of accomplishments from page 2 of his resume (Figure 10.1c). This completes "Employment History."

*Step 12:* Bob quickly fills in the education and references section of ResumeBuilder (Figure 10.7d) and does not change the default settings for Layout and Format. The input form is complete. Bob clicks the "Build Resume" icon (Figure 10.7d).

*Step 13:* Bob thoroughly reviews the completed Resume and Background Brief (Figures 10.8a to 10.8d). He makes no changes and fills in the e-mail Address and Password at the bottom of the completed resume (Figure 10.8d). Bob clicks the "Update" icon.

*Step 14:* Bob reads a confirmation message indicating that his resume has been updated (and stored). The registration is now complete: Bob can now use his registered resume to respond to recruiters and many of the open jobs listed by CareerJournal .com.

## Case History Continues: Client Registers with CareerJournal.com's Job Agent

To activate CareerJournal's job agent feature, Bob clicks the "Home" icon, returning him to CareerJournal's home page (Figures 10.2a and 10.2b). He clicks on the "Site Map" link in the left-hand column. On the site map Web page (Figure 10.4a), Bob clicks the "Job Agent" link, which takes him to the "Job Seek Agents" sign up page (Figures 10.9a and 10.9b). He enters duration/frequency parameters, search criteria (including keywords, location, and job category), and his e-mail address. He clicks the "Save" icon. Bob receives new job listings from the job agent daily based on his specific search criteria.

FIGURE 10.8a. Power of the Internet: Real-Life Client Registers with www.CareerJournal.com: Completed "ResumeBuilder" Resume: CareerJournal.com from *The Wall Street Journal*

WSJ.com **CareerJournal**
*from* THE WALL STREET JOURNAL

*The Premier Career Site For Executives, Managers and Professionals*

| HOME | SALARY & HIRING INFO | CAREER COLUMNISTS | WHO'S NEWS | JOB-HUNTING ADVICE | MANAGE YOUR CAREER | EXECUTIVE RECRUITERS | HR CENTER |

Our Partners: **Artemis** | **Bookstore** | **Who's Hiring** | **Marketplace**

**POST A JOB:** POST individual positions on CareerJournal.com

**FIND A HEADHUNTER:** SEARCH our directory of Executive Recruiters

## Resume Builder

*Account Info/Contact Info*

**First Name:**
Robert

**Last Name:**
Gordon

**Address:**
One Sutton Place

**City:**
New York

**Country:**
United States

**Zip:**
10022

NY

**Home Phone:**
(212)555-1234

**Work Phone:**
(212)555-2345

## Resume:

Contact Information:

Robert Gordon
rgmanager@aol.com
One Sutton Place
New York, NY 10022
Home:(212)555-1234
Work: (212)555-2345

Miscellaneous Information:

I am interested in pursuing a senior management position in the Financial Industry.

I am currently working as a Manager of Risk and Portfolio Management for Agra Financial Services (AFS).

————continued————

**FIGURE 10.8b. Power of the Internet: Real-Life Client Registers with www.CareerJournal.com: Completed "ResumeBuilder" Resume: CareerJournal.com from *The Wall Street Journal***

**Resume:**

Career Skills/Key Words Include:

Risk management skills: Leasing/retail financing; Quality/reengineering; P&L management/systems; Balance sheet management/systems; Portfolio risk management; Leveraged leasing; Residual value analysis/reserves; Loss reserves; Provision for reserves; Delinquency analysis/monitoring; Inventory monitoring/remarketing; Inventory write-downs; Write-offs and loss recovery.

Additional Skills/Key Words:

Auditing/financial management skills: General portfolio accounting; Marketing support/subvention; Portfolio systems accounting security; Business planning/aviation/ABL; Annual audit plan development/budgeting; Computerized audit department startup; Manpower planning/staff development; Year-end audits/outside auditor controls; Major operational and financial audits; Financial controls/collections turnaround; Process improvement/compliance audits; IT operational reviews/security; Cost reductions and productivity growth.

I am elibible to work in the United States.

I need 200k/year to consider leaving my current position.

Employment History:

Agra Financial Services (AFS) (4/97–Present)

Job Title: Manager of Risk and Portfolio Management

Accomplishments/Responsibilities:

- Exposed and assuaged serious downside risks; based on huge inventory of used agricultural equipment, poor remarketing, and scant reserves, persuaded management to take drastic measures including major organizational changes and a $92 million lump sum write-off followed by monthly charges to P&L of $12 million to build reserves; failure to act would have doubled the losses recorded between 1997 and 2001.

- In spite of losses generated by AFS, forestalled downgrading of credit rating by preparing and delivering strong reports to Moody's and S&P detailing corrective action plans; added $125 million to the bottom-line by producing a study that allowed AFS to reduce residual reserves for key products from 7% to 6%.

- Shifted $78.9 million from deferred income to P&L by completing—and negotiating approval for—complex analysis of residual supports paid to AFS by N.A. subsidiaries; negotiated early end to payment supports allowing AFS to shift over $60 million from deferred income to the P&L over a three-year period.

- In response to massive volume of lease maturities engulfing the Seattle CSC, initiated and managed a temporary remarketing phone bank at our New York City HQ: aggressive remarketing eliminated backlog and quickly produced over 400 lease extensions. 190 customer purchases, and 212 continued billings.

- After AFS merger with Deere & Company, was offered promotion to Manager of Portfolio Risk Management with responsibility for JD Financial lease portfolios for U.S. and Europe: accountabilities included profit maximization, policies, reporting, and strategic projects related to business development, residual financing and remarketing; based on factors that precluded relocation to the Midwest. declined the offer.

—continued—

**FIGURE 10.8c.   Power of the Internet: Real-Life Client Registers with www.CareerJournal.com: Completed "ResumeBuilder" Resume: CareerJournal.com from *The Wall Street Journal***

**Resume:**

Global Resource Corporation (GRC) (4/91–3/97)

Job Title: Director of Corporate Internal Audit

Accomplishments/Responsibilities:

Expanded IA's charter and radically restructured annual audit plans: shifted focus from compliance to unstructured operational audits as chief investigative arm of senior management; introduced state-of-the-art auditing techniques and computerized manual operations in spite of strong resistance from IT.

Exposed and resolved potentially disastrous legal and financial exposures related to noncompliance with state and local taxes applied to customer lease payments; automated out-of-control processes; initiated much needed systems integration; and effected major organizational and policy changes.

Worked with GRC and C&L senior management in scheduling and executing year-end audits: saved tens of thousands of dollars in fees by developing new CAAT applications for use by C&L; created automated account confirmation process; expanded the year-end audits to include GRC subsidiaries.

Exposed and fixed weak controls over multimillion dollar streams of cash flowing between GRC and its equipment dealers; stopped big dollar overpayments to dealers cause by untrained staffers who failed to net current and overdue amounts owed to GRC by dealers against amounts owed to dealers.

Saved failed remarketing program by forcing GRC Quebec to establish a corporate office with new staff; fixed weak controls over Repo Inventory that had caused inventory aged over 90 days to rise from 17% to 56% of total assets; rectified weak controls over Loss Recovery that had caused doubling of write-offs.

Sunbeam Corporation (4/89–4/91)

Job Title: Senior Operational Auditor

Accomplishments/Responsibilities:

Government division audits exposed: millions of dollars in committed-yet-unapproved appropriations; out-of-control inventory; unjustified project delays; high-dollar purchases without valid POs. Manufacturing audits exposed major discrepancies between the actual parts, BOM, and engineering drawings.

Education:

Attended University of Illinois from 1985 to 1989 and received a(n) Bachelor's degree with a 3.5 G.P.A.

References:

John Everhardt - VP Business Development - Bear Stearns (212)555-3456
Richard Abernathy - Director of Finance - KPMG (212)555-4567

**FIGURE 10.8d. Power of the Internet: Real-Life Client Registers with www.CareerJournal.com: Completed "ResumeBuilder" Resume: CareerJournal.com from *The Wall Street Journal***

**Background Brief:**

Career Skills/Key Words Include:

Risk management skills: Leasing/retail financing; Quality/reengineering; P&L management/systems; Balance sheet management/systems; Portfolio risk management; Leveraged leasing; Residual value analysis/reserves; Loss reserves; Provision for reserves; Delinquency analysis/monitoring; Inventory monitoring/remarketing; Inventory write-downs; Write-offs and loss recovery.

Additional Skills/Key Words:

Auditing/financial management skills: General portfolio accounting; Marketing support/subvention; Portfolio systems accounting security; Business planning/aviation/ABL; Annual audit plan development/budgeting; Computerized audit department startup; Manpower planning/staff development; Year-end audits/outside auditor controls; Major operational and financial audits; Financial controls/collections turnaround; Process improvement/compliance audits; IT operational reviews/security; Cost reductions and productivity growth.

**Current Employer*:**
Agra Financial Services (A

**Job Title*:**
Manager of Risk and Portfo

**Function:**
Finance

**Years at Present Company:**
4

**Industry:**

**Years at Present Position:**
4

**Total years of experience:**
11–15

☑ **I am willing to relocate to:**
Open

**Salary Range:**
150–200k

**Citizenship:**
US Citizen

**Language(s):**
English
Arabic
Cantonese
Chinese

**Education:**
Bachelors

**Email Address*:**
rgmanager@aol.com

**Password*:**
*******

**Confirm Password*:**
*******

**Secret Question*:**
Mother's Maiden Name

**Answer*:**
Ross

[ Update ]    [ Delete ]

**FIGURE 10.9a. Power of the Internet: Real-Life Client Registers with www.CareerJournal.com: "Job Seek Agents" Sign Up Form: CareerJournal.com from *The Wall Street Journal***

*from* THE WALL STREET JOURNAL.

CareerJournal

WSJ.com

*The Premier Career Site*
*For Executives, Managers*
*and Professionals*

POST A JOB: POST individual positions on CareerJournal.com

FIND A HEADHUNTER: SEARCH our directory of Executive Recruiters

| HOME | SALARY & HIRING INFO | CAREER COLUMNISTS | WHO'S NEWS | JOB-HUNTING ADVICE | MANAGE YOUR CAREER | EXECUTIVE RECRUITERS | HR CENTER |

*Our Partners:* Artemis | Bookstore | Who's Hiring | Marketplace

## Job Seek Agents

Create a new customized e-mail Job Seek Agent here. Simply fill out the form below, and we will automatically send you, by e-mail, new job listings for the specific search criteria you choose.

*Duration/Frequency:*

E-mail results every [ 1 ◆ ] day(s) and keep sending them [ Forever ◆ ]

*Search Criteria:*

**Search**
○ Job Titles  ● Full Text

**Search jobs by keyword:**
risk, auditing
(eg., sales, CFO, Germany, "vice president")

**Find jobs with:**
● Any words  ○ All of the words

[ Save ]

**Sort by**
● Date  ○ Relevance

**FIGURE 10.9b.    Power of the Internet: Real-Life Client Registers with www.CareerJournal.com: "Job Seek Agents" Sign Up Form: CareerJournal.com from *The Wall Street Journal***

Location:

New York

(eg., New York, Paris, Tokyo OR 10027)

☐ Search CareerJournalEurope.com jobs only

Corporate Partners:

All
Abbott Laboratories
AIG-Valic Financial
Allstate Financial

Willing to commute:

Optional

☐ Search CareerJournalAsia.com jobs only

Category:

All
Accounting
Administrative/Support Services
Advertising

E-mail results to*:

rgmanager@aol.com

☑ Send Job Seek Agent as a web page

☑ I would like to receive occasional important information by e-mail

If I am outside the U.S., by submitting this request, I consent to the transfer to the U.S. of all of the information I am providing.

[Save]

## Case History Wrap: Client Explores Managing Your Career and Job-Hunting Advice

After registering his resume and signing up for the job agent, Bob decides to explore and capitalize on other CareerJournal features including "Manage Your Career" (Figures 10.10a and 10.10b) and "Job-Hunting Advice" (Figures 10.11a and 10.11b). The career management site offers over a dozen categories of professional advice covering such issues as climbing the corporate ladder, retirement planning, surviving a crisis, working abroad, returning to school, legal concerns, work and family, and age discrimination. The job-hunting site offers advice in a dozen categories including career change, networking, negotiation tips, the net, job loss, relocation, interviewing, options and benefits, and resumes. Bob routinely visits both sites.

Now that you are registered with CareerJournal.com, it's time to capitalize further on the megapower of the World Wide Web. The *24/7 Online Job Search Directory* in Chapter 11 facilitates and expedites this process.

FIGURE 10.10a. Power of the Internet: Real-Life Client Registers with www.CareerJournal.com: "Manage Your Career" Resource Center: CareerJournal.com from *The Wall Street Journal*

## Reach Your Career Goals
## By Managing Your Boss

Climbing the Ladder: Do you and your manager seem to clash over every idea or proposal you present? Maybe you aren't speaking the same language. Here's how to recognize and deliver what your boss wants.

## Motivating Your Staff
## Through the Downturn

Management Style: In the wake of the dot-com bubble, companies are struggling to keep employees happy -- and driven -- with stock options. Find out how top managers are boosting morale and productivity despite the economic obstacles.

## How Employees Adapt
## To Workplace Changes

Office Life: For countless professionals across the country, office life has changed since Sept. 11. Find out how people are dealing with both mundane and profound alterations.

**FIGURE 10.10b. Power of the Internet: Real-Life Client Registers with www.CareerJournal.com: "Manage Your Career" Resource Center: CareerJournal.com from *The Wall Street Journal***

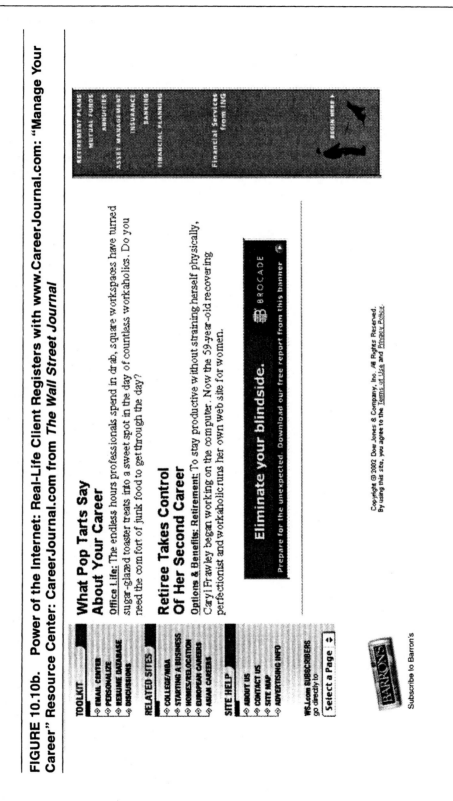

TOOLKIT
- EMAIL CENTER
- PERSONALIZE
- RESUME DATABASE
- DISCUSSIONS

RELATED SITES
- COLLEGE/MBA
- STARTING A BUSINESS
- HOMES/RELOCATION
- EUROPEAN CAREERS
- ASIAN CAREERS

SITE HELP
- ABOUT US
- CONTACT US
- SITE MAP
- ADVERTISING INFO

WSJ.com SUBSCRIBERS
go directly to

Select a Page ◆

Subscribe to Barron's

## What Pop Tarts Say About Your Career

Office Life: The endless hours professionals spend in drab, square workspaces have turned sugar-glazed toaster treats into a sweet spot in the day of countless workaholics. Do you need the comfort of junk food to get through the day?

## Retiree Takes Control Of Her Second Career

Options & Benefits: Retirement: To stay productive without straining herself physically, Caryl Frawley began working on the computer. Now the 59-year-old recovering perfectionist and workaholic runs her own web site for women.

**Eliminate your blindside.**   ❖ BROCADE

Prepare for the unexpected. Download our free report from this banner

**FIGURE 10.11a.** Power of the Internet: Real-Life Client Registers with www.CareerJournal.com: "Job-Hunting Advice" Resource Center: CareerJournal.com from *The Wall Street Journal*

WSJ.com

**CareerJournal**

*from* **THE WALL STREET JOURNAL.**

*The Premier Career Site*
*For Executives, Managers*
*and Professionals*

| HOME | SALARY & HIRING INFO | CAREER COLUMNISTS | WHO'S NEWS | FIND A JOB! | JOB-HUNTING ADVICE | MANAGE YOUR CAREER | EXECUTIVE RECRUITERS | HR CENTER |

Artemis | Bookstore | Who's Hiring | Marketplace

**ARTICLE SEARCH**
- KEYWORD
- Site  Section
- Advanced Search · GO

Our Partners:

> Home > Job-Hunting Advice

**JOB-HUNTING ADVICE**
- RESUMES / COVER LETTERS
- INTERVIEWING
- CHANGING CAREERS
- NETWORKING
- SEARCH STRATEGIES
- USING THE NET
- AFTER A JOB LOSS
- WORKING ABROAD
- NEGOTIATION TIPS
- HELP WANTED
- RELOCATION INFO
- OPTIONS & BENEFITS

**TOOLKIT**
- EMAIL CENTER
- PERSONALIZE
- RESUME DATABASE
- DISCUSSIONS

FIND A JOB!
Keyword [        ] GO

## Why Resume Revision Means Never Being Done

After a Job Loss: Few exercises can be as frustrating and bewildering as rewriting your resume. Tim Johnston shares his account of this never-ending process as he chronicles his hunt for employment.

## Finding the Truth Behind Online Job-Search Myths

Using the Net: If you expect to be offered job opportunities simply for posting your resume on the Web, think again. Here's how to avoid falling victim to common myths about taking your hunt to the Internet.

## Build Your Own Brand To Rev Up Your Career

Search Strategies: Smart executives use the principles of branding to advance their careers and companies. These practical steps will help you create your own brand statement.

POST A JOB: POST individual positions on CareerJournal.com

FIND A HEADHUNTER: SEARCH our directory of Executive Recruiters

**Marketplace**
- Free Resume Critique
- Career Counseling
- Contact Recruiter
- Search HR Directors
- Find $100K+ Jobs
- Reference Checking
- Executives Inside
- Networking Members
- Tip of the Week
- More...

**Executive Education**
- Search for Programs
- View Business Schools

**FIGURE 10.11b.** Power of the Internet: Real-Life Client Registers with www.CareerJournal.com: "Job-Hunting Advice" Resource Center: CareerJournal.com from *The Wall Street Journal*

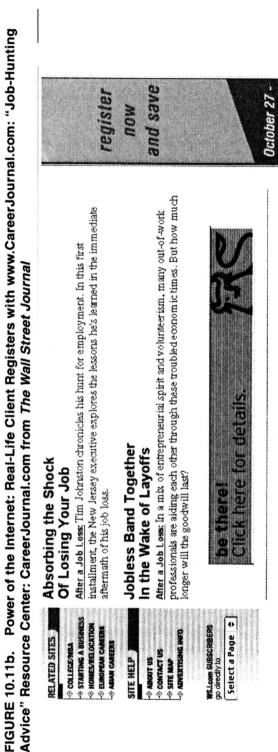

RELATED SITES

◇ COLLEGE/MBA
◇ STARTING A BUSINESS
◇ HOMES/RELOCATION
◇ EUROPEAN CAREERS
◇ ASIAN CAREERS

SITE HELP

◇ ABOUT US
◇ CONTACT US
◇ SITE MAP
◇ ADVERTISING INFO

WSJ.com SUBSCRIBERS
go directly to

Select a Page ◆

## Absorbing the Shock
## Of Losing Your Job

After a Job Loss: Tim Johnston chronicles his hunt for employment. In this first installment, the New Jersey executive explores the lessons he's learned in the immediate aftermath of his job loss.

## Jobless Band Together
## In the Wake of Layoffs

After a Job Loss: In a mix of entrepreneurial spirit and volunteerism, many out-of-work professionals are aiding each other through these troubled economic times. But how much longer will the goodwill last?

be there!
Click here for details.

register
now
and save

October 27 -
November 1

# 11

The 24/7 Online
Job Search Directory:
Market-Tested
Career and Job
Search Web Sites

---

**THE INTERNET HONOR ROLL; JOB SEARCH
ICONS OF THE WORLD WIDE WEB**

**Margaret F. Dikel:** *The Riley Guide: Employment Job Resources on the Internet* (www.rileyguide.com)

**Pam Dixon:** *The Dixon Report: The Online Job Search Companion* (www.pamdixon.com)

**Dr. Randall Hansen:** Publisher/Webmaster: *Quintessential Careers: Job Guide* (www.careerdoctor.org)

**Dave Opton:** Executive Director-ExecuNet, Inc.: Center for Executive Careers (www.execunet.com)

**Peter D. Weddle:** *WEDDLE's: Internet Resources for Job Seekers/Career Activists* (www.weddles.com)

---

## A BRIEF WORD ABOUT SOME TRUE ICONS OF THE INTERNET

Before discussing *The 24/7 Online Job Search Directory*—which is based on intense online research one Web site at a time—I want to pay tribute to a select few whose contributions to the Internet have made them true icons. In drafting this directory, I navigated and researched countless Web sites in search of the best. This research not only revealed the quality Web sites in the directory—it also revealed names of trailblazers who have made the Web an essential job search tool. In alphabetical order, these icons are Margaret Dikel, Pam Dixon, Randall Hansen, Dave Opton, and Peter Weddle. Their early vision brought critically needed organization, creativity, and discipline to the untamed Web. Margaret Dikel is a noted author, columnist, and Internet consultant for HR industry leader Drake Beam Morin. Her milestone Web site, *The Riley Guide,* is a pioneering guide (www.rileyguide.com) to job search resources on the Internet. Veteran Internet authority Pam Dixon is a respected journalist, speaker, and award-winning author of online job search and other technology-related books. Her *Dixon Report/Online Job Search Companion* Web site (www.pamdixon.com) includes weekly updates and select lists of career and job search sites. Dr. Randall Hansen is Webmaster and Publisher of *Quintessential Careers,* a milestone career center (www.quintcareers.com) where he is a career advisor and commentator. Dave Opton is Executive Director of ExecuNet, Inc., a veteran, membership-based executive networking and job search center (www.execunet.com). Mr. Opton is among the earliest visionaries to identify and harness the untapped potential of the Internet. As an Internet luminary, Peter Weddle is a senior executive turned commentator and author whose business career, books, and career Web sites have established him as a true icon. *WEDDLE's Guide to Employment Resources on the Internet* (www.weddles.com) is a milestone Web site.

## INTRODUCTION: THE 24/7 ONLINE JOB SEARCH DIRECTORY: MARKET-TESTED CAREER AND JOB SEARCH WEB SITES

*The 24/7 Online Job Search Directory* starting on page 319 was researched—via the online research sources listed at the front of the directory—and developed from the bottom up. Each and every Web site was visited, revisited, researched, and probed before a final decision was made—if there were any doubts about a Web site, it was deleted from the directory. As of this writing, all of the Web sites in the directory are active. Of course, this does not guarantee that the ongoing consolidations and business failures within the dot-com business sector won't claim some of the Web sites in the directory. However, many of the sites listed are owned and operated by some of the most dynamic and durable names in the job search industry— including such premium names as Korn/Ferry International, Heidrick & Struggles, Spencer Stuart, A. T. Kearney, Whitehead Mann Group, The Whitney Group, DHR International, Management Recruiters International, and TMP Worldwide Executive Search. Other enduring names in the *24/7 Directory* include the Riley Guide, Quintessential Careers, Kennedy Information, Pam Dixon's Online Job Search Companion, Peter Weddle, Hunt-Scanlon, CareerJournal from the *Wall Street Journal*, and ExecuNet—an executive career center affiliated with CareerJournal. As for the consolidations taking place in the industry, CareerBuilder recently acquired the Headhunter Web site (CareerBuilder's new web address is www.headhunter.net). You will be able to keep up with such changes through the real-time career centers (e.g., www.rileyguide .com and www.quintcareers.com) included in the 24/7 directory— which will serve you well now and in the coming years.

## THE 24/7 ONLINE JOB SEARCH DIRECTORY: SIX GROUPS AND 19 CATEGORIES

The directory names and addresses are broken down into 19 major categories and organized into six major group headings. The 19 categories are further broken down into subcategories to make the directory as user-friendly as possible.

### Group One: Career and Job Search Sites for Senior Executives and Professionals

I. Online Job Search Sites/Job Listings/Select Recruiters
II. Specialty Job Search Sites/Job Listings/Select Recruiters
III. International Job Search Sites/Job Listings/Select Recruiters
IV. Fee-Based Career Services and Contact Information Resources

*Group One* consists of many of the most respected names in senior level executive placement:

*Category I (Online Job Search Sites)* includes such top tier players as e-Korn/Ferry (http://ekornferry.com), Spencer Stuart Talent Network (www.spencerstuart.com), A.T. Kearney (www.executivesearch.atkearney.com), Russell Reynolds (www.rresweb.russreyn.com), Christian & Timbers (www.ctnet.com/contact/contact2.asp), Hunt Howe Partners (www.hunthowe.com), Conboy, Sur & Associates (www .conboysur.com/Why.htm), Ethos Consulting (www .ethosconsulting.com), Ogden Partnership (www.ogdon.com), ExecuNet (www.execunet.com), Quintessential Careers (http://quintcareers.com/executive_jobs.html), Riley Guide (www.rileyguide.com), Kennedy Information (www .kennedyinfo.com), WEDDLE's (www.weddles.com/jobcatalog .htm), and CareerJournal.com (careerjournal.com/partners /advsearch.html). *Category I* also includes such respected executive job boards as Futurestep (www.futurestep.com), Heidrick & Struggles Management Search (http://msp.heidrick.com/home .asp), BrilliantPeople (www.brilliantpeople.com), CFO Magazine (www.cfo.com/careers), CIO Magazine (www.cio.com/career), CEO Update (www.associationjobs.com), CareerJournal Europe (careerjournaleurope.com), 6FigureJobs (www.6figurejobs.com), HotJobs2000 (www.hotjobs2000.com), and ChiefMonster (www.chief.monster.com)—a Web site for senior executives owned and operated by TMP Worldwide and their Monster Division.

*Category II (Specialty Job Search Sites)* includes such industry leaders as Heidrick & Struggles (www.heidrick.com /industry_expertise.htm), Herbert Mines Associates (www .herbertmines.com/credentials.html), Preng & Associates (www.preng.com/experience.htm), Wyatt & Jaffe (www.wyattjaffe .com), DHR International (www.dhrintl.net/index3.html), Plummer & Associates (www.plummersearch.com), BTS Executive Search (www.btssearch.com), Atlantic Research Technologies (www.atlanticresearch.com), Gilreath Search (www.gilreathsearch .com), Bloomberg (www.bloomberg.com/careers), ET Search (www.etsearch.com/searches.html), Ray & Berndtson (www .rayberndtson.com), Solomon-Page Group (http://company .monster.com/solpage), JobLink for Journalists (newslink.org/newjoblinksearch.html), J. Robert Scott (j-robert-scott.com/aboutus.html), Legalstaff (www.legalstaff .com), MedHunters (www.medhunters.com), USAJOBS (www .usajobs.opm.gov/a3.htm), DRG Nonprofit Executive Search (www.drgnyc.com), Quintessential Careers (http://quintcareers .com/former_military_networking.html), and Transition Assistance Online (www.taonline.com).

*Category III (International Job Search Sites)* includes such prestigious firms as Amrop Hever Group (www.amrop.com/home.html),

Egon Zehnder (www.zehnder.com), Ward Howell Euroselect (www.wardhowell.at/html/index_flash.htm), IIC Partners (www .iicpartners.com/focus), Stanton Chase International (www.stantonchase.com), Austin McGregor International (www.amidallas.com), and Raines International (www .rainesinternational.com/resumeform.cfm). Other resources in *Category III* include CareerJournal Asia (www.careerjournalasia .com) and StepStone's European Career Portal (www .stepstone.com).

*Category IV (Fee-Based Career Services and Contact Information Resources)* includes such names as ExecuNet (www.execunet.com), Kennedy Information (www.kennedyinfo.com/db/db_dhr_bas .html), BlueSteps (www.bluesteps.com), 6FigureJobs (www .6figurejobs.com), ExecutivesOnly (www.executivesonly.com), WEDDLE's (www.weddles.com/jobcatalog.htm), Hunt-Scanlon (www.hunt-scanlon.com/shop), CEO UPDATE (www .associationjobs.com), and CareerJournal Marketplace (www.careerjournal.com/marketplace)—comprised of select fee-based executive job search, networking, outplacement, counseling, reference-checking, and contact information services.

The powerhouse Web sites in Group One will be the nucleus of your executive job search campaign.

## Group Two: Career Centers and Multicultural Resource Centers

    V.  Career and Job Search Resource Centers
   VI.  Diversity and Multicultural Career Resource Centers

*Group Two* includes some of the most respected career and multicultural resource centers on the Web:

*Category V (Career and Job Search Resource Centers)* is composed of such respected names as the Riley Guide (www.rileyguide.com), Quintessential Careers (www.quintcareers.com/general_resources .html), Job-Hunt (www.job-hunt.org), Online Job Search Companion (www.pamdixon.com/jobsearch.htm), CareerInfoNet (www.acinet.org/acinet/library.htm), About.com (www.about .com/careers), CIO Magazine (www.cio.com), Yahoo! Executive Career Center (http://executive.yahoo.com), and JobHuntersBible (www.jobhuntersbible.com/sitemap.shtml) from the distinguished author of *What Color Is Your Parachute.*

*Category VI (Diversity and Multicultural Career Resource Centers)* is composed of several diversity Web sites including Quintessential Careers Diversity Career Resources (www.quintcareers.com

/diversity_resources.html), CareerCity Diversity Job Center (http://djb.jobcontrolcenter.com/search/index.cfm), Minority Executive Search (www.minorityexecsearch.com), iVillage (www.ivillage.com/work/job), Native American Jobs (www.nativeamericanjobs.com), The Black Collegian On-line (www.black-collegian.com), National Black MBA Association (www.nbmbaa.org), Hispanic Alliance for Career Enhancement (www.hace-usa.org), LatPro (www.latpro.com), and the National Association of Asian American Professionals (www.naaap.org/naaap/contact.html). Sites for the disabled include Quintessential Career's Career Resources for the Disabled (www.quintcareers.com/disabled_career_resources.html), the Riley Guide's Resources for the Disabled (www.rileyguide.com/vets.html), JobAccess (www.jobaccess.org), National Business & Disability Council (www.businessdisability.com), and Careers and the dis-ABLED (www.eop.com/compcd.html). Sites for older candidates include FortyPlus (www.fp.org/chapters.htm), ThirdAgeCareers (www.thirdage.com/money/careers), CareerJournal's 50+ Profes-sionals Web site (www.careerjournal.com/myc/fifty), and Quin-tessential Careers Job Resources for Mature and Older Jobseekers (www.quintcareers.com/mature_jobseekers.html).

## Group Three: Career and Job Search Sites for Executives/Managers/Professionals

> VII. Online Job Search Sites/Job Listings/Select Recruiters
> VIII. Specialty Job Search Sites/Job Listings/Select Recruiters
> IX. International Job Search Sites/Job Listings/Select Recruiters

*Group Three* includes more of the best names in the job search industry:

*Category VII (Online Job Search Sites)* is composed of such re-spected firms as Kensington International (www.kionline.com/p&s_rs.htm), D.E. Foster Partners (www.fosterpartners.com), Boyden Global Search (www.boyden.com), LucasCareers (www.lucascareers.com), and WJM Associates (www.wjmassoc.com), a search firm founded by outplacement industry icon William J. Morin. Other recruiter Web sites in this category include Korn/Ferry International's Futurestep (www.futurestep.com) and Management Recruiters' BrilliantPeople (www.brilliantpeople.com). Major career portals and job boards in *Category VII* include CareerJournal.com (careerjournal.com/partners/advsearch.html),

Monster (www.monster.com), JobStar.org (http://jobstar.org
/jobstar.cfm), Flipdog (www.flipdog.com), CareerBuilder
(www.headhunter.net), HotJobs (www.hotjobs.com), JobBankUSA
(www.jobbankusa.com), Career.com (www.career.com), Employment 911 (www.employment911.com/asp/JobSeekersEnter.asp),
and EmployersOnline (www.employersonline.com).

*Category VIII (Specialty Job Search Sites)* includes Diversified
Search (www.diversifiedsearch.com/about.htm), NationJob
(www.nationjob.com/frqsrc.html), Kenzer Corporation (www
.kenzer.com), SalesJobs (www.salesjobs.com), Dice
(www.dice.com), Boston Search Group (www.bsgweb.com),
HotJobs2000 (www.hotjobs2000.com), Techies (www.techies.com),
ITcareers (www.itcareers.com), IEEE.org (www.ieee.org
/membership/benefits/careers.html), American Association
of Finance and Accounting (www.aafa.com), BankJobs (www
.bankjobs.com), K. Russo Associates (www.krussoassociates.com),
LawJobs (www.lawjobs.com), HealthCareerWeb
(www.healthcareerweb.com/jobseeker), JournalismJobs
(www.journalismjobs.com), and JobsInSports
(www.jobsinsports.com). Additional sites in *Category VIII*
include USAJOBS (www.usajobs.opm.gov), FedWorld (www
.fedworld.gov/jobs/jobsearch.html), DRG Nonprofit Executive
Search (www.drgnyc.com), Military.com (www.military.com
/Careers/JobSearch), Riley Guide Resources for Military Personnel
(www.rileyguide.com/vets.html), and Quintessential Careers Job
Search Resources by Specialty and Industry (www.quintcareers
.com/indres.html).

*Category IX (International Job Search Sites)* includes World Search
Group (www.worldsearchgroup.com), Michael Page International
(www.michaelpage.com.au), Maxwell Executive Search
(http://maxwellsearch.netfirms.com), EMA Partners International
(www.ema-partners.net/offices/window.html), PEAT Executive
Search (www.peat.ch/eng.htm), and Global Search USA
(www.globalsearchusa.net). International job boards in *Category IX*
include CareerJournal Europe (careerjournaleurope.com), Career-
Journal Asia (www.careerjournalasia.com), CareerBuilder International Gateway (www.headhunter.net/jobseeker/jobs
/jobfindil.asp?CH=IL), Financial Job Network (www.fjn.com
/default.asp), JobsDB Interactive Recruitment Network (www
.jobsdb.com), BrassRing International Sites (www.brassring.com),
OverseasJobs (www.overseasjobs.com), GoJobsite (www.jobsite
.co.uk), CareerOne (www.careerone.com.au), and GlobalGateway

(http://globalgateway.monster.com), which is owned and operated by TMP Worldwide Executive Search and their Monster Division.

**Group Four: Job Search Contact Information Resources**

      X. Recruiter Contact Resources: Executive Recruiter Listing Directories/Databases
     XI. Recruiter Contact Resources: Select Recruiter Listing
    XII. Online Classified Ads: Global Newspaper Listing Directories
   XIII. Online Classified Ads: Major U.S. Regional and National Newspapers
   XIV. Direct Company Contacts: Company Listing Web Sites
    XV. Mass Mailing Services: Fee-Based Online Resume Distribution Services

*Group Four* includes some of the best reference material and contact information Web sites:

*Category X (Executive Recruiter Listing Directories)* includes directories and databases from such names as ExecutiveAgent (www.executiveagent.com/about/about.html), Kennedy Information (www.kennedyinfo.com/db/db_der_bas.html), Recruiters Online Network (www.recruitersonline.com/match/search.phtml), Top Echelon (www.topechelon.com/employers/findrecr.asp), Hunt-Scanlon's RecruiterLink (www.recruiterlink.com), and BlueSteps (www.bluesteps.com), a fee-based service of the Association of Executive Search Consultants (AESC).

*Category XI (Select Recruiter Listing)* includes such names as Korn/Ferry International (www.kornferry.com), Heidrick & Struggles (www.heidrick.com), Spencer Stuart (www.spencerstuart.com), Russell Reynolds (www.russreyn.com/firmprofile/index.asp), McCray, Hewitt & Associates (www.mccray-inc.com), Graystone Partners (www.graystonepartners.com/frames_exec.asp), J.B. Homer Associates (www.jbhomer.com/submit.html), Sanford Rose Associates (www.sanfordrose.com), KPMM International (www.kpmm.net/page2.html), and Westerberg and Associates (www.westerberginc.com/page4.html).

*Category XII (Global Newspaper Listing Directories)* includes comprehensive, up-to-date, and easy to navigate global directories (www.newsdirectory.com) listing newspapers and magazines for North America, Europe, Asia, South America, Africa, and Oceania.

*Category XIII (Major U.S. Regional and National Newspapers)* is a select listing of newspaper career center Web sites for more than a dozen major U.S. metropolitan cities.

*Category XIV (Company Listing Web Sites)* includes updated listings from Hoover's Online (www.hoovers.com/company/all/list/0,2504,116,00.html), Quintessential Careers (www.quintcareers.com/career_centers), Job-Hunt (www.job-hunt.org/companies.shtml), WetFeet (www.wetfeet.com/asp/companies_atoz.asp), Monster (http://company.monster.com), e-CareerCenter (www.e-careercenter.com/jobsearch), Kennedy Information (www.kennedyinfo.com/db/db_dhr_bas.html), U.S. Chamber of Commerce (www.uschamber.org/Chambers), and U.S. Hispanic Chamber of Commerce (www.ushcc.com/hyperlinks.htm).

*Category XV (Fee-Based Online Resume Distribution Services)* includes resume mass mailing sites listed by and/or affiliated with Quintessential Careers (www.quintcareers.com/resume_distribution_sites.html), Kennedy Information (www.executiveagent.com/about/about.html), and JobBankUSA (www.resumebroadcaster.com/ourstor.asp?id=ResumeBroadcaster).

## Group Five: Interim, Temporary, and Contract Employment Resources

XVI. Interim Management/Temporary Employment Web Sites
XVII. Independent Consultant/Contract/Freelance Employment Web Sites

*Group Five* is composed of leaders in interim, temporary, and contract employment:

*Category XVI (Interim Management/Temporary Employment Web Sites)* includes such directories as the Riley Guide list of temporary employment agencies (www.rileyguide.com/misc.html), Kennedy Information's *Directory of Executive Temporary Placement Firms* (www.kennedyinfo.com/js/xtemp.html), and Quintessential Careers listing of temporary employment agencies (www.quintcareers.com/temp_jobs.html). *Category XVI* also includes such interim executive management firms as RHI Management Resources (www.rhimr.com), CFOs2GO (www.cfos2go.com/candidatespage.htm), Manpower Professional (www.manpowerprofessional.com), and Spherion Interim Executives (www.spherion.com/professionalrecruiting), which was formerly known as IMCOR. Temp employment agency Web sites—covering diverse mix of specialties and disciplines—include Net-Temps (www.net-temps.com), Manpower (www.us.manpower.com),

Robert Half International (www.rhii.com/divisions/index.html), MBA FreeAgents (www.mbaglobalnet.com/freeagents.html), Accountemps (www.accountemps.com), CoreStaff (www.corestaff.com/fastflex), The Affiliates (www.affiliates.com), RHI Consulting (www.rhic.com), Adecco International (www.adecco.com), TAC Worldwide Companies (www.1tac.com), CTS International (www.ctstech.com), Creative Group (www.creativegroup.com), AQUENT (www.aquent.com), and Temp Art (www.tempart.com).

*Category XVII (Independent Consultant/Contract/Freelance Employment Web Sites)* includes Quintessential Careers listing of consultant and freelance job sites (www.quintcareers.com /consultant_jobs.html). Other names in this category are eWork (www.ework.com/index.cfm), AllFreelance (www.allfreelance .com), Guru (www.guru.com), and Monster Contract & Temporary (http://ct.monster.com)—a self-described marketplace for free agents.

## Group Six: Additional Career Planning, Job Search, and Relocation Resources

XVIII. Other Web Sites to Facilitate and Expedite the Job Search Process
 XIX. Web Sites to Facilitate and Expedite the Relocation Process

*Group Six* includes Web sites that will expedite your job search and relocation:

*Category XVIII (Other Web Sites to Facilitate and Expedite the Job Search Process)* is populated by such names as CareerJournal (www.careerjournal.com/marketplace/bookstore), Quintessential Careers (www.quintcareers.com/career_change_resources.html), Kennedy Information (www.kennedyinfo.com/mc/dmc.html), CEOExpress (www.ceoexpress.com/default.asp), Refdesk (www.refdesk.com), Bureau of Labor Statistics (www.bls.gov/oco), CyberTimes Navigator (www.nytimes.com/library/cyber /reference), and the Cybernet Chamber of Commerce Guide to the Internet (www.ccc.net).

*Category XIX (Web Sites to Facilitate and Expedite the Relocation Process)* includes Homestore (www.homestore.com), MonsterMoving (www.monstermoving.com), DigitalCity (www.digitalcity.com), MapBlast (www.mapblast.com), Career-Journal's salary calculator (www.careerjournal.com/salaries /calculator/index.html), and the *Wall Street Journal's*

RealEstateJournal (www.realestatejournal.com)—a comprehensive real estate and relocation center. International relocation Web sites include EscapeArtist (www.escapeartist.com), RealEstateJournal (http://www.realestatejournal.com/distinctiveprops/), CitySearch (www.citysearch.com), MapQuest (www.mapquest .com), HomeFair's International Salary Calculator (www .homefair.com/homefair/calc/intsalcalc.html), and OANDA's currency converter (www.oanda.com/convert/classic), which provides up-to-date exchange rates for 164 currencies.

## A FINAL THOUGHT

Armed with the *24/7 Online Directory* starting on page 319, the Expansionist Theory™ in Chapter 9, and your power resume package developed in earlier chapters, nothing can stop you from achieving your career and life planning objectives. Feel free to contact me at authorbill@aol.com to let me know how your job search is progressing. I look forward to hearing from you.

# The 24/7 Online Job Search Directory: Market-Tested Career and Job Search Web Sites

## CONTENTS

*Note:* Unless otherwise indicated, the listings herein are in the order/sequence determined by the author based on research findings; listings in alphabetical order are so indicated.

## RESEARCH SOURCES

*Note:* The author would like to express his deepest gratitude to the following online research sources—whose excellence and thoroughness made the past months of research both interesting and informative.

| Major Online Research Sources: Alphabetical Order | Internet Address |
| --- | --- |
| About.com Career Center | www.about.com/careers |
| American Online (AOL): Online Search | www.aol.com |
| CareerJournal.com from *The Wall Street Journal* | www.careerjournal.com |
| Careers.org: Career Resource Center | www.careers.org |
| CEOExpress.com: Career Center | www.ceoexpress.com |
| Hunt-Scanlon.com: RecruiterLink.com | www.hunt-scanlon.com |
| Hoover's Online Home Page | www.hoovers.com |
| Job-Hunt.org: Career Center | www.job-hunt.org |
| JobHuntersBible.com: *What Color Is Your Parachute* Career Center | www.jobhuntersbible.com /sitemap.shtml |
| Kennedy Information.com: Contact Information Resources | www.kennedyinfo.com |
| Lycos: Online Search | www.lycos.com |
| Monster.com Career Center | http://content.monster.com |
| Netscape: Online Search | www.netscape.com |
| NewsDirectory.com: Global Newspaper Directory | www.newsdirectory.com |
| The Online Job Search Companion.com: Career Center | www.pamdixon.com |
| Oya's Recruiter Directory.com | http://i-recruit.com/drecruiters.htm |
| Quintessential Careers.com: Career Center | www.quintcareers.com |
| The Riley Guide: Career Center | www.rileyguide.com |
| Yahoo!: Online Search | www.yahoo.com |

## GROUP ONE: CAREER AND JOB SEARCH SITES FOR SENIOR EXECUTIVES AND PROFESSIONALS

**I. Online Job Search Sites/Job Listings/Select Recruiters for Senior Executives**

**CareerJournal.com: Career Management and Job Search Resources**

| Web Site | Web Address |
| --- | --- |
| CareerJournal.com from *The Wall Street Journal:* Online Job Search | careerjournal.com/partners /advsearch.html |
| CareerJournal.com Marketplace: Fee-Based Executive Job Search Services | careerjournal.com/marketplace |
| CareerJournal.com: Online Executive Job-Hunting Advice | careerjournal.com/jobhunting/index .html |
| CareerJournal.com: Online Executive Career Management Advice | careerjournal.com/myc/index.html |
| CareerJournal.com: Salary and Hiring Information by Industry and Job Function | careerjournal.com/salaries/index .html |
| JobStar.org: In Alliance with CareerJournal.com: Job Search Guide | http://jobstar.org/jobstar.cfm |

# The 24/7 Online Job Search Directory:
## Market-Tested Career and Job Search Web Sites

**Select Executive Resources: Icons of the World Wide Web (Alphabetical Order)**

| Web Site | Web Address |
| --- | --- |
| CEOExpress.com: CEO Career and Job Search Center: Created by a CEO | ceoexpress.com/html/careerframed.asp |
| ExecuNet: Personalized Networking/Job Search: Alliance with CareerJournal | execunet.com |
| Job-Hunt.org: Job Hunter's Online Super-List: Veteran Job Search Center | job-hunt.org |
| JobHuntersBible.com: *What Color is Your Parachute* Career Center | www.jobhuntersbible.com/sitemap.shtml |
| Online Job Search Companion: From Noted Web Expert/Author Pam Dixon | pamdixon.com/jobsearch.htm |
| Online Executive Recruiter Database: Kennedy Information: Database Search | kennedyinfo.com/db/db_der_bas.html |
| Quintessential Careers: Executive Job Web Sites: Publisher: Dr. Randall Hansen | quintcareers.com/executive_jobs.html |
| RecruiterLink.com: Recruiter Database: Powered by Hunt-Scanlon.com | recruiterlink.com |
| The Riley Guide: Margaret F. Dikel's Milestone Job Resources Site | rileyguide.com |
| WEDDLES.com: Catalog for Job Seekers: From Internet Guru Peter Weddle | weddles.com/jobcatalog.htm |

**Top Tier Executive Search Firms**

| | |
| --- | --- |
| e-Korn/Ferry: Korn/Ferry International: Online Registration and Job Search | ekornferry.com |
| Spencer Stuart Global Talent Network: Online Registration and Feedback | www.spencerstuart.com |
| Russell Reynolds Associates: Candidate Profile System: Online Registration | www.rresweb.russreyn.com |
| A.T. Kearney Executive Search: An EDS Company: Online Registration | www.executivesearch.atkearney.com |
| Christian & Timbers: CEO, Board, Senior Level Search: Online Registration | www.ctnet.com/contact/contact2.asp |
| Hunt Howe Partners LLC: CEO, COO, Board, and Division Head Searches | www.hunthowe.com |
| Conboy, Sur & Associates: Contact Information: Successful Placement List | www.conboysur.com/Why.htm |
| TMP Worldwide Executive Search: Recruiter Listing and Contact Information | www.tmpsearch.com/recruiter_search.asp |
| BoardSeat.com: Executive Search: Board Directors/ Advisory Board Members | www.boardseat.com |
| SPANUSA: Recruits Spanish-English Speaking Executives and Professionals | www.spanusa.net |
| Whitehead Mann Group: Global Search: Average Candidate Salary: $450,000 | www.wmann.com |
| The Whitney Group: Global Search: Average Candidate Salary: $400,000 | www.whitneygroup.com |

| Web Site | Web Address |
|---|---|
| Ethos Consulting: Senior Talent Search: Average Candidate Salary: $300,000 | www.ethosconsulting.com |
| Cendea: Executive Search: Job Listings: Average Candidate Salary: $250,000 | www.cendea.com/opportun.html |
| Ogden Partnership: Select Searches: Average Candidate Salary: $250,000 | www.ogdon.com |
| Callan Associates, Ltd.: Select Searches: Average Candidate Salary: $200,000 | www.callanassociates.com/main.htm |

**Executive Job Boards/Open Job Listings**

| | |
|---|---|
| Futurestep.com: Executive Recruiting Firm from Korn/Ferry International | www.futurestep.com |
| Heidrick & Struggles: Management Search: Formerly LeadersOnline | msp.heidrick.com |
| BrilliantPeople.com: Management Recruiters' Web Site: Online Registration | www.brilliantpeople.com |
| ChiefMonster: Monster.com for Senior Executives: TMP Worldwide Division | www.chief.monster.com |
| 6FigureJobs.com: Executive Center: Free Job Board after Registration | www.6figurejobs.com |
| Quintessential Careers: Directory of Company Career Centers: Job Postings | quintcareers.com/career_centers |
| CFO.com: CFO Magazine Online Career Center: Senior Financial Job Listings | www.cfo.com/careers |
| CIO.com: CIO Magazine Executive Career Resources: Job Openings: Senior IT | www.cio.com/career |
| HotJobs2000.com: High Technology Executive Search: Online Job Search | www.hotjobs2000.com |
| MarketingPower.com: American Marketing Association: AMA Career Center | www.marketingpower.com |
| SalesJobs.com: Online Recruiting Site: Sales Executives and Professionals | www.salesjobs.com |
| Legalstaff.com: Center for Legal Professionals: Online Registration/Job Search | www.legalstaff.com |
| MedHunters.com: M.D./Other Healthcare: Online Search/Position Postings | www.medhunters.com |
| CEO UPDATE: Senior Nonprofit Opportunities: Pay Subscription Service | www.associationjobs.com |
| The Internet Job Source: State Government Jobs: Online Job Search by State | statejobs.com/gov.html |
| USAJOBS.gov: Senior Executive Positions at Top Levels of U.S. Government* | www.usajobs.opm.gov/a3.htm |
| GlobalGateway: Monster.com's International Site: A TMP Worldwide Division | globalgateway.monster.com |

*This official government site is managed by the Office of Personnel Management (OPM): The USAJOBS.gov Web site is the "Government's official source of job and employment information provided to the public at no cost."

# The 24/7 Online Job Search Directory:
## Market-Tested Career and Job Search Web Sites

| Web Site | Web Address |
| --- | --- |
| CareerJournal Europe from *The Wall Street Journal Europe:* Find a Job | careerjournaleurope.com |
| CareerJournal Asia from *The Asian Wall Street Journal:* Find a Job | careerjournalasia.com |

## II. Specialty Job Search Sites/Job Listings/Select Recruiters for Senior Executives

### Multiple Specialties and Industries

| Web Site | Web Address |
| --- | --- |
| Heidrick & Struggles International: Multiple Specialty Practices Web Site | www.heidrick.com /industry_expertise.htm |
| Herbert Mines Assoc.: Consumer Products, e-Commerce, and Retail Search | www.herbertmines.com /credentials.html |
| The Dieck Group: Forest Products, Chemical, Packaging, and Food Search | www.dieckgroup.com/served.htm |
| Preng & Associates: Energy, Chemical, and Natural Resources Search | www.preng.com/experience.htm |
| MRI Worldwide: Global Search: Hotel, Hospitality, and Leisure Sectors | www.mri-london.com |
| Villeneuve Associates: Retained Search: Retail, e-Business, and Food Service | www.vaisearch.com |

### Senior Sales/Marketing, General Management, and CEOs

| Web Site | Web Address |
| --- | --- |
| Wyatt & Jaffe: Senior Sales/General Management Search: High Technology | www.wyattjaffe.com |
| DHR International: Retained Executive Search: Sales Executives/CEOs/CFOs | www.dhrintl.net/index3.html |
| Bishop Partners Search: Senior Sales/General Management: Online Contact | www.bishoppartners.com/contact .html |
| Plummer & Associates Executive Search: Marketing, Retail, and e-Commerce | www.plummersearch.com |
| MarketingPower.com: American Marketing Association: AMA Career Center | www.marketingpower.com |

### Senior Level Information Technology (IT)

| Web Site | Web Address |
| --- | --- |
| CIO.com: CIO Magazine Executive Career Resources: Job Openings: Senior IT | www.cio.com/career |
| BTS Executive Search: Senior Level IT, CIO, CTO, Financial, and e-Business | www.btssearch.com |
| Atlantic Research Technologies: Senior IT, CIO, CTO, CEO, and CFO Searches | www.atlanticresearch.com |

### Senior Finance/Accounting/Banking/Tax

| Web Site | Web Address |
| --- | --- |
| Gilreath Search: Retained Searches: Senior Financial/General Management | www.gilreathsearch.com |
| CFO.com: CFO Magazine Online Career Center: Senior Financial Job Listings | www.cfo.com/careers |

# The 24/7 Online Job Search Directory:
## Market-Tested Career and Job Search Web Sites

| Web Site | Web Address |
| --- | --- |
| Bloomberg.com: Senior Financial: Online Job Search/Company Job Postings | www.bloomberg.com/careers |
| ET Search, Inc.: Executive Search for Tax Professionals: Current Search List | www.etsearch.com/searches.html |
| National Banking & Financial Services Network: Online Registration/Job Search | www.nbn-jobs.com |

### Senior Human Resources and Communications

| | |
| --- | --- |
| Ray & Berndtson: Senior HR Search: Average Candidate Salary: $265,000 | www.rayberndtson.com |
| Kelly and Company: Senior HR Search: Average Candidate Salary: $200,000 | www.kellyandco.com |

### Attorneys and Other Legal Professionals

| | |
| --- | --- |
| Legalstaff.com: Center for Legal Professionals: Online Registration/Job Search | www.legalstaff.com |
| FindLaw: Attorneys and Other Legal Professionals: Online Job Search/Postings | www.jobs.findlaw.com |

### Senior Level Healthcare Specialty

| | |
| --- | --- |
| Solomon-Page Group LLC: Healthcare Executive Search | http://company.monster.com/solpage |
| International Medical Placement: Global Healthcare: Online Search/Postings | intlmedicalplacement.com |
| MedHunters.com: M.D./Other Healthcare: Online Search/Position Postings | www.medhunters.com |
| Blau Mancino Associates: Pharmaceutical and Medical Technology Searches | www.blaumancino.com |

### Senior Publishing and Media

| | |
| --- | --- |
| Ariel Associates: Executive Search: Publishing and New Media Industries | www.arielassociates.com |
| JobLink for Journalists: NewsLink Associates | newslink.org/newjoblinksearch.html |

### Specialty: Leaders Who Think "Outside the Box"

| | |
| --- | --- |
| J. Robert Scott Executive Search: Candidates Who Think "Outside the Box" | j-robert-scott.com/aboutus.html |

### Federal and State Government: Senior Executive Positions

| | |
| --- | --- |
| USAJOBS.gov: Senior Executive Positions at Top Levels of U.S. Government* | www.usajobs.opm.gov/a3.htm |
| The Internet Job Source: State Government Jobs: Online Job Search by State | statejobs.com/gov.html |

---

* This official government site is managed by the Office of Personnel Management (OPM): The USAJOBS.gov Web site is the "Government's official source of job and employment information provided to the public at no cost."

**Nonprofit Sector: Senior Executive and Professional Positions**

| Web Site | Web Address |
| --- | --- |
| DRG Executive Search: Recruitment of Nonprofit Executives: Online Job List | www.drgnyc.com |
| CEO UPDATE: Senior Nonprofit Opportunities: Pay Subscription Service | www.associationjobs.com |

**Military Transition to Civilian Sector**

| Web Site | Web Address |
| --- | --- |
| Quintessential Career Center: Networking for Transitioning Military Personnel | quintcareers.com/ former_military_networking.html |
| The Riley Guide: Resources for Military Personnel: Career and Job Web Sites | rileyguide.com/vets.html |
| TransitionAssistanceOnline.com: Division of LucasGroup: Networking Center | taonline.com |
| Military.com: Career, Networking, Service Center for the Military Community | military.com |

## III. International Job Search Sites/Job Listings/Select Recruiters for Senior Executives

### CareerJournal.com: Global Resources

| Web Site | Web Address |
| --- | --- |
| CareerJournal Europe from *The Wall Street Journal Europe:* Find a Job | careerjournaleurope.com |
| CareerJournal Asia from *The Asian Wall Street Journal:* Find a Job | careerjournalasia.com |
| CareerJournal: International Executive Recruiters: Fee-based Database Search | careerjournal.com/marketplace /international |

### Top Tier International Executive Search Firms

| Web Site | Web Address |
| --- | --- |
| The Amrop Hever Group: Global Executive Search: Over 80 Offices in 50 Countries | www.amrop.com/home.html |
| Egon Zehnder International: Recruits Business Leaders: European/Asian Jobs | www.zehnder.com |
| Ward Howell Euroselect: Executive Search: Central and Eastern Europe | www.wardhowell.at/html /index_flash.htm |
| Ward Howell International: Offices: Moscow and St. Petersburg: Russian Jobs | www.wardhowell.ru/contacts.html |
| IIC Partners: Executive Search Worldwide: Top 20 Global Search Firm | www.iicpartners.com/focus |
| Stanton Chase International: Search: Average Candidate Salary: $200,000 | www.stantonchase.com |
| Austin McGregor International: Retained Executive Search: Global Clients | www.amidallas.com |

# The 24/7 Online Job Search Directory:
## Market-Tested Career and Job Search Web Sites

| Web Site | Web Address |
|---|---|
| Raines International: Global Talent Search: Online Candidate Registration | www.rainesinternational.com /resumeform.cfm |
| Allied Global Partners Search: Tokyo: Jobs at Multinational Firms in Japan | www.agpjapan.com |
| International Executive Search: Latin America and North America | www.international-executive-search .com |
| Resolve Associates International: Retainer Search: Central/Latin America | www.resolveassociates.com /jobseek.htm |

**International Job Boards**

| Web Site | Web Address |
|---|---|
| StepStone: Europe's Career Portal: Online Registration and Job Search | www.stepstone.com |
| JobPilot.com: Europe's Career Market on the Internet: Online Job Search | www.jobpilot.com |
| Cyber-CV.com: U.K. Job Search: Online Registration and Job Search by Sector | www.cyber-cv.com |
| OverseasJobs.com: For Professionals and Adventure Seekers: Online Search | www.overseasjobs.com |
| JobsDB.com: Global Job Opportunities: Online Registration and Job Search | www.jobsdb.com |
| BrassRing.com: Global Online Job Search and Career Fair Portal: High Tech | www.brassring.com |
| JobNet: Australia: Center for IT Professionals: Online Registration/Job Search | www.jobnet.com.au |
| MedHunters.com: M.D./Other Healthcare: Online Search/Position Postings | www.medhunters.com |

**IV. Fee-Based Career Services and Contact Information Resources for Senior Executives**

**CareerJournal.com Marketplace: Fee-Based Executive Job Search Resources**

| Web Site | Web Address |
|---|---|
| CareerJournal: Kennedy Information Online Executive Recruiter Search | careerjournal.com/marketplace /contactrecruiters |
| CareerJournal: Kennedy Online International Executive Recruiter Search | careerjournal.com/marketplace /international |
| CareerJournal: Kennedy Information Online Corporate HR Director Search | careerjournal.com/marketplace /searchhr |
| CareerJournal: Reference Check: Assesses Quality of Your References | careerjournal.com/marketplace /refservice |
| CareerJournal: CareerXroads Directory: Reference Guide to Employment Web Sites | careerxroads.com |

# The 24/7 Online Job Search Directory:
# Market-Tested Career and Job Search Web Sites

**Fee-Based Executive Career Centers: For $100K+ Executives**

| Web Site | Web Address |
| --- | --- |
| ExecuNet: Personalized Career/Search Services: Alliance with CareerJournal | execunet.com |
| BlueSteps: Assoc. of Executive Search Consultants: Fee-Based Registration | www.bluesteps.com |
| 6FigureJobs.com: Executive Center: Both Free and Fee-Based Services | www.6figurejobs.com |
| International Career Employment Center: Pay Services: Membership Fee | www.internationaljobs.org/index.html |
| Business and Professional Women/USA: Networking and Career Center* | www.bpwusa.org |
| CEO UPDATE: Senior Level Nonprofit Opportunities: Pay Subscription | www.associationjobs.com |

**Fee-Based Resume Distribution: Through U.S. Postal Service**

| | |
| --- | --- |
| WSA Corporation: Fee: $2.25 + Postage Per Package: Laser-Printed/Mailed | www.wsacorp.com/services.asp |
| ExecutivesOnly.com: Fee: $2.15 + Postage Per Package: Laser-Printed/Mailed | www.executivesonly.com |
| Career Marketing Services: Fee: $2.50 Per Package: Laser-Printed/Mailed | yourcareerservices.com |

**Fee-Based Contact Information Resources**

| | |
| --- | --- |
| Kennedy Information: Hiring Company Listing: Online Database Pay Service | kennedyinfo.com/db/db_dhr_bas.html |
| Directory of Executive Recruiters: Kennedy Information (The "Red Book") | kennedyinfo.com/js/der.html |
| International Directory of Executive Recruiters: Kennedy Information | kennedyinfo.com/er/ider.html |
| Executive Recruiters of North America: Retained Firms: Hunt-Scanlon.com | hunt-scanlon.com/shop |
| WEDDLES.com: Catalog of Products for Job Seekers: From Peter D. Weddle | weddles.com/jobcatalog.htm |

**Fee-Based Executive Outplacement and Counseling: Services, Directories, Databases, and Consumer Guides**

| | |
| --- | --- |
| CareerJournal Marketplace: Outplacement Firm Database Search | careerjournal.com/marketplace/outplacement |
| Directory of Outplacement and Career Management Firms: Career Counselors | kennedyinfo.com/hr/dof.html |
| CareerJournal Marketplace: Career Development Services (CDS): Counseling | careerjournal.com/marketplace/career/index.html |

---

* This 80-year-old Washington DC-based organization charges an annual membership fee: 2000 local chapters nationwide.

# The 24/7 Online Job Search Directory: Market-Tested Career and Job Search Web Sites

| Web Site | Web Address |
|---|---|
| National Career Development Assoc.: Counselor Selection Consumer Guide | www.ncda.org/about/polscc.html |
| American Counseling Association: Consumer Guide to Counselor Selection | www.counseling.org /consumers_media |

## GROUP TWO: CAREER CENTERS AND MULTICULTURAL RESOURCE CENTERS

### V. Career and Job Search Resource Centers

**The Riley Guide and The Online Job Search Companion**

| Web Site | Web Address |
|---|---|
| Riley Guide: Margaret F. Dikel's Milestone Career Center | www.rileyguide.com |
| Riley Guide: Preparing for a Job Search: Options/ Job Search/Internet Services | www.rileyguide.com/prepare.html |
| Riley Guide: Executing the Job Search: Using the Internet to Find Job Leads | www.rileyguide.com/jobleads.html |
| Riley Guide: Job Listings: Job Banks and Recruiting Sites: Listed A-Z | www.rileyguide.com/multiple.html |
| Riley Guide: Online Libraries and Engines: Tools for Finding More Information | www.rileyguide.com/search.html |
| Online Job Search Companion: From Noted Web Expert/Author Pam Dixon | www.pamdixon.com/jobsearch.htm |

**Quintessential Career Center and CareerShop.com**

| Web Site | Web Address |
|---|---|
| Quintessential Careers: General Job Search Web Site Listing A to Z | quintcareers.com/general_resources .html |
| Quintessential Careers: The Top 50 Job Search Resources | quintcareers.com/top_50_sites.html |
| Quintessential Careers: Job Expos and Career Fair Resources | quintcareers.com /career_fair_resources.html |
| Quintessential Careers: Resource Guide for Employers (and Candidates) | quintcareers.com/employer_guide .html |
| Quintessential Careers: The Best Career Resource Sites | quintcareers.com/best_career_sites .html |
| CareerShop.com: Online Job Search; Dr. Randall S. Hansen's Q&A Web Site | careershop.com/careerdr/index.asp |

**Other Online Career Centers**

| Web Site | Web Address |
|---|---|
| JobHuntersBible.com: *What Color Is Your Parachute* Career Center | www.jobhuntersbible.com/sitemap .shtml |
| Job-Hunt.org: Job Hunter's Online Super-List: Veteran Job Search Center | job-hunt.org |
| CEOExpress.com: CEO Career and Job Search Center: Created by a CEO | ceoexpress.com/html/careerframed .asp |

# The 24/7 Online Job Search Directory:
## Market-Tested Career and Job Search Web Sites

| Web Site | Web Address |
|---|---|
| NETSHARE.com: Fee-Based Career Management for Executive Job Seekers | www.netshare.com |
| America's CareerInfoNet: Career Resource Library: Global Job Search Sites | www.acinet.org/acinet/library.htm |
| Monster.com Career Center: Career and Job Search Resources | content.monster.com |
| About.com Career Center: Operated by Veteran Online Company About.com | www.about.com/careers |
| CIO.com: Resources for Information Technology Executives | www.cio.com |
| Vault Career Network: Insider Company Information: Job Search by Industry | www.vault.com/admin2/sitemap.jsp |
| Careers.org: Career Resource Center: Featuring the Web Career Directory | www.careers.org |
| Lycos Career Center: Career Planning, Job Search, and Relocation Resources | careers.lycos.com |
| Yahoo! Executive Career Center: In Alliance with Korn/Ferry International | executive.yahoo.com |
| The World Wide Web Employment Office: Company Job Listings by State | www.employmentoffice.net/city.htm |
| Freeality.com: Up-to-date Listings of Online Job and Career Search Engines | www.freeality.com/jobs.htm |
| WorkTree.com: Job Search Portal: Proprietary Search Platform: Member Fees | www.worktree.com/careerpages /pricing.cfm |

## VI. Diversity and Multicultural Career Resource Centers

### General Diversity Web Sites

| Web Site | Web Address |
|---|---|
| Quintessential Career Center: Diversity Jobseeker Career and Job Resources | quintcareers.com/diversity_resources .html |
| CareerCity: Diversity and Minority Job Center: Online Registration/Job Search | djb.jobcontrolcenter.com/search /index.cfm |

### Diversity Web Sites for Women

| Web Site | Web Address |
|---|---|
| Quintessential Career Center: Career and Job Resources for Women | quintcareers.com /women_career_resources.html |
| MinorityExecutiveSearch.com: Female/Minority Job Placements Nationwide | www.minorityexecsearch.com |
| iVillage.com: The Women's Network: Job Resource Center: Online Job Search | www.ivillage.com/work/job |
| Careers USA: Woman-Owned Business Enterprise: Diversity Staffing | www.careersusa.com/about.htm |
| Advancing Women: Career Center: Online Registration and Job Search | www.advancingwomen.com /awcareer.html |
| CareerIntelligence.com: Online Career Center for Women: Online Job Search | www.career-intelligence.com /jobs.html |

## Diversity Web Sites for Native Americans

| Web Site | Web Address |
| --- | --- |
| NativeAmericanJobs.com: Career Center: Jobs Listed by State: Online Search | www.nativeamericanjobs.com |
| The Tribal Employment Newsletter: Jobs for Native Americans: Online Search | nativejobs.com/jobannou.htm |

## Diversity Web Sites for African Americans

| Web Site | Web Address |
| --- | --- |
| The Black Collegian Online: Career Center: Online Job Search/Company List | www.black-collegian.com |
| National Black MBA Association: Employment Network: Membership Fee | www.nbmbaa.org |
| BlackEnterprise.com: Virtual Desktop For African Americans: Career Center | www.blackenterprise.com/S0 /CareersTab.asp |
| BlackEOEJournal.com: Employment Journal: Career and Business Connection | www.blackeoejournal.com /Linkspage.html |
| NAACP Diversity Job Fair: Best Diversity Employers Job Board: Online Search | www.naacpcareerfair.com |
| Diversity Job Fairs Schedule: Major Employment Fairs Managed by PSI, Inc. | www.psijobfair.com |
| National Urban League: Career Center Powered by Monster.com: Job Search | nul.monster.com |
| BlackVoices.com: Employment/Job Search Powered by CareerCast.com | new.blackvoices.com/classified/jobs |
| Blackworld: Diversity Career Center/Job Search Powered by CareerBuilder | www.blackworld.com/careers.htm |
| National Organization of Black Law Enforcement Executives: Career Center | noblenatl.org |

## Diversity Web Sites for the Hispanic Community

| Web Site | Web Address |
| --- | --- |
| Quintessential Career Center: Career and Job Resources for Hispanics | quintcareers.com /Hispanic_career_resources.html |
| Hispanic Alliance For Career Enhancement (HACE): Online Job Search Center | www.hace-usa.org |
| LatPro Career Center: Jobs for Spanish/ Portuguese-Speaking Professionals | www.latpro.com |
| JobCentro: Official Career Site of the U.S. Hispanic Chamber of Commerce | www.jobcentro.com |
| U.S. Hispanic Chamber of Commerce: Network Links to Hispanic Organizations | www.ushcc.com/hyperlinks.htm |
| Saludos: Hispanic Employment Center: Online Registration and Job Search | www.saludos.com |
| TodoLatino: Hispanic Career Center: Latino/ Hispanic Portal for Professionals | www.todolatino.com/careercenter |
| DiversiLink: Innovative Human Resources Solution (IHRS) Employment Web Site | www.diversilink.com |

# The 24/7 Online Job Search Directory:
## Market-Tested Career and Job Search Web Sites

**Diversity Web Sites for the Asian Community**

| Web Site | Web Address |
| --- | --- |
| Quintessential Career Center: Career and Job Resources for Asian-Americans | quintcareers.com /Asian_career_resources.html |
| National Association of Asian American Professionals (NAAAP): Networking | www.naaap.org/naaap/contact.html |
| Organization of Chinese Americans: Online Job Search: Membership Fees | www.ocanatl.org/jobbank.htm |

**Diversity Web Sites for the DisABLED**

| Web Site | Web Address |
| --- | --- |
| Riley Guide: Resources for the Disabled: Career and Job Search Information | www.rileyguide.com/vets.html |
| Quintessential Career Center: Career Resources for Disabled Americans | quintcareers.com /disabled_career_resources.html |
| JobAccess.org: Powered by CareerBuilder: For Candidates with Disabilities | www.jobaccess.org |
| National Business & Disability Council: Jobs for Candidates with Disabilities | www.businessdisability.com |
| Careers and the disABLED: Listing of Companies Actively Recruiting/Hiring | www.eop.com/compcd.html |
| American Council of the Blind: ACB Job Connection: Online Job Listings | www.acb.org/acbjobs/index.html |
| American Sign Language Teachers Association: Open Teaching Positions | aslta.org/national/announcements /job/index.html |

**Diversity Web Sites for Older Candidates**

| Web Site | Web Address |
| --- | --- |
| Quintessential Careers: Job Resources for Mature and Older Jobseekers | quintcareers.com /mature_jobseekers.html |
| CareerJournal.com: Career Management Advice: Age 50+ Professionals | careerjournal.com/myc/fifty |
| Senior Job Bank: Links to Networking, Job Search, and Life Planning Sites | www.seniorjobbank.org/links /index.html |
| FortyPlus.com: Non-Profit Career, Networking, and Job Search Centers | www.fp.org/chapters.htm |
| ThirdAge/Careers: Career and Job Search Site for the Baby Boom Generation | www.thirdage.com/money/careers |

## GROUP THREE: CAREER AND JOB SEARCH SITES FOR EXECUTIVES/MANAGERS/PROFESSIONALS

### VII. Online Job Search Sites/Job Listings/Select Recruiters for Executives/Managers

**Online Executive Search Firms**

| Web Site | Web Address |
| --- | --- |
| Futurestep: Korn/Ferry International: Online Registration: Executives/Managers | www.futurestep.com |
| BrilliantPeople.com: Management Recruiters' Web Site: Online Registration | www.brilliantpeople.com |

# The 24/7 Online Job Search Directory:
# Market-Tested Career and Job Search Web Sites

| Web Site | Web Address |
| --- | --- |
| Kensington International: Retainer Firm: Average Candidate Salary: $170,000 | www.kionline.com/p&s_rs.htm |
| D.E. Foster Partners: Search Firm: Average Candidate Salary: $150,000 | www.fosterpartners.com |
| Executive Manning Corp.: Search: Average Candidate Salary: $100,000 | www.exmanning.com |
| Boyden Global Search: Registration: Average Candidate Salary: $100,000 | www.boyden.com |
| WJM Associates Search: Founded by HR Industry Icon William J. Morin | www.wjmassoc.com |
| LucasCareers.com: Lucas Group Executive Search: Online Job Search | www.lucascareers.com |

**Online Career Portals and Job Boards**

| | |
| --- | --- |
| CareerJournal.com from *The Wall Street Journal:* Online Job Search | careerjournal.com/partners /adsearch.html |
| Monster.com: Veteran Online Job Search Site: Owned by TMP Worldwide, Inc. | www.monster.com |
| JobStar.org: In Alliance with CareerJournal.com: Job Search Guide | http://jobstar.org/jobstar.cfm |
| FlipDog.com: TMP Worldwide: Lists Jobs Directly from Employer Sites | www.flipdog.com |
| CareerBuilder.com: In Partnership with Knight-Ridder/Tribune Company | www.headhunter.net |
| QuintCareers.com and Flip.dog.com Alliance: Quintessential Careers Job Board | quintcareers.com/jobres.html |
| HotJobs.com: A Yahoo! Service: Online Registration and Job Search | www.hotjobs.com |
| GrassIsGreener.com: Online Search: Millions of Jobs Posted by Thousands of Web Sites | www.grassisgreener.com |
| JobOptions.com: In Alliance with TMP Worldwide's Flipdog.com Site | joboptions.com |
| Career.com: Veteran Career Web Site: Online Registration and Job Search | www.career.com |
| JobBankUSA.com: Free Online Job Search and Fee-Based Support Services | www.jobbankusa.com |
| Job.com: Free Online Job Search and Fee-Based Support Services | www.job.com |
| A True Job-Search-Engine: Global Jobs From Over 400 Job Boards | www.job-search-engine.com |
| Employment911.com: In Partnership with Wanted Technologies Corporation | employment911.com/asp /JobSeekersEnter.asp |
| EmployersOnline: Online Registration and Job Search: Salaries to Six Figures | www.employersonline.com |

# The 24/7 Online Job Search Directory:
## Market-Tested Career and Job Search Web Sites

## VIII. Specialty Job Search Sites/Job Listings/Select Recruiters for Executives/Managers

### Multiple Specialties and Industries

| Web Site | Web Address |
|---|---|
| Quintessential Career Center: Job Search Resources by Specialty/Industry | quintcareers.com/indres.html |
| Diversified Search: Multiple Specialty Practices; Online Search; EEO Focus | www.diversifiedsearch.com/about.htm |
| NationJob.com: Targeted Web Sites in Specific Employment Categories A-Z | www.nationjob.com/frqsrc.html |

### Sales/Marketing Specialty: Search Firms and Job Boards

| | |
|---|---|
| Kenzer Corporation: Search Firm: Senior Sales Management/Other Specialties | www.kenzer.com |
| SalesJobs.com: Online Recruiting Site: Sales Executives and Professionals | www.salesjobs.com |
| MarketingJobs.com: Sales Management/ Marketing/Advertising Jobs Nationwide | www.marketingjobs.com |

### Information Technology (IT): Search Firms

| | |
|---|---|
| Boston Search Group: Focus: Internet and Other Technology-Driven Industries | www.bsgweb.com |
| Huntington Group Search: Specializing in Emerging Technology Industries | www.hgllc.com |
| Talent Intelligence Agency: Executive Search: CIOs, CTOs, and Technical VPs | www.talent-llc.com |
| The Stevens Group: Search Specialties Include IT and Telecommunications | www.thestevensgroup.com |

### Information Technology (IT): Job Boards

| | |
|---|---|
| HotJobs2000.com: High Technology Executive Search; Online Job Search | www.hotjobs2000.com |
| CareerCity: Computer and High-Tech Careers: Online Registration/Job Search | www.careercity.com/channels/comp/index.cfm |
| Dice.com: High Tech Jobs: Veteran Information Technology Job Board | www.dice.com |
| ComputerJobs.com: Online Registration and Job Search by Skills and Location | www.computerjobs.com |
| Techies.com: Technology Career Center: Online Registration and Job Search | www.techies.com |
| OperationIT: Center for IT Professionals: In Partnership with CareerBuilder, Inc. | www.operationit.com/IndexCC.asp |
| ComputerWork.com: Veteran Site for Computer Professionals: IT/IS Jobs | www.computerwork.com |
| ITcareers.com: Career Corner and Global IT Careers: Online Registration/Jobs | www.itcareers.com |
| Women in Technology International: Career Center: Including Senior IT Jobs | www.witi4hire.com |

# The 24/7 Online Job Search Directory:
# Market-Tested Career and Job Search Web Sites

## Engineering Specialty

| Web Site | Web Address |
| --- | --- |
| Institute of Electrical and Electronics Engineers (IEEE): Dues Paying Job Site | www.ieee.org/membership /benefits/careers.html |
| Society of Women Engineers: Membership Includes Job Search Resources | www.swe.org |
| Diversity/Careers in Engineering and IT: List of Companies Actively Recruiting | www.diversitycareers.com |
| National Society of Black Engineers: Networking and Job Search Resources | www.nsbe.org/woozone |
| DiversiLink: Official Career Site of Society of Hispanic Professional Engineers | www.diversilink.com |

## Finance/Accounting/Banking

| | |
| --- | --- |
| W.L. Handler & Associates Search: Senior Financial and General Management | www.wlhandler.com |
| American Association of Finance and Accounting (AAFA): Online Job Search | www.aafa.com |
| National Association of Black Accountants: Career Center: Online Job Search | nabainc.jobcontrolcenter.com |
| BankJobs.com: Financial Services Careers: Online Registration and Job Search | www.bankjobs.com |

## Human Resources/Communications

| | |
| --- | --- |
| K. Russo Associates: Search Specialties: Senior HR and PR Executives | www.krussoassociates.com |
| TRRG, Inc.: Corporate Communications/Investor Relations Search: Job Listing | www.trrg.com |

## Attorneys and Other Legal Specialties

| | |
| --- | --- |
| LawJobs.com: Careers: Attorneys/Other Legal Positions: Online Job Search | www.lawjobs.com |
| LawInfo.com: Job Center: Attorneys/Other Legal Positions; Online Job Search | jobs.lawinfo.com |

## Healthcare Specialty

| | |
| --- | --- |
| Michael E. Marion & Associates: Recruiters Serving the Healthcare Industry | www.marionsearch.com/pages /expertise.htm |
| HealthCareerWeb.com: Healthcare Careers: Online Registration/Job Search | www.healthcareerweb.com /jobseeker |
| MedSearch.com: Monster.com Healthcare Jobs: Online Registration/Job Search | www.medsearch.com |

# The 24/7 Online Job Search Directory: Market-Tested Career and Job Search Web Sites

**Publishing and Media Jobs**

| Web Site | Web Address |
| --- | --- |
| JournalismJobs.com: Job Board for Media Professionals: Online Job Search | www.journalismjobs.com |

**Sports Related Jobs**

| | |
| --- | --- |
| JobsInSports.com: Pay Service: Monthly Subscription: Jobs in Sports Market | www.jobsinsports.com |
| OnlineSports.com: Career Center: Sports Related Jobs; Online Job Search | www.onlinesports.com/pages /CareerCenter.html |

**Federal and State Government Jobs**

| | |
| --- | --- |
| USAJOBS.gov: Federal Employment: Managers and Professionals* | www.usajobs.opm.gov |
| FedWorld: U.S. Government Federal Job Search: Online Job Search by State** | www.fedworld.gov/jobs/jobsearch .html |
| The Internet Job Source: State Government Jobs: Online Job Search by State | statejobs.com/gov.html |

**Nonprofit Sector Jobs**

| | |
| --- | --- |
| DRG Executive Search: Recruitment of Nonprofit Executives: Online Job List | www.drgnyc.com |
| ExecSearches.com: Online Executive Search: Nonprofit and Public Jobs | www.execsearches.com |

**Military Transition to Civilian Sector Jobs**

| | |
| --- | --- |
| Riley Guide: Resources for Military Personnel: Career and Job Web Sites | www.rileyguide.com/vets.html |
| Riley Guide: Information for Activated Reservists/ Reassigned Military Personnel | www.rileyguide.com/vets.html |
| Quintessential Career Center: Job Transitioning: Military to Civilian Sector | quintcareers.com/former_military .html |
| Quintessential Career Center: Networking for Transitioning Military Personnel | quintcareers.com /former_military_networking.html |
| TransitionAssistanceOnline.com: A Division of LucasGroup: Online Job Search | taonline.jobcontrolcenter.com/ccn /search.cfm |
| Military.com: Career Center: Civilian Jobs for Military: Online Job Search | military.com/Careers/JobSearch |
| Career Development: Junior Military Officer Placement: Individualized Services | cdc-va.com/introduction.htm |

* This official government site is managed by the Office of Personnel Management (OPM): The USAJOBS.gov Web site is the "Government's official source of job and employment information provided to the public at no cost."

** The National Technical Information Service, an agency of the U.S. Department of Commerce, operates this government job site.

# The 24/7 Online Job Search Directory:
## Market-Tested Career and Job Search Web Sites

**IX. International Job Search Sites/Job Listings/Select Recruiters for Executives/Managers**

**International Recruiters**

| Web Site | Web Address |
|---|---|
| World Search Group: Global Alliance of Retained Executive Search Firms | www.worldsearchgroup.com |
| Michael Page International: Executive Search: Over 100 Offices in 14 Countries | www.michaelpage.com |
| Maxwell Executive Search International: Asia and Europe: Online Contact | http://maxwellsearch.netfirms.com |
| EMA Partners International Search: Asia-Pacific, Europe, and Latin America | www.ema-partners.net/offices /window.html |
| PEAT Executive Search AG, Zurich: Online Registration and Job Listings | www.peat.ch/eng.htm |
| Global Search USA: U.S., Japan, and Korea: Online Contact | www.globalsearchusa.net |

**International Job Boards**

| Web Site | Web Address |
|---|---|
| CareerJournal Europe from *The Wall Street Journal Europe:* Find a Job | careerjournaleurope.com |
| CareerJournal Asia from *The Asian Wall Street Journal:* Find a Job | careerjournalasia.com |
| GlobalGateway: Monster.com's International Jobs Site: TMP Worldwide Division | globalgateway.monster.com |
| CareerBuilder International Gateway: Major Global Job Search Site | headhunter.net/jobseeker/jobs /jobfindil.asp?CH=IL |
| FinancialJobNetwork.com: Global Job Search Listings for Financial Executives | www.fjn.com/default.asp |
| JobsDB.com: Global Job Opportunities: Online Registration and Job Search | www.jobsdb.com |
| BrassRing.com: Global Online Job Search and Career Fair Portal: High Tech | www.brassring.com |
| OverseasJobs.com: For Professionals and Adventure Seekers: Online Search | www.overseasjobs.com |
| GoJobsite.com: Veteran Site: U.K./European-Wide Jobs: Online Job Search | www.jobsite.co.uk |
| CraigsList.org: Online Job Search: Vancouver, BC, Australia, and 13 U.S. Cities | vancouver.craigslist.org |
| CareerOne.com: Online Registration/Job Search: Australia and New Zealand | www.careerone.com.au |
| NetJobs.com: Online Registration and Job Search: Canadian Job Openings | www.netjobs.com |
| FreeJobSearchEngines.com: Online Search: U.K., Hong Kong, and Australia | www.free-job-search-engines.com |

## GROUP FOUR: JOB SEARCH CONTACT INFORMATION RESOURCES

### X. Recruiter Contact Resources: Executive Recruiter Listing Directories/Databases

**No-Charge Recruiter Listing Resources**

| Web Site | Web Address |
| --- | --- |
| RecruiterLink.com: Recruiter Database: Powered by Hunt-Scanlon Corporation | www.recruiterlink.com |
| Recruiters Online Network: FindARecruiter: Recruiter Search/Job Listings | www.recruitersonline.com/match /search.phtml |
| Top Echelon: Network of Executive Recruiters: Listings by State/Specialty | www.topechelon.com/employers /findrecr.asp |
| Oya's Directory of Recruiters: Online Listings by Specialty and Location | i-recruit.com/drecruiters.htm |

**Fee-Based Recruiter Listing Services***

| | |
| --- | --- |
| ExecutiveAgent.com/Kennedy Information: Recruiter Listing/e-Mail Service** | www.executiveagent.com/about /about.html |
| Online Executive Recruiter Database: Kennedy Information | www.kennedyinfo.com/db /db_der_bas.html |
| SearchSelect 3.0®: Executive Search Firm Listings: Kennedy Information | www.kennedyinfo.com/js/ss.html |
| Directory of Executive Recruiters: Kennedy Information (The "Red Book") | www.kennedyinfo.com/js/der.html |
| International Directory of Executive Recruiters: Kennedy Information | www.kennedyinfo.com/er/ider.html |
| Executive Recruiters of NA: Contingency Firms: From Hunt-Scanlon Direct | hunt-scanlon.com/shop |
| BlueSteps: Assoc. of Executive Search Consultants: Fee-Based Registration | www.bluesteps.com |
| The Directory of Legal Recruiters: Kennedy Information | www.kennedyinfo.com/er/dlr.html |

### XI. Recruiter Contact Resources: Select Recruiter Listing

| Web Site | Web Address |
| --- | --- |
| Korn/Ferry International: Senior/ Mid-Level Searches: Offices in 38 Countries | www.kornferry.com |
| Heidrick & Struggles International: Offices in Over 75 Locations Worldwide | www.heidrick.com |
| Spencer Stuart, Inc.: Top Tier Firm: Over 50 Offices in 25 Countries | www.spencerstuart.com |

\* Prices for directories/databases range from under $50 up to several hundred dollars depending on products/services selected.

\*\* Fixed-price recruiter listing and e-mail service (Fee: $100 range): An average of 400+ resumes are e-mailed to targeted recruiters who are chosen based on candidate's specific selection criteria.

## The 24/7 Online Job Search Directory: Market-Tested Career and Job Search Web Sites

| Web Site | Web Address |
|---|---|
| Russell Reynolds Associates: Veteran Firm: Over 30 Offices Worldwide | www.russreyn.com/firmprofile /index.asp |
| McCray, Hewett & Associates: Retained Search: Senior Officer Level | www.mccray-inc.com |
| Gilbert Tweed Associates: Multiple-Industry Searches: Diverse Clientel | www.gilberttweed.com/who.html |
| Graystone Partners LLC: Retained Executive Search: Online Registration | www.graystonepartners.com /frames_exec.asp |
| J.B. Homer Associates: Senior Level IT Executives: Online Contact | www.jbhomer.com/submit.html |
| Paradigm Associates: International Executive Search: Sales and Technical | www.paradigm-assoc.com |
| GlocapSearch.com: Recruiting for Leading Investment Funds and Corporations | www.glocap.com/gs_home.jsp |
| KPMM International: Specializes in Attorneys, Banking, and Finance | www.kpmm.net/page2.html |
| Sanford Rose Associates: Proprietary Search Process: Online Job Search | www.sanfordrose.com |
| Westerberg and Associates: Retained Search: Senior Executives/Managers | www.westerberginc.com/page4.html |
| Valerie Frederickson & Co.: Retained Executive Search: Online Job Listing | www.vfandco.com/retained /index.html |
| Spherion Workforce Architects: Global Recruiting: Senior/Mid-Level/Staff Jobs | www.spherion.com /professionalrecruiting |
| Management Recruiters International: BrilliantPeople.com Site: Online Search | www.mrinet.com |
| JobPlex.com: Affiliated with DHR Intl.: Retained Search: Managers/Technical | www.jobplex.com/about.htm |

## XII. Online Classified Ads: Global Newspaper Listing Directories

| Web Site | Web Address |
|---|---|
| NewsDirectory.com: United States Newspaper Directory* | newsdirectory.com |
| NewsDirectory.com: North America Newspaper Directory | newsdirectory.com |
| NewsDirectory.com: European Newspaper Directory | newsdirectory.com |
| NewsDirectory.com: Asian Newspaper Directory | newsdirectory.com |
| NewsDirectory.com: South American Newspaper Directory | newsdirectory.com |
| NewsDirectory.com: African Newspaper Directory | newsdirectory.com |
| NewsDirectory.com: Oceania Newspaper Directory | newsdirectory.com |

* See listing of major U.S. metropolitan and national newspapers in Section XIII.

**XIII. Online Classified Ads: Major U.S. Regional and National Newspapers***

| Web Site | Web Address |
|---|---|
| *The Arizona Republic:* Classifieds: Job Search: USA Today Careers Network | azcentral.com |
| *The Atlanta Journal-Constitution:* Career Center: Virtual Career Fair | ajcclassifieds.com/search/employ |
| *The Chicago Tribune:* Job Search Powered by CareerBuilder.com | chicagotribune.com/classified/jobs |
| *The Dallas Morning News:* Job Search Powered by CareerBuilder.com | careerbuilder.dallasnews.com |
| *The Detroit News:* Job Search Powered by USA Today Careers Network | detnews.com/careers/index.htm |
| *The Hartford Courant:* Job Search Center Powered by CareerBuilder.com | hartfordcourant.com/adinfo /classonline.stm |
| *The Houston Chronicle:* ChronicleJobs.com Online Registration/Job Search | www.chron.com/jobs |
| *The Los Angeles Times:* Job Search Powered by CareerBuilder.com | latimes.com/class/employ |
| *The Miami Herald:* Job search Powered by CareerBuilder.com | careers.miami.com |
| *New York Newsday:* Job Search Powered by CareerBuilder.com | newsday.com/RedirectServlet /classified/jobs |
| *The New York Times:* Career Resource Center and Online Job Search | nytimes.com/yr/mo/day /jobmarket |
| *The Philadelphia Inquirer:* Job Search Powered by CareerBuilder.com | www.philly.com/mld/philly /classifieds/employment |
| *The San Diego Union-Tribune:* SignOnSanDiego.com Career Center | joblink.uniontrib.com |
| *USA Today:* Money Section: Job Search: USA Today Careers Network | usatoday.com/money/mfront.htm |
| *The Wall Street Journal:* CareerJournal.com: Career and Job Search Center | careerjournal.com/partners /advsearch.html |

**XIV. Direct Company Contacts: Company Listing Web Sites**

**No-Charge Company Contact Information Listings**

| Web Site | Web Address |
|---|---|
| Hoover's Online: Hoover's Companies A-Z: Contact Information** | hoovers.com/company/all/list /0,2504,116,00.html |
| Quintessential Careers: Directory of Company Career Centers: Job Openings | quintcareers.com/career_centers |

---

* See global directories in Category XII. for a complete listing of domestic and international newspapers.

** Hoover's Online offers nonsubscribers sufficient free contact information to satisfy most job search requirements; more detailed information requires annual subscriptions starting at $399.

# The 24/7 Online Job Search Directory:
# Market-Tested Career and Job Search Web Sites

| Web Site | Web Address |
|---|---|
| Quintessential Careers: Guide to Researching Companies: Online Sources | quintcareers.com /researching_companies.html |
| Monster.com: Research Companies: Company Profiles by Alphabet A-Z | http://company.monster.com |
| Job-Hunt.org: Company Employment Pages: Online Company Job Postings | www.job-hunt.org/companies .shtml |
| Job-Hunt.org: Reference Information Resources: Employer Listing Sites | www.job-hunt.org/reference |
| WetFeet.com: Companies A to Z: Company Job Centers/Contact Information | wetfeet.com/asp/companies_atoz.asp |
| Directory of Corporate Affiliations: Over 130,000 Parent/Affiliated Companies* | corporatelinkage.com |
| CareerJournal.com: Who's Hiring: Employers: Links to Employer Web Sites | careerjournal.com/whoshiring /index.html |
| e-CareerCenter.com: Company Career Center Web Sites: A to Z Listing | e-careercenter.com/jobsearch |
| U.S. Hispanic Chamber of Commerce: Directory of Hispanic Businesses** | www.ushcc.com |
| U.S. Hispanic Chamber of Commerce: Links to Hispanic Organizations/Resources | www.ushcc.com/hyperlinks.htm |

**Fee-Based Company Contact Information Listings**

| | |
|---|---|
| Kennedy Information: Hiring Company Listing: Online Database Pay Service*** | kennedyinfo.com/db/db_dhr_bas .html |
| U.S. Chamber of Commerce: National Directory of Local Chambers**** | www.uschamber.org/Chambers |

**XV. Mass Mailing Services: Fee-Based Online Resume Distribution Services**

**Mass Mailing: Resume Packages Prepared and Mailed Via U.S. Postal Service**

| Web Site | Web Address |
|---|---|
| WSA Corporation: $2.25 + Postage Per Package: Laser-Printed/Mailed | www.wsacorp.com/services.asp |
| ExecutivesOnly.com: $2.15 + Postage Per Package: Laser-Printed/Mailed | www.executivesonly.com |
| Career Marketing Services: $2.50 Per Resume Package: Laser-Printed/Mailed | yourcareerservices.com |

---

* Hard copies of directory available free of charge at local libraries; CD-ROM/download options cost between $1,000 and $2,000.

** In 2002, the U.S. Hispanic Chamber of Commerce—in concert with sponsor Ford Motor Company—announced the launching of a National Online Directory of Hispanic Businesses: The directory is a work in progress.

*** Kennedy Information database search service: Price of targeted company contact information is $0.50 per listing.

**** Contact information for small/mid-size firms can be found in company-listing directories published and sold by local Chambers.

# The 24/7 Online Job Search Directory:
## Market-Tested Career and Job Search Web Sites

**Mass E-Mailing: Listed by or Affiliated with Quintessential Careers, Kennedy Information, JobBank USA**

| Web Site | Web Address |
| --- | --- |
| ExecutiveAgent: Powered by Kennedy Information: Recruiter List/e-Mailing* | www.executiveagent.com/about /about.html |
| Quintessential Careers: Resume Distribution Services: Listing of Web Sites | quintcareers.com /resume_distribution_sites.html |
| BlastMyResume.com: $49–79: Alliance with Quintessential Careers: Guarantee | blastmyresume.com/cobrand /main.cfm?affiliate |
| JobSearchPage.com: $24–50: Global Distribution: Listed by QuintCareers | www.jobsearchpage.com |
| ResumeBlaster.com: $49–89 + Options: Guarantee: Listed by QuintCareers | www.resumeblaster.com |
| ResumeBroadcaster.com: $79 + Options: Targeted Mailing: From JobBankUSA | www.resumebroadcaster.com |
| ResumeBooster.com: $30–60 + Options: Targets Thousands of Employers/Recruiters | www.resumebooster.com/boost.asp |
| ResumeZapper: $50 + $80 in Options: Targeted Mailing: Listed by QuintCareers | resumezapper.com |
| RocketResume.com: $100–150: Targeted Distribution: Listed by QuintCareers | rocketresume.com /eresume_dist_service.htm |
| ResumeTrader.com: $30 + Optional Services: Posts to 70 Job Boards | www.careerweb.com/resumetrader |

**Mass E-Mailing: Additional Web Sites**

| Web Site | Web Address |
| --- | --- |
| ResumeXposure.com: $49–89: Offers Unlimited Resume Resends for $19 | resumexposure.com |
| SeeMeResumes: $39–69: Competitor Comparison Chart: Guarantee | www.seemeresumes.com |
| CareerXpress.com: ResumeSubmit Pricing: $79–289 + Optional Services | www.careerxpress.com |
| ResumeAgent.com: $40–60: Targeted Job Sites/ Employers/Recruiters | www.resumeagent.com |
| SoftForces.com: $40–100: Distribution Service for IT Professionals | www.softforces.com/resume.htm |
| RecruiterConnection.com: $19–99: Offers Multiple Service Levels | recruiterconnection.com |
| Resume Rabbit: $59.95: Posts to Over 75 Career Sites/Job Boards | www.resumerabbit.com |
| Xpostit.com: $49–149: Service Options: From 450 up to 2000 Contacts | crosspostit.com/js_promo.asp |
| Distinctive Documents: Variable Fees Based on Volume of Contacts | www.distinctiveweb.com/services .htm |

* Fixed-price recruiter listing and e-mail service ($100 range): An average of 400+ resumes are e-mailed to targeted recruiters.

# The 24/7 Online Job Search Directory: Market-Tested Career and Job Search Web Sites

## GROUP FIVE: INTERIM, TEMPORARY, AND CONTRACT EMPLOYMENT RESOURCES

### XVI. Interim Management/Temporary Employment Web Sites

**Interim Management/Temporary Employment Agency Directories**

| Web Site | Web Address |
|---|---|
| Directory of Executive Temporary Placement Firms: Lists by Industry/Geography | www.kennedyinfo.com/js/xtemp .html |
| Riley Guide: List of Temporary Employment Agencies: Also Seasonal/Other Sites | www.rileyguide.com/misc.html |
| Quintessential Careers: Listing of Temporary Employment Agency Web Sites | quintcareers.com/temp_jobs.html |

**Interim Management Firms**

| | |
|---|---|
| Spherion Interim Executives: Interim/Project Jobs (Formerly IMCOR) | spherion.com /professionalrecruiting |
| RHI Management Resources: Interim Senior Accounting/Financial Management | www.rhimr.com |
| CFOs2GO.com: Source for Senior Financial Executives: Online Application | cfos2go.com/candidatespage.htm |
| Manpower Professional: Staffing Services: IT, Engineering, Finance, and Other | www.manpowerprofessional.com |

**Temp Employment Agencies: Multiple Specialties**

| | |
|---|---|
| Net-Temps.com: Job Seekers Desktop and Career Center: Online Job Search | www.net-temps.com |
| Manpower Inc: Fortune 500 Global Recruiter: Online Registration/Job Search | www.us.manpower.com |
| WorkNow.com: Olsten Staffing Services Online Recruiting: Temporary/Full-Time | www.worknow.com/future |
| Robert Half Int'l.: Multiple Specialized Divisions: Financial, Legal, and Creative | www.rhii.com/divisions/index.html |
| MBAFreeAgents.com: Offers Basic Service and Fee-Based Subscriber Services | www.mbaglobalnet.com/freeagents .html |

**Temp Employment Agencies: Financial/Accounting/Legal/HR**

| | |
|---|---|
| Accountemps: Specialized Temp Staffing: Accounting/Finance/Bookkeeping | www.accountemps.com |
| CoreStaff.com: Specialties: Accounting, Finance, and Information Technology | www.corestaff.com/fastflex |
| The Affilates: Attorneys/Paralegals/Support Staff: Project-Based/Permanent | www.affiliates.com |
| HRCS: Provider of Outsourced Recruitment Services: Candidate Job Search | www.hrcs.com/cgi-local /jobsearch.cgi |
| Administaff: Professional Employer Organization (PEO): Online Application | www.administaff.com/careers /resume.htm |

## Temp Employment Agencies: Information Technology (IT) and Engineering

| Web Site | Web Address |
| --- | --- |
| RHI Consulting: Deploys Technology Professionals: Contract or Full-Time | www.rhic.com |
| Adecco International: Temporary or Full-Time Industrial and Technical Staffing | www.adecco.com |
| TAC Worldwide Companies: Provider of Technical and Software Staff | www.1tac.com |
| CTS International: Global High-Tech Recruiting: Online Registration/Job Lists | www.ctstech.com |
| National Technical Employment Services: Online Search/Optional Services | www.ntes.com |
| Contract Employment Weekly: Engineering/IT/ Technical: Membership Fee | www.ceweekly.com |

## Temp Employment Agencies: Creative and Technical Talent

| Web Site | Web Address |
| --- | --- |
| The Creative Group: Marketing, Advertising, Copywriter, and Web Professionals | www.creativegroup.com |
| AQUENT.com: Talent Agency: Creative/Technical Professionals: Online Search | www.aquent.com |
| SunOasis.com: Jobs for Writers, Editors, and Copywriters: Online Job Search | www.sunoasis.com |
| Creative Freelancers: Designers, Illustrators, Editors, and More: Online Search | www.freelancers.com |
| TempArt.com: Designers/Web Developers/ Illustrators/Other: Online Job Search | www.tempart.com |

## XVII. Independent Consultant/Contract/Freelance Employment Web Sites

### Independent Consultant Web Sites

| Web Site | Web Address |
| --- | --- |
| Quintessential Careers: Listing of Consultant and Freelance Job Sites | quintcareers.com/consultant_jobs .html |
| eWork: Online Marketplace Where Independent Professionals Find Projects | www.ework.com/index.cfm |

### Contract/Freelance Web Sites

| | |
| --- | --- |
| Monster Contract & Temporary: Online Marketplace for Free Agents | http://ct.monster.com |
| All Freelance: Resource Center for Freelancers and Independent Contractors | www.allfreelance.com |
| Guru: Talent Marketplace: Connecting Independent Talent with Opportunities | www.guru.com |
| Freelance Work Exchange: Fee-Based Services for Freelance Professionals | www.freelanceworkexchange.com |

## GROUP SIX: ADDITIONAL CAREER PLANNING, JOB SEARCH, AND RELOCATION RESOURCES

### XVIII. Other Web Sites to Facilitate and Expedite the Job Search Process

**CareerJournal.com: Bookstore and Executive Education**

| Web Site | Web Address |
| --- | --- |
| CareerJournal.com: Bookstore: Career and Job Search Books/Tapes | careerjournal.com/marketplace/bookstore |
| CareerJournal.com: Executive Education Center: Premier Business Programs: Global Listing | cj.ce.com |
| CareerJournal.com: Return to School: Peterson's Higher Education Databases | careerjournal.com/myc/school/index.html |

**Quintessential Career Center: Career Planning and Research Sites**

| | |
| --- | --- |
| Quintessential Careers: The Best Companies for Jobseekers: Rankings | quintcareers.com/best_places_to_work.html |
| Quintessential Careers: Career Resources Toolkit: Best Internet Resources | quintcareers.com/career_resources.html |
| Quintessential Careers: Job and Career Resources for Career Changers | quintcareers.com/career_change_resources.html |
| Quintessential Careers: Ask The Career Doctor Dr. Randall S. Hansen | careerdoctor.org |
| Quintessential Careers: Free Career and Job-Related Tutorials | quintcareers.com/tutorials.html |

**Online Reference Materials and Internet Resource Guides**

| | |
| --- | --- |
| CEOExpress: Executive Business Portal: Career Planning Resource Center | ceoexpress.com/default.asp |
| Occupational Outlook Handbook: Bureau of Labor Statistics: Career Information | www.bls.gov/oco |
| The Directory of Management Consultants: Profiles 2,400 Firms: North America | kennedyinfo.com/mc/dmc.html |
| Refdesk.com: Online Reference Library: Desktop Resources: Veteran Web Site | www.refdesk.com |
| CyberTimes Navigator: New York Times: Selective Guide to the Internet | www.nytimes.com/library/cyber/reference |
| Cybernet Chamber of Commerce: Comprehensive Guide to the Internet | www.ccc.net |

### XIX. Web Sites to Facilitate and Expedite the Relocation Process

**Domestic Relocation Assistance**

| Web Site | Web Address |
| --- | --- |
| RealEstateJournal.com: *Wall Street Journal* Property Guide: Relocation Tools | realestatejournal.com |
| Homestore.com: House and Home Network: Multiple Relocation Tools | homestore.com |

# The 24/7 Online Job Search Directory:
# Market-Tested Career and Job Search Web Sites

| Web Site | Web Address |
| --- | --- |
| Homestore.com: Apartments and Rentals: Online Rental Guide | springstreet.com/apartments |
| MonsterMoving.com: From Monster.com: Online Relocation Management | monstermoving.com |
| MSN HomeAdvisor.com: Relocation Center: Online Relocation Management | homeadvisor.msn.com |
| DigitalCity.com: Guide to U.S. Cities: Business, Shopping, and Entertainment | www.digitalcity.com |
| MapBlast: Maps, Driving Directions, and Yellow Pages On the Web | mapblast.com |
| Salary Calculator: Compare the Cost of Living in Hundreds of U.S. Cities | careerjournal.com/salaries /calculator/index.html |

**International Relocation Assistance**

| Web Site | Web Address |
| --- | --- |
| RealEstateJournal.com: *Wall Street Journal* Guide: International Properties | http://www.realestatejournal.com /distinctiveprops/ |
| EscapeArtist.com: Overseas Living for Global Job Seekers: Resource Center | escapeartist.com |
| CitySearch.com: Domestic and International City Guides: 128 Cities Worldwide | citysearch.com |
| MapQuest: Global Maps, Driving Directions, and Road Trip Planner | mapquest.com |
| International Salary Calculator: Compare Cost of Living in Cities Worldwide | homefair.com/calc/intsalcalc.html |
| FXConverter: Currency Converter: Up-to-date Exchange Rates: 164 Currencies | www.oanda.com/convert/classic |

# Appendix I

Conversion from the Recommended
Combination Functional and
Chronological Format
to a Chronological Format

# JAMES A. SMITH                                    R&D/Engineering/Marketing

123 Any Street, Any City, NY XXXXX (914) 555-1234

B.S.E.E.    University of Rochester    Self-financed    1985

Honors:    o Earned top grade for Senior project: designed hand-held scanner
           o Who's Who Among Students in American Colleges
           o Graduated with Honors; Dean's List

## CAREER SKILLS/KNOWLEDGE

o Product development
o Project management
o System engineering
o Electronics/mechanical
o Digital/analog technology
o PCB design/development
o Computer science/programming
o Biomedical engineering

o Sales/marketing
o Product creation/introduction
o Revenue/profit growth
o Client development
o Cold-calling/telemarketing
o Proposals/presentations
o Closing/customer service
o Business start-up

## CAREER ACHIEVEMENTS

o As Director of a key development group at XYZ, a subsidiary of ABC Company, developed several state-of-the-art communication products in five years creating one of the company's most profitable ventures: ground-breaking systems overcame restrictive limitations permitting peripherals to be located 70 miles away from a computer mainframe.

o As Cofounder of a start-up venture, led development of Single Board Computer, a processor board for industrial applications requiring less coding than other processor boards: protected product through legal means and marketed it to major Fortune 500 clients.

o As Founder of an E.E. consulting firm, developed a proprietary computer-based device called the "XYZ Product" for the Chairman of a market research firm under contract to the Executive Branch: earned fees based on the development, usage, and subsequent sale of the product.

o Started and marketed two business ventures during the past year generating six-figure sales: expanded an E.E. consulting firm; started a hazardous material consulting service.

o Directed a software-intensive group in executing state-of-the-art changes to a major machine at Acme Company: led development of coding printer executing all of the complex software and hardware tasks in harnessing the speed-printing technology.

o Successfully developed, for a major automotive company, the 4066 product which provided tape drive channels for customers without dedicated communications facilities: required complete restructuring of XYZ's 6088 product line.

## CAREER EXPERIENCE

**JAMES SMITH ASSOCIATES, Any Town, NY    1990–Present**
E.E. Consulting: Developed feeder mechanism critical to development of a mail machine to be marketed by an electronics firm. Created "XYZ Product" proprietary computer-based data-entry device used to measure responses to words, phrases, and ideas. Worked on a computer-based automated routing system for Essex Corporation.

**HAZARDOUS WASTE CONSULTING CORPORATION, Any Town, NY    1994–Present**
Started and manage consulting business.

**ACME COMPANY, Any City, NY    1992–1994**
Directed a product development effort aimed at instituting critical changes to a major machine: introduced speed-printing technology to new code printer.

**XYZ SUBSIDIARY, ABC COMPANY, Any Town, NY    1987–1992**
Director: Developed high-speed data communications equipment for mainframes; designed PC compatible interface card for serial and parallel transfer to proprietary product. Codeveloped high-speed logic board using FAST series logic and programmable devices; implemented 64K deep high-speed FIFO capable of a 5 Mega word throughput; employed error detection and correction with the RAM array.

**COMPUTER START-UP VENTURE, Any Town, NY    1987–1988**
Cofounder/Partner: Designed and marketed a single board computer using the Intel 8051 microcomputer: incorporated ROM memory mapping, 8155 I/O ports/RAM/Timers, Electronically Erasable PROM, and RS-232 serial communication using the on-board UART of the 8051.

**A FORTUNE 500 ELECTRONICS COMPANY, Any Town, NY    1986–1987**
Electronic Engineer: Earned positive feedback for systems testing and authoring critical test sections of major proposal.

**A SMALLER ELECTRONICS COMPANY, Any City, NY    1985–1986**
Electronic Engineer: Developed control system software for custom molding machines; generated assembly language and PLM programs for the Intel 8085 processor.

## REFERENCES PROVIDED UPON REQUEST

## JAMES A. SMITH                          R&D/Engineering/Marketing

123 Any Street, Any City, NY XXXXX (914) 555-1234

B.S.E.E.   University of Rochester   Self-financed   1985

Honors:   o Earned top grade for Senior project: designed hand-held scanner
          o Who's Who Among Students in American Colleges
          o Graduated with Honors; Dean's List

## CAREER EXPERIENCE

**JAMES SMITH ASSOCIATES, Any Town, NY   1990–Present**
E.E. Consulting: One of two ventures started during the last year. Developed feeder mechanism critical to development of a mail machine to be marketed by an electronics firm.

Also developed a proprietary computer-based device called the "XYZ Product" for the Chairman of a market research firm under contract to the Executive Branch: earned fees based on the development, usage, and subsequent sale of the product.

**HAZARDOUS WASTE CONSULTING CORPORATION, Any Town, NY   1994–Present**
Started and manage consulting business.

**ACME COMPANY, Any City, NY   1992–1994**
Directed a product development effort aimed at instituting critical changes to a major machine.

Led development of coding printer executing all of the complex software and hardware tasks in harnessing the speed-printing technology.

**XYZ SUBSIDIARY, ABC COMPANY, Any Town, NY   1987–1992**
Director: Developed high-speed data communications equipment for mainframes; designed PC compatible interface card for serial and parallel transfer to proprietary product. Codeveloped high-speed logic board using FAST series logic and programmable devices; implemented 64K deep high-speed FIFO capable of a 5 Mega word throughput; employed error detection and correction with the RAM array. Selected accomplishments include:

o As Director of a key development group, developed several state-of-the-art communication products in five years creating one of the company's most profitable ventures: groundbreaking systems overcame restrictive limitations permitting peripherals to be located 70 miles away from a computer mainframe.

o Successfully developed, for a major automotive company, the 4066 product which provided tape drive channels for customers without dedicated communications facilities: required complete restructuring of XYZ's 6088 product line.

## COMPUTER START-UP VENTURE, Any Town, NY    1987–1988
Cofounder/Partner: Designed and marketed a single board computer using the Intel 8051 microcomputer: incorporated ROM memory mapping, 8155 I/O ports/RAM/Timers, Electronically Erasable PROM, and RS-232 serial communication using the on-board UART of the 8051.

Processor board for industrial applications required less coding than other processor boards: protected product through legal means and marketed it to major Fortune 500 clients.

## A FORTUNE 500 ELECTRONICS COMPANY, Any Town, NY    1986–1987
Electronic Engineer: Earned positive feedback for systems testing and authoring critical test sections of major proposal.

## A SMALLER ELECTRONICS COMPANY, Any City, NY    1985–1986
Electronic Engineer: Developed control system software for custom molding machines; generated assembly language and PLM programs for the Intel 8085 processor.

## REFERENCES PROVIDED UPON REQUEST

# Appendix II

## Time-Tested Observations about the Job Interview

---

**REALITY CHECK**

Be yourself, inform yourself, and subtly take control. Remember that the interviewer is not God and that you are not a slave—it's a 50–50 dialogue, period.

---

As a brief supplement to the plethora of interview books, audiotapes, videos, and on-line guidance, the following are time-tested observations regarding the interview process.

1. At the risk of sounding naive, it's my strong opinion that the truth is the best interview script. Being prepared, truthful, and forthright in responding to questions eliminates the need to "get your story straight." It also mitigates the need to role-play and "act" your way through interviews. Not getting the job is a secondary problem compared to the problems created by pretending to be somebody you're not. Be yourself, period.

2. Remember that the interviewer isn't God and you're not a slave. Be respectful, but recognize that interviews are a 50–50 proposition. You're also there to screen them. It's better to

identify the worst now. Prevention is much less painful than the cure.

3. Regarding salary negotiations, remember that if they try to nickel and dime you now, they will nickel and dime you later. If at all possible, discuss salary last so that you can properly assess the value of the job. Once you know that they are interested, you can request a fair to premium salary based on the job's scope of responsibility.

4. Turn rejection into alternative opportunities. If the offer is dead, ask about other jobs in the company or other leads. You have nothing to lose and everything to gain.

5. In follow-up letters or calls, communicate interest, restate contributions you'll make, and, most importantly, reference specific key points from the interview. Never send a boiler-plate letter. It should be from the heart. Failure to do so can cost you the job.

6. Don't become discouraged. Learn from, but try not to obsess about, interview gaffes. You will do better in future inter-views.

7. Always remember that you have a major competitive edge. Unlike most interviewees, you are conducting an aggressive, multistep job search campaign armed with market-tested re-sumes and cover letter packages. The Expansionist Theory works, period.

## A FINAL THOUGHT: INTERVIEWER QUESTIONS

Candidates sometimes encounter off-center questions designed to test their temperament—don't take the bait. Here are a dozen exam-ples heard over the years.

1. Are we just a stopover for you? Does this job really measure up to your goals?
2. Isn't the team player stuff a lot of nonsense? Contrast coop-eration with taking charge.
3. What negatives soured you on past employers? How do you know we're any better?
4. What past criticism really angered you? How did you re-solve your hostility?

5. How do you correct lousy morale? When push comes to shove, isn't theory X better?

6. What types of personalities rub you the wrong way? How do you react emotionally?

7. Contrast working smarter with working harder. How do you really feel about overtime?

8. How do you respond to intense pressure, deadlines, or adversity? How angry do you get?

9. How do you feel about constant fire fighting? constant crises? midnight meetings?

10. Would you take a cut in pay? Don't you agree that it's cheaper to live in the South?

11. What can you do that other more skilled candidates can't? Why should we hire you?

12. Don't you think that you might be better off in another company?

Printed in the United States
27351LVS00001BA/115-132

9 780471 232872